Beginning Apache Spark 2

With Resilient Distributed Datasets, Spark SQL, Structured Streaming and Spark Machine Learning library

Hien Luu

Apress®

Beginning Apache Spark 2: With Resilient Distributed Datasets, Spark SQL, Structured Streaming and Spark Machine Learning library

Hien Luu
SAN JOSE, California, USA

ISBN-13 (pbk): 978-1-4842-3578-2   ISBN-13 (electronic): 978-1-4842-3579-9
https://doi.org/10.1007/978-1-4842-3579-9

Library of Congress Control Number: 2018953881

Managing Director, Apress Media LLC: Welmoed Spahr
Acquisitions Editor: Steve Anglin
Development Editor: Matthew Moodie
Coordinating Editor: Mark Powers

Cover designed by eStudioCalamar

Cover image designed by Freepik (www.freepik.com)

Distributed to the book trade worldwide by Springer Science+Business Media New York, 233 Spring Street, 6th Floor, New York, NY 10013. Phone 1-800-SPRINGER, fax (201) 348-4505, e-mail orders-ny@ springer-sbm.com, or visit www.springeronline.com. Apress Media, LLC is a California LLC and the sole member (owner) is Springer Science + Business Media Finance Inc (SSBM Finance Inc). SSBM Finance Inc is a **Delaware** corporation.

For information on translations, please e-mail editorial@apress.com; for reprint, paperback, or audio rights, please email bookpermissions@springernature.com.

Apress titles may be purchased in bulk for academic, corporate, or promotional use. eBook versions and licenses are also available for most titles. For more information, reference our Print and eBook Bulk Sales web page at www.apress.com/bulk-sales.

Any source code or other supplementary material referenced by the author in this book is available to readers on GitHub via the book's product page, located at www.apress.com/9781484235782. For more detailed information, please visit www.apress.com/source-code.

Printed on acid-free paper

Table of Contents

About the Author

Hien Luu has extensive working experience in designing and building big data applications and scalable web-based applications. He is particularly passionate about the intersection between big data and machine learning. Hien enjoys working with open source software and has contributed to Apache Pig and Azkaban. Teaching is one of his passions, and he serves as an instructor at the UCSC Silicon Valley Extension school teaching Apache Spark. He has given presentations at various conferences such a QCon SF, QCon London, Seattle Data Day, Hadoop Summit, and JavaOne.

About the Technical Reviewer

Karpur Shukla is a research fellow at the Centre for
Mathematical Modeling at FLAME University in Pune, India.
His current research interests focus on topological quantum
computation, nonequilibrium and finite-temperature
aspects of topological quantum field theories, and
applications of quantum materials effects for reversible
computing. He received an M.Sc. in physics from Carnegie
Mellon University, with a background in theoretical analysis
of materials for spintronics applications as well as Monte
Carlo simulations for the renormalization group of
finite-temperature spin lattice systems.

CHAPTER 1

Introduction to Apache Spark

There is no better time to learn Spark than now. Spark has become one of the critical components in the big data stack because of its ease of use, speed, and flexibility. This scalable data processing system is being widely adopted across many industries by many small and big companies, including Facebook, Microsoft, Netflix, and LinkedIn. This chapter provides a high-level overview of Spark, including the core concepts, the architecture, and the various components inside the Apache Spark stack.

Overview

Spark is a general distributed data processing engine built for speed, ease of use, and flexibility. The combination of these three properties is what makes Spark so popular and widely adopted in the industry.

The Apache Spark website claims it can run a certain data processing job up to 100 times faster than Hadoop MapReduce. In fact, in 2014, Spark won the Daytona GraySort contest, which is an industry benchmark for sorting 100TB of data (one trillion records). The submission from Databricks claimed Spark was able to sort 100TB of data three times faster and using ten times fewer resources than the previous world record set by Hadoop MapReduce.

Since the inception of the Spark project, the ease of use has been one of the main focuses of the Spark creators. It offers more than 80 high-level, commonly needed data processing operators to make it easy for developers, data scientists, and data analysts to build all kinds of interesting data applications. In addition, these operators are available in multiple languages, namely, Scala, Java, Python, and R. Software engineers, data scientists, and data analysts can pick and choose their favorite language to solve large-scale data processing problems with Spark.

© Hien Luu 2018
H. Luu, *Beginning Apache Spark 2*, https://doi.org/10.1007/978-1-4842-3579-9_1

In terms of flexibility, Spark offers a single unified data processing stack that can be used to solve multiple types of data processing workloads, including batch processing, interactive queries, iterative processing needed by machine learning algorithms, and real-time streaming processing to extract actionable insights at near real-time. Before the existence of Spark, each of these types of workload required a different solution and technology. Now companies can just leverage Spark for most of their data processing needs. Using a single technology stack will help with dramatically reducing the operational cost and resources.

A big data ecosystem consists of many pieces of technology including a distributed storage engine called HDFS, a cluster management system to efficiently manage a cluster of machines, and different file formats to store a large amount of data efficiently in binary and columnar format. Spark integrates really well with the big data ecosystem. This is another reason why Spark adoption has been growing at a really fast pace.

Another really cool thing about Spark is it is open source; therefore, anyone can download the source code to examine the code, to figure out how a certain feature was implemented, or to extend its functionalities. In some cases, it can dramatically help with reducing the time to debug problems.

History

Spark started out as a research project at Berkeley AMPLab in 2009. At that time, the researchers of this project observed the inefficiencies of the Hadoop MapReduce framework in handling interactive and iterative data processing use cases, so they came up with ways to overcome those inefficiencies by introducing ideas such as in-memory computation and an efficient way of dealing with fault recovery. Once this research project proved to be a viable solution that outperformed MapReduce, it was open sourced in 2010 and became the Apache top-level project in 2013. A group of researchers working on this research project got together and founded a company called Databricks; they raised more than $43 million in 2013. Databricks is the primary commercial steward behind Spark. In 2015, IBM announced a major investment in building a Spark technology center to advance Apache Spark by working closely with the open source community and building Spark into the core of its company's analytics and commerce platforms.

Two popular research papers about Spark are "Spark: Cluster Computing with Working Sets" and "Resilient Distributed Datasets: A Fault-Tolerant Abstraction for In-Memory Cluster Computing." These papers were well received at academic conferences and provide good foundations for anyone who would like to learn and understand Spark. You can find them at `http://people.csail.mit.edu/matei/papers/2010/hotcloud_spark.pdf` and `http://people.csail.mit.edu/matei/papers/2012/nsdi_spark.pdf`, respectively.

Since its inception, the Spark open source project has been an active project with a vibrant community. The number of contributors has increased to more than 1,000 in 2016, and there are more than 200,000 Apache Spark meetups. In fact, the number of Apache Spark contributors has exceeded the number of contributors of one of the most popular open source projects called Apache Hadoop. Spark is so popular now that it has its own summit called Spark Summit, which is held annually in North America and Europe. The summit attendance has doubled each year since its inception.

The creators of Spark selected the Scala programming language for their project because of the combination of Scala's conciseness and static typing. Now Spark is considered to be one of the largest applications written in Scala, and its popularity certainly has helped Scala to become a mainstream programming language.

Spark Core Concepts and Architecture

Before diving into the details of Spark, it is important to have a high-level understanding of the core concepts and the various core components in Spark. This section will cover the following:

- Spark clusters

- The resource management system

- Spark applications

- Spark drivers

- Spark executors

Spark Clusters and the Resource Management System

Spark is essentially a distributed system that was designed to process a large volume of data efficiently and quickly. This distributed system is typically deployed onto a collection of machines, which is known as a Spark *cluster*. A cluster size can be as small as a few machines or as large as thousands of machines. The largest publicly announced Spark cluster in the world has more than 8,000 machines. To efficiently and intelligently manage a collection of machines, companies rely on a resource management system such as Apache YARN or Apache Mesos. The two main components in a typical resource management system are the *cluster manager* and the *worker*. The cluster manager knows where the workers are located, how much memory they have, and the number of CPU cores each one has. One of the main responsibilities of the cluster manager is to orchestrate the work by assigning it to each worker. Each worker offers resources (memory, CPU, etc.) to the cluster manager and performs the assigned work. An example of the type of work is to launch a particular process and monitor its health. Spark is designed to easily interoperate with these systems. Most companies that have been adopting big data technologies in recent years usually already have a YARN cluster to run MapReduce jobs or other data processing frameworks such as Apache Pig or Apache Hive.

Startup companies that fully adopt Spark can just use the out-of-the-box Spark cluster manager to manage a set of dedicated machines to perform data processing using Spark. Figure 1-1 depicts this type of setup.

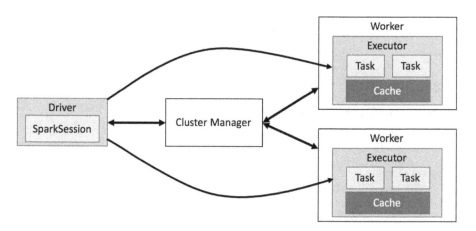

Figure 1-1. *Interactions between a Spark application and a cluster manager*

Spark Application

A Spark application consists of two parts. The first is the application data processing logic expressed using Spark APIs, and the other is the Spark driver. The application data processing logic can be as simple as a few lines of code to perform a few data processing operations or can be as complex as training a large machine learning model that requires many iterations and could run for many hours to complete. The Spark *driver* is the central coordinator of a Spark application, and it interacts with a cluster manager to figure out which machines to run the data processing logic on. For each one of those machines, the Spark driver requests that the cluster manager launch a process called the Spark *executor*. Another important job of the Spark driver is to manage and distribute Spark tasks onto each executor on behalf of the application. If the data processing logic requires the Spark driver to display the computed results to a user, then it will coordinate with each Spark executor to collect the computed result and merge them together. The entry point into a Spark application is through a class called `SparkSession`, which provides facilities for setting up configurations as well as APIs for expressing data processing logic.

Spark Driver and Executor

Each Spark executor is a JVM process and is exclusively allocated to a specific Spark application. This was a conscious design decision to avoid sharing a Spark executor between multiple Spark applications in order to isolate them from each other so one badly behaving Spark application wouldn't affect other Spark applications. The lifetime of a Spark executor is the duration of a Spark application, which could run for a few minutes or for a few days. Since Spark applications are running in separate Spark executors, sharing data between them will require writing the data to an external storage system like HDFS.

As depicted in Figure 1-2, Spark employs a master-slave architecture, where the Spark driver is the master and the Spark executor is the slave. Each of these components runs as an independent process on a Spark cluster. A Spark application consists of one and only one Spark driver and one or more Spark executors. Playing the slave role, each Spark executor does what it is told, which is to execute the data processing logic in the form of tasks. Each task is executed on a separate CPU core. This is how Spark can speed up the processing of a large amount of data by processing it in parallel. In addition to executing assigned tasks, each Spark executor has the responsibility of caching a portion of the data in memory and/or on disk when it is told to do so by the application logic.

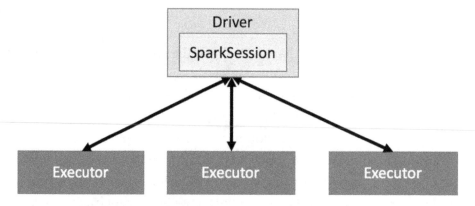

Figure 1-2. *A small Spark cluster with three executors*

At the time of launching a Spark application, you can request how many Spark executors an application needs and how much memory and the number of CPU cores each executor should have. Figuring out an appropriate number of Spark executors, the amount of memory, and the number of CPU requires some understanding of the amount of data that will be processed, the complexity of the data processing logic, and the desired duration by which a Spark application should complete the processing logic.

Spark Unified Stack

Unlike its predecessors, Spark provides a unified data processing engine known as the *Spark stack*. Similar to other well-designed systems, this stack is built on top of a strong foundation called Spark Core, which provides all the necessary functionalities to manage and run distributed applications such as scheduling, coordination, and fault tolerance. In addition, it provides a powerful and generic programming abstraction for data processing called *resilient distributed datasets* (RDDs). On top of this strong foundation is a collection of components where each one is designed for a specific data processing workload, as shown in Figure 1-3. Spark SQL is for batch as well as interactive data processing. Spark Streaming is for real-time stream data processing. Spark GraphX is for graph processing. Spark MLlib is for machine learning. Spark R is for running machine learning tasks using the R shell.

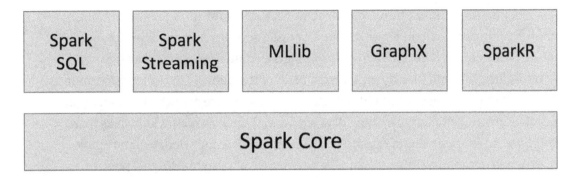

Figure 1-3. *Spark unified stack*

This unified engine brings several important benefits to the task of building scalable and intelligent big data applications. First, applications are simpler to develop and deploy because they use a unified set of APIs and run on a single engine. Second, it is way more efficient to combine different types of data processing (batch, streaming, etc.) because Spark can run those different sets of APIs over the same data without writing the intermediate data out to a storage system. Finally, the most exciting benefit is Spark enables new applications that were not possible before because of its ease of composing different sets of data processing types within a Spark application. For example, it can run interactive queries over the results of machine learning predictions of real-time data streams. An analogy that everyone can relate to is the smartphone, which consists of a powerful camera, cell phone, and GPS device. By combining the functions of these components, a smartphone enables innovative applications such as Waze, a traffic and navigation application.

Spark Core

Spark Core is the bedrock of the Spark distributed data processing engine. It consists of two parts: the distributed computing infrastructure and the RDD programming abstraction.

The distributed computing infrastructure is responsible for the distribution, coordination, and scheduling of computing tasks across many machines in the cluster. This enables the ability to perform parallel data processing of a large volume of data efficiently and quickly on a large cluster of machines. Two other important responsibilities of the distributed computing infrastructure are handling of computing task failures and efficiently moving data across machines, which is known as *data shuffling*. Advanced users of Spark need to have intimate knowledge of the Spark distributed computing infrastructure to be effective at designing highly performant Spark applications.

The key programming abstraction in Spark is called RDD, and it is something every Spark developer should have some knowledge of, especially its APIs and main concepts. The technical definition of an RDD is that it is an immutable and fault-tolerant collection of objects partitioned across a cluster that can be manipulated in parallel. Essentially, it provides a set of APIs for Spark application developers to easily and efficiently perform large-scale data processing without worrying where data resides on the cluster or dealing with machine failures. For example, say you have a 1.5TB log file that resides on HDFS and you need to find out the number of lines containing the word *Exception*. You can create an instance of RDD to represent all the log statements in that log file, and Spark can partition them across the nodes in the cluster such that filtering and counting logic can be executed in parallel to speed up the search and counting logic.

The RDD APIs are exposed in multiple programming languages (Scala, Java, and Python), and they allow users to pass local functions to run on the cluster, which is something that is powerful and unique. RDDs will be covered in detail in Chapter 3.

The rest of the components in the Spark stack are designed to run on top of Spark Core. Therefore, any improvements or optimizations done in Spark Core between versions of Spark will be automatically available to the other components.

Spark SQL

Spark SQL is a component built on top of Spark Core, and it is designed for structured data processing at scale. Its popularity has skyrocketed since its inception because it brings a new level of flexibility, ease of use, and performance.

Structured Query Language (SQL) has been the lingua franca for data processing because it is fairly easy for users to express their intent, and the execution engine then performs the necessary intelligent optimizations. Spark SQL brings that to the world of data processing at the petabyte level. Spark users now can issue SQL queries to perform data processing or use the high-level abstraction exposed through the DataFrames APIs. A DataFrame is effectively a distributed collection of data organized into named columns. This is not a novel idea; in fact, this idea was inspired by data frames in R and Python. An easier way to think about a DataFrame is that it is conceptually equivalent to a table in a relational database.

Behind the scenes, Spark SQL leverages the Catalyst optimizer to perform the kinds of the optimizations that are commonly done in many analytical database engines.

Another feature Spark SQL provides is the ability to read data from and write data to various structured formats and storage systems, such as JavaScript Object Notation (JSON), comma-separated value (CSV) files, Parquet or ORC files, relational databases, Hive, and others. This feature really helps in elevating the level of versatility of Spark because Spark SQL can be used as a data converter tool to easily convert data from one format to another.

According to a 2016 Spark survey, Spark SQL was the fastest-growing component. This makes sense because Spark SQL enables a wider audience beyond big data engineers to leverage the power of distributed data processing (i.e., data analysts or anyone who is familiar with SQL).

The motto for Spark SQL is to write less code, read less data, and let the optimizer do the hard work.

Spark Structured Streaming and Streaming

It has been said that "Data in motion has equal or greater value than historical data." The ability to process data as it arrives is becoming a competitive advantage for many companies in highly competitive industries. The Spark Streaming module enables the ability to process real-time streaming data from various data sources in a high-throughput and fault-tolerant manner. Data can be ingested from sources such as Kafka, Flume, Kinesis, Twitter, HDFS, or TCP sockets.

The main abstraction in the first generation of the Spark Streaming processing engine is called *discretized stream* (DStream), which implements an incremental stream processing model by splitting the input data into small batches (based on a time interval) that can regularly combine the current processing state to produce new results. In other words, once the incoming data is split into small batches, each batch is treated as an RDD and replicated out onto the cluster so they can be processed accordingly.

Stream processing sometimes involves joining with data at rest, and Spark makes it easy to do so. In other words, combining batch and interactive queries with streaming processing can be easily done in Spark because of the unified Spark stack.

A new scalable and fault-tolerant streaming processing engine called Structured Streaming was introduced in Spark 2.1, and it was built on top of the Spark SQL engine. This engine further simplifies the life of streaming processing application developers by treating streaming computation the same way as one would express a batch computation on static data. This new engine will automatically execute the streaming processing logic incrementally and continuously as new streaming data continues to arrive. A new and important feature that Structured Streaming provides is the ability to process incoming streaming data based on the event time, which is necessary for many of the new streaming processing use cases. Another unique feature in the Structured Streaming engine is the end-to-end, exactly once guarantee, which will make a big data engineer's life much easier than before in terms of saving data to a storage system such as a relational database or a NoSQL database.

As this new engine matures, undoubtedly it will enable a new class of streaming processing applications that are easy to develop and maintain.

According to Reynold Xin, Databricks' chief architect, the simplest way to perform streaming analytics is not having to reason about streaming.

Spark MLlib

In addition to providing more than 50 common machine learning algorithms, the Spark MLlib library provides abstractions for managing and simplifying many of the machine learning model building tasks, such as featurization, pipeline for constructing, evaluating and tuning model, and persistence of models to help with moving the model from development to production.

Starting with Spark 2.0, the MLlib APIs will be based on DataFrames to take advantage of the user friendliness and many optimizations provided by the Catalyst and Tungsten components in the Spark SQL engine.

Machine learning algorithms are iterative in nature, meaning they run through many iterations until a desired objective is achieved. Spark makes it extremely easy to implement those algorithms and run them in a scalable manner through a cluster of machines. Commonly used machine learning algorithms such as classification, regression, clustering, and collaborative filtering are available out of the box for data scientists and engineers to use.

Spark Graphx

Graph processing operates on data structures consisting of vertices and edges connecting them. A graph data structure is often used to represent real-life networks of interconnected entities, including professional social networks on LinkedIn, networks of connected web pages on the Internet, and so on. Spark GraphX is a component that enables graph-parallel computations by providing an abstraction of a directed multigraph with properties attached to each vertex and edge. The GraphX component includes a collection of common graph processing algorithms including page ranks, connected components, shortest paths, and others.

SparkR

SparkR is an R package that provides a light-weight front end to use Apache Spark. R is a popular statistical programming language that supports data processing and machine learning tasks. However, R was not designed to handle large datasets that can't fit on a single machine. SparkR leverages Spark's distributed computing engine to enable large-scale data analysis using the familiar R shell and popular APIs that many data scientists love.

Apache Spark Applications

Spark is a versatile, fast, and scalable data processing engine. It was designed to be a general engine since the beginning days and has proven that it can be used to solve various use cases. Many companies in various industries are using Spark to solve real-life use cases. The following is a small list of applications that were developed using Spark:

- Customer intelligence applications
- Data warehouse solutions
- Real-time streaming solutions
- Recommendation engines
- Log processing
- User-facing services
- Fraud detection

Example Spark Application

In the world of big data processing, the canonical example application is a word count application. This tradition started with the introduction of the MapReduce framework. Since then, every big data processing technology book must follow this unwritten tradition by including this canonical example. The problem space in the word count example application is easy for everyone to understand since all it does is count how many times a particular word appears in a given set of documents, whether that is a chapter of a book or hundreds of terabytes of web pages from the Internet. Listing 1-1 contains the word count example written in Spark using Scala APIs.

Listing 1-1. Word Count Example Application in Spark in the Scala Language

```
val textFiles = sc.textFile("hdfs://<folder contains text files")
val words = textFiles.flatMap(line => line.split(" "))
val wordTuples = words.map(word => (word, 1))
val wordCounts = wordTuples.reduceByKey(_ + _)
wordCounts.saveAsTextFile("hdfs://<outoupt folder>")
```

There is a lot going on behind these five lines of code. The first line is responsible for reading in the text files in the specified folder. The second line iterates through each line in each of the files, tokenizes each line into an array of words, and finally flattens each array into one word per line. To count the number of words across all the documents, the third line attaches a count of 1 to each word. The fourth line performs the summation of the count of each word. Finally, the last line saves the result in the specified folder. Ideally this gives you a general sense of the ease of use of Spark to perform data processing. Future chapters will go into much more detail about what each of these lines of code does.

Summary

In this chapter, you learned the following:

- Apache Spark has certainly produced many sparks since its inception. It has created much excitement and many opportunities in the world of big data. More important, it allows you to create many new and innovating big data applications to solve a diverse set of use cases.

- The three important properties of Spark to note are ease of use, speed, and flexibility.

- The Spark distributed computing infrastructure employs a master-slave architecture. Each Spark application consists of a driver, which plays the master role, and one or more executors, which are the slaves, to process data in parallel.

- Spark provides a unified scalable and distributed data processing engine that can be used for batch processing, interactive and exploratory data processing, real-time streaming processing, training machine learning models and performing predictions, and graph processing.

- Spark applications can be written in multiple programming languages including Scala, Java, Python, and R.

CHAPTER 2

Working with Apache Spark

This chapter provides details about the different ways of working with Spark, including using the Spark shell, submitting a Spark application from the command line, and using a hosted cloud platform called Databricks. The last part of this chapter is geared toward software engineers who want to set up the Apache Spark source code on a local machine to examine the Spark code and learn how certain features were implemented.

Downloading and Installing Spark

For the purposes of learning or experimenting with Spark, it is good to install Spark locally on your computer. This way you can easily try the Spark features or test your data processing logic with small datasets. By having Spark locally installed on your laptop, you can learn Spark from anywhere, including in your comfortable living room, on the beach, or at a bar in Mexico.

Spark is written in the Scala programming language, and it is packaged in such a way that it can be run on both Windows and Unix-like systems (e.g., Linux and macOS). All that is needed is to have Java installed on your computer.

Setting up a multitenant Spark production cluster requires a lot more details and resources and is beyond the scope of this book.

Downloading Spark

The Download section of the Apache Spark website (`http://spark.apache.org/downloads.html`) has detailed instructions for downloading the prepackaged Spark binary file. At the time of writing this book, the latest version is 2.3.0. In terms of the package type, choose the one with the latest version of Hadoop. Figure 2-1 shows the various options for downloading Spark. The important thing is to download the prepackaged binary file because it contains the necessary JAR files to run Spark on your

15

© Hien Luu 2018
H. Luu, *Beginning Apache Spark 2*, https://doi.org/10.1007/978-1-4842-3579-9_2

computer. Clicking the link on line 4 will trigger the binary file download process. There is a way to manually package the Spark binary from source code, and the instructions for how to do that will be available later in the chapter.

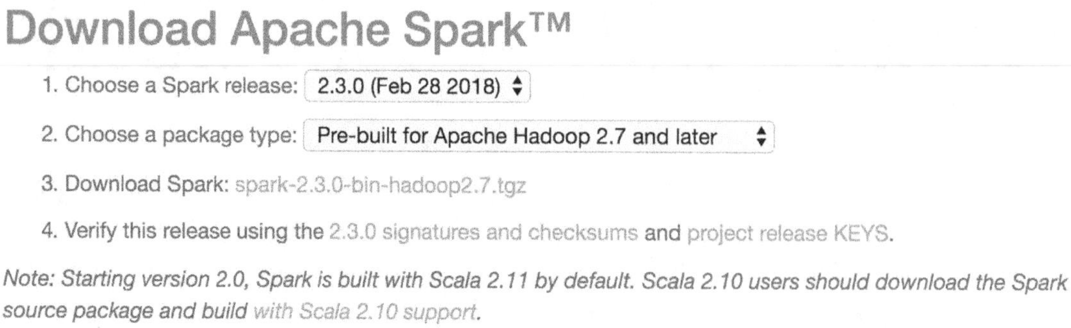

Download Apache Spark™

1. Choose a Spark release: 2.3.0 (Feb 28 2018) ⬍

2. Choose a package type: Pre-built for Apache Hadoop 2.7 and later   ⬍

3. Download Spark: spark-2.3.0-bin-hadoop2.7.tgz

4. Verify this release using the 2.3.0 signatures and checksums and project release KEYS.

Note: Starting version 2.0, Spark is built with Scala 2.11 by default. Scala 2.10 users should download the Spark source package and build with Scala 2.10 support.

Figure 2-1. *Apache Spark download options*

Installing Spark

Once the binary file is successfully downloaded onto your computer, the next step is to uncompress it. The downloaded file, `spark-2.x.x-bin-hadoop2.7.tgz`, is in a GZIP-compressed tar archive file, so you need to use the right tool to uncompress it.

For Linux or Mac computers, the `tar` command should already exist. So, run the following command to uncompress the downloaded file:

```
tar xvf spark-2.x.x-bin-hadoop2.7.tgz
```

For Windows computers, you can use either the WinZip or 7-zip tool to unzip the downloaded file.

Once the uncompressing is successfully finished, there should be a directory called `spark-2.x.x-bin-hadoop2.7`. From here on, this directory is referred to as the *Spark directory*.

Note   If a different version of Spark was downloaded, the directory name will be slightly different.

There are about a dozen directories underneath the Spark directory. Table 2-1 lists the ones you should know.

Table 2-1. *Subdirectories Inside the spark-2.1.1-bin-hadoop2.7 Directory*

Name	Description
bin	Contains the various executable files to bring up a Spark shell in Scala or Python, submit Spark applications, and run Spark examples
data	Contains small sample data files for various Spark examples
examples	Contains both the source code and binary file for all Spark examples
jars	Contains the necessary binaries that are needed to run Spark
sbin	Contains the executable files to manage the Spark cluster

After the uncompressing step, the next step is to test the installation by bringing up the Spark shell.

A Spark shell is like a Unix shell, but it is for Spark. It provides an interactive environment to make it easy to learn the Spark APIs and to analyze data interactively. The cool thing is that it is available in either Scala or Python. If you are a data scientist and Python is your cup of tea, then you will be at home. The following sections will show how to bring up the Spark Scala and Spark Python shells.

Note   The Scala programming language is a JVM language, and thus it is easy for Scala to use existing Java libraries.

Spark Scala Shell

To start a Spark Scala shell, enter this command in the Spark directory:

```
./bin/spark-shell
```

After a few seconds, you should see something similar to Figure 2-2.

```
Spark context available as 'sc' (master = local[*], app id = local-1528320587772).
Spark session available as 'spark'.
Welcome to
      ____              __
     / __/__  ___ _____/ /__
    _\ \/ _ \/ _ `/ __/  '_/
   /___/ .__/\_,_/_/ /_/\_\   version 2.3.0
      /_/

Using Scala version 2.11.8 (Java HotSpot(TM) 64-Bit Server VM, Java 1.8.0_121)
Type in expressions to have them evaluated.
Type :help for more information.

scala> 
```

Figure 2-2. *Scala Spark shell output*

To exit the Scala Spark shell, type :quit or :q.

Note   The Spark Scala shell requires Java 1.8.*x* installed on your machine.

Spark Python Shell

To start up a Spark Python shell, enter this command in the Spark directory:

```
./bin/pyspark
```

After a few seconds, you should see something similar to Figure 2-3.

```
Python 3.6.1 (v3.6.1:69c0db5050, Mar 21 2017, 01:21:04)
[GCC 4.2.1 (Apple Inc. build 5666) (dot 3)] on darwin
Type "help", "copyright", "credits" or "license" for more information.
18/06/06 14:31:19 WARN NativeCodeLoader: Unable to load native-hadoop library for your platform...
 using builtin-java classes where applicable
Welcome to
      ____              __
     / __/__  ___ _____/ /__
    _\ \/ _ \/ _ `/ __/  '_/
   /__ / .__/\_,_/_/ /_/\_\   version 2.3.0
      /_/

Using Python version 3.6.1 (v3.6.1:69c0db5050, Mar 21 2017 01:21:04)
SparkSession available as 'spark'.
>>> 
```

Figure 2-3. *Output of the Python Spark shell*

To exit the Python Spark shell, press Ctrl+D.

Note   The Spark Python shell requires Python 2.6.*x* or newer installed on your machine.

Both the Spark Scala shell and the Spark Python shell are extensions of Scala REPL and Python REPL, respectively. REPL is an acronym for *read-eval-print loop*. It is basically an interactive computer programming environment that takes user input, evaluates it, and returns the result to the user. Once a line of code is entered, the REPL will immediately provide feedback about whether there was a syntactic error. If there are no syntactic errors, that line of code will evaluated, and the output is displayed in the shell if there is any. The interactive and immediate feedback environment allows developers to be very productive by bypassing the code compilation step in the normal software development process.

For the purpose of learning Spark, the Spark shell is a convenient tool to use on your local computer anytime and anywhere. It doesn't have any external dependencies, other than the data files you would like to process. However, if you have an Internet connection, then it is possible to access those remote data files, but it will be slow.

The remaining chapters of this book will use the Spark Scala shell.

Having Fun with the Spark Scala Shell

This section will provide detailed information about the Scala Spark shell and a set of useful commands to know to be effective at using it for exploratory data analysis or for building Spark applications interactively.

The command `./bin/spark-shell` effectively starts a Spark application and provides an environment where you can interactively call Spark Scala APIs to easily perform exploratory data processing. Since the Spark Scala shell is an extension of the Scala REPL, it is a great way to use it to learn Scala and Spark at the same time.

Useful Spark Scala Shell Commands and Tips

Once a Spark Scala shell is started, it puts you in an interactive environment where you can enter shell commands and Scala code. This section will cover the various useful commands and a few tips for working with this shell.

Once you are inside the Spark shell, type the following to bring up a complete list of available commands:

```
scala>   :help
```

Figure 2-4 shows the output of the previous command.

```
scala> :help
All commands can be abbreviated, e.g., :he instead of :help.
:edit <id>|<line>         edit history
:help [command]           print this summary or command-specific help
:history [num]            show the history (optional num is commands to show)
:h? <string>              search the history
:imports [name name ...]  show import history, identifying sources of names
:implicits [-v]           show the implicits in scope
:javap <path|class>       disassemble a file or class name
:line <id>|<line>         place line(s) at the end of history
:load <path>              interpret lines in a file
:paste [-raw] [path]      enter paste mode or paste a file
:power                    enable power user mode
:quit                     exit the interpreter
:replay [options]         reset the repl and replay all previous commands
:require <path>           add a jar to the classpath
:reset [options]          reset the repl to its initial state, forgetting all session entries
:save <path>              save replayable session to a file
:sh <command line>        run a shell command (result is implicitly => List[String])
:settings <options>       update compiler options, if possible; see reset
:silent                   disable/enable automatic printing of results
:type [-v] <expr>         display the type of an expression without evaluating it
:kind [-v] <expr>         display the kind of expression's type
:warnings                 show the suppressed warnings from the most recent line which had any
```

Figure 2-4. *List of available shell commands*

Some commands are used more often than others because of their usefulness. Table 2-2 describes the commonly used commands.

Table 2-2. *Useful Spark Shell Commands to Know*

Name	Description
:history	This command displays what was entered during the previous Spark shell session as well as the current session. It is useful for copying purposes.
:load	This command loads and executes the code in the provided file. This is particular useful when the data processing gets a bit long. It is a bit easier to keep track of the logic and what's going in a file than in the shell.
:reset	After experimenting with the various Scala or Spark APIs for a while, you may lose track of the value of various variables. This command resets the shell to a clean state to make it easy to reason about.

(*continued*)

Table 2-2. (*continued*)

Name	Description
:silent	This is for an advanced user who is a bit tired at looking at the output of each Scala or Spark API that was entered in the shell. The command will stop the shell from displaying the default output after evaluating an expression. To re-enable the output, simply type :silent again.
:quit	This is a pretty self-explanatory command but useful to know. Oftentimes, people try to quit the shell by entering :exit, which doesn't work.
:type	This command displays the type of a variable, for example, :type <variable name>.

In addition to these commands, a helpful feature for improving developer productivity is the code completion feature. Similar to popular integrated development environments (IDEs) like Eclipse or IntelliJ, the code completion feature helps developers by exploring the possible options and reducing typing errors.

Inside the shell, type spa and then hit the Tab key. The environment will add characters to transform spa to spark. In addition, it will show a list of possible matches for *spark*, as shown in Figure 2-5.

```
scala> spa <tab>

                 scala> spark
                 spark    spark_partition_id
```

Figure 2-5. *Tab completion output of spa*

In addition to completing the name of a partially entered word, the tab completion feature can show the available member variables and functions of an object.

Inside the shell, type spark. and then hit the Tab key. This will display a list of available member variable and functions of the Scala object represented by the spark variable, as shown in Figure 2-6.

21

```
scala> spark.
baseRelationToDataFrame     createDataFrame     experimental      range           sql             table
catalog                     createDataset       implicits         read            sqlContext      time
close                       emptyDataFrame      listenerManager   readStream      stop            udf
conf                        emptyDataset        newSession        sparkContext    streams         version
```

Figure 2-6. *List of available member variables and functions of the object called spark*

The command :history displays the previously entered commands or lines of code. This suggests that the Spark shell maintains a record of what was entered. One way to quickly display or recall what was entered recently is by pressing the up arrow key. Once you scroll up to the line you would like to execute, simply just hit Enter to execute it.

Basic Interactions with Scala and Spark

Now that you know how to navigate around the Spark shell, this section will introduce a few fundamental ways of working with Scala and Spark in the Spark shell. This fundamental knowledge will be really helpful in future chapters, which go into much deeper details of topics such as Spark RDDs, Spark SQL, and so on.

Basic Interactions with Scala

Let's start working with Scala in the Spark Scala shell, which provides a full-blown environment for learning Scala. Think of the Spark Scala shell as a Scala application with an empty body, which is where you come in. You fill this empty body with Scala functions and logic for your application. The intention of this section is to demonstrate a few simple Scala examples in the Spark shell. Scala is a fascinating programming language that is powerful, concise, and elegant. (Please refer to Scala-related books to learn more about the Scala programming language.)

Let's begin with some basic Scala. The canonical example for learning any programming language is the "Hello World" example, which entails printing out a message, so let's do that. Enter the following line into the Spark Scala shell; the output should look something like Figure 2-7:

```
scala> println("Hello from Spark Scala shell")
```

```
scala> println("Hello from Spark Scala shell")
Hello from Spark Scala shell

scala>
```

Figure 2-7. *Output of the "Hello World" example*

The next example is to define an array of ages and print those element values in the Spark shell. In addition, this example illustrates the code completion feature that was mentioned in the previous section.

To define an array of ages and assign it to an immutable variable, enter the following into the Spark shell. See Figure 2-8 for the evaluation output.

```
scala> val ages = Array(20, 50, 35, 41)
```

```
scala> val ages = Array(20, 50, 35, 41)
ages: Array[Int] = Array(20, 50, 35, 41)
```

Figure 2-8. *Output of defining an array of ages*

Now you can refer to the variable ages, as in the following line of code. Let's pretend that you can't exactly remember a function name in the Array class that you can use to iterate through the elements in the array, but you know it starts with fo. Then you can just enter the following and hit Tab to see how the Spark shell can help you:

```
scala> ages.fo
```

After you press the Tab key, the Spark shell displays the output shown in Figure 2-9.

```
scala> ages.fo
fold    foldLeft    foldRight    forall    foreach    formatted
```

Figure 2-9. *Output of code completion*

Aha—what you need is the foreach function to iterate through the elements in the array. Let's use it to print the ages.

```
scala> ages.foreach(println)
```

Figure 2-10 shows the expected output.

```
scala> ages.foreach(println)
20
50
35
41
```

Figure 2-10. *Output from printing the ages*

The previous line of code may look a bit cryptic for those who are new to Scala; however, you can intuitively guess what it does. As the function `foreach` iterates through each element in the `ages` array, it passes that element to the `println` function to print the value to the console. You will use this style quite a bit in the coming chapters.

The last example in this section is to define a Scala function to determine whether an age is an odd or even number, and then you will use it to find out what the odd-number ages are in the array.

```
scala> def isOddAge(age:Int) : Boolean = {
  (age % 2) == 1
}
```

If you are coming from a Java programming background, the previous function signature may look a bit strange, but it is not too difficult to decipher what the function does. Notice the function doesn't use the `return` keyword to return the value of the expression in its body. In Scala, it is not necessary to add the `return` keyword. The output of the last statement in a function body will be returned to the caller (if that functions was defined to return a value). See Figure 2-11 for the output from the Spark shell.

```
scala> def isOddAge(age:Int) : Boolean = {
     |     (age % 2) == 1
     | }
isOddAge: (age: Int)Boolean
```

Figure 2-11. *If there is not a syntax error, the Spark shell returns the function signature*

To figure out what the odd-number ages are in the `ages` array, you will leverage the `filter` function in the `Array` class.

```
scala> ages.filter(age => isOddAge(age)).foreach(println)
```

The previous line of code does the filtering and then iterates through the result to print out the odd ages. It is a common practice in Scala to use function chaining to make the code concise. See Figure 2-12 for the output from the Spark shell.

```
scala> ages.filter(age => isOddAge(age)).foreach(println)
35
41
```

Figure 2-12. *Output of filtering and printing only the ages that are odd numbers*

Now let's try the shell command called :type on a Scala variable and function that was defined earlier. This command comes in handy after you have been using the Spark shell for a while and lose track of the data type of a certain variable or the return type of a function. See Figure 2-13 for examples of using the:type command.

```
scala> :type ages
Array[Int]

scala> :type isOddAge(100)
Boolean
```

Figure 2-13. *Output of the :type command*

For the purpose of learning Spark, it is not absolutely necessary to master the Scala programming language. However, you must be comfortable with knowing and working with the basics of Scala. Here is a good resource about learning just enough Scala to learn Spark: https://github.com/deanwampler/JustEnoughScalaForSpark. This resource was presented at various Spark-related conferences.

Spark UI and Basic Interactions with Spark

In the previous section, I mentioned the Spark shell is a Scala application. That is only partially true. The Spark shell is actually a Spark application written in Scala. When the Spark shell is started, a few things are initialized and set up for you to use, including Spark UI and a few important variables.

Spark UI

If you carefully examine the Spark shell output in either Figure 2-2 or Figure 2-3, you will see a line that looks something like the following. The URL may look a bit different for your Spark shell, but the important thing is the URL.

```
Spark context Web UI available at http://192.168.1.73:4042
```

If you point your browser to that URL in your Spark shell, your browser will display something like Figure 2-14.

Figure 2-14. *The Spark UI*

The Spark UI is a web application designed to help with monitoring and debugging Spark applications. It contains detailed runtime information and various resource consumptions of a Spark application. The runtime includes various metrics that are tremendously helpful in diagnosing performance issues in your Spark applications. One thing to note is that the Spark UI is available only while a Spark application is running.

The navigation bar at the top of the Spark UI contains links to the various tabs including jobs, stages, storage, environment, executors, and SQL. For now, I will briefly cover the Environment and Executors tabs and will describe the remaining tabs in later chapters.

The Environment tab contains the basic information about the environment that a Spark application is running in. The sections are Runtime Information, Spark Properties, System Properties, and Classpath Entries. Table 2-3 provides some details about each of these areas.

Table 2-3. *Information About the Various Sections Inside the Environment Tab*

Name	Description
Runtime Information	This section contains the locations and versions of the various components that Spark depends on, including Java and Scala.
Spark Properties	This area contains the basic and advanced properties that are configured in a Spark application. The basic properties include the basic information about an application such as application ID, name, etc. The advanced properties are meant to turn on or off certain features of Spark or to tweak them in certain ways that are best for a particular application. See `https://spark.apache.org/docs/latest/configuration.html` for a comprehensive list of configurable properties.
System Properties	These properties are mainly at the OS and Java level and are not Spark specific.
Classpath Entries	This area contains a list of classpaths and JAR files that are used in a Spark application.

The Executors tab contains the summary and breakdown information for each of the executors that is supporting a Spark application. This information includes the capacity of certain resources as well as how much is being used in each executor. The resources include memory, disk, CPU, and so on. The Summary section provides a bird's-eye view of the resource consumption across all the executors in a Spark application. See Figure 2-15 for more details.

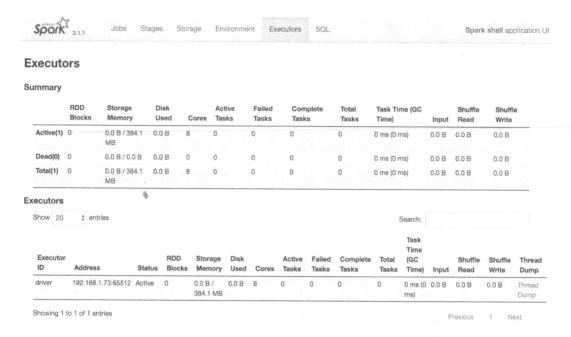

Figure 2-15. *Executors tab of a Spark application that uses only a single executor*

Basic Interactions with Spark

Once a Spark shell is successfully started, a notable variable called `spark` is initialized and ready to be used in the Spark shell. This `spark` variable is an instance of a class called `SparkSession`. Let's use the `:type` command to verify this.

```
scala>:type spark
```

The Spark shell displays its type, as shown in Figure 2-16.

```
[scala> :type spark
org.apache.spark.sql.SparkSession
```

Figure 2-16. *Showing the type of the spark variable*

The SparkSession class was introduced in Spark 2.0 to provide a single point of entry to interact with underlying Spark functionalities. This class has APIs for reading data from an unstructured text file as well as structured and binary data in various formats including JSON, CSV, Parquet, ORC, and so on. In addition, SparkSession provides a facility for retrieving and setting Spark-related configurations.

Let's start interacting with the spark variable in the Spark shell to print out a few useful pieces of information, such as the version and existing configurations. From the Spark shell, type the following code to print the Spark version (see Figure 2-17 for the output):

```
scala> spark.version
```

```
scala> spark.version
res1: String = 2.1.1
```

Figure 2-17. *Spark version output*

To be a little more formal, you can use the println function that you learned in the previous section to print out the Spark version, as shown in Figure 2-18.

```
scala> println("Spark version:" + spark.version)
```

```
scala> println("Spark version: " + spark.version)
Spark version: 2.1.1
```

Figure 2-18. *Displaying the Spark version using the println function*

To see the default configuration that was configured in the Spark shell, you access the conf variable of spark. Here is the code to display the default configuration in the Spark shell (the output is shown in Figure 2-19):

```
scala> spark.conf.getAll.foreach(println)
```

```
scala> spark.conf.getAll.foreach(println)
(spark.driver.host,192.168.1.73)
(spark.driver.port,54812)
(hive.metastore.warehouse.dir,file:/Users/spark-user/spark-2.1.1-bin-hadoop2.7/spark-warehouse)
(spark.repl.class.uri,spark://192.168.1.73:54812/classes)
(spark.jars,)
(spark.repl.class.outputDir,/private/var/folders/h1/9msx26wd1lj_hgcn5l5xpnxr0003g5/T/spark-e617f983-7c43-
53040/repl-25e6f76e-add5-47bd-bc5a-c19803ff64bf)
(spark.app.name,Spark shell)
(spark.executor.id,driver)
(spark.submit.deployMode,client)
(spark.master,local[*])
(spark.home,/Users/spark-user/spark-2.1.1-bin-hadoop2.7)
(spark.sql.catalogImplementation,hive)
(spark.app.id,local-1496548726845)
```

Figure 2-19. *Default configuration in the Spark shell application*

To see the complete set of available objects you can access from spark, you can leverage the Spark shell code completion features.

```
scala> spark.<tab>
```

Figure 2-20 contains the result of the previous command.

```
scala> spark.
!=                      catalog         ensuring      implicits        range          streams        wait
##                      close           eq            isInstanceOf     read           synchronized   →
+                       conf            equals        listenerManager  readStream     table
->                      createDataFrame experimental  ne               sparkContext   time
==                      createDataset   formatted     newSession       sql            toString
asInstanceOf            emptyDataFrame  getClass      notify           sqlContext     udf
baseRelationToDataFrame emptyDataset    hashCode      notifyAll        stop           version
```

Figure 2-20. *A complete list of variables that can be accessed from the spark variable*

Future chapters will have more examples of using spark to interact with the underlying Spark functionalities.

Introduction to Databricks

Databricks is a commercial product that is offered by a company called Databricks, which is the main driving force behind Apache Spark. According to its product documentation, Databricks is a just-in-time data platform that runs in the cloud and is fully managed. The main goal of this platform is to make big data simple and empower anyone to easily build and deploy advanced analytics solutions. It is built around Apache Spark and provides four main value propositions to customers around the world. See Figure 2-21 for more details.

- Fully managed Spark clusters

- An interactive workspace for exploration and visualization

- A production pipeline scheduler

- A platform for powering your favorite Spark-based applications

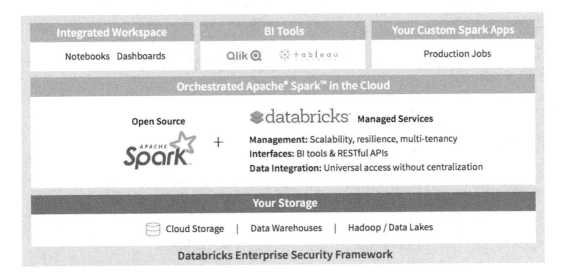

Figure 2-21. *Databricks platform*

The Databricks product has two versions, the full platform and the community edition. The full platform is a paid product for companies to leverage all the advanced features in the Databricks product. The community edition is free and ideal for those who want to try Databricks and to learn Apache Spark.

The following section will cover the basic features of the Databricks community edition so you can use Databricks to learn Apache Spark. Once you are familiar with Databricks, you will find it easy and intuitive to learn Spark, to perform data analysis, or to build Spark applications. This section is not intended to be a comprehensive guide about the Databricks product. All future examples will be done in a Spark shell. For a comprehensive guide about DataBricks, please refer to `https://docs.databricks.com/user-guide/index.html`.

The first step to use Databricks is to sign up for a free account on the Databricks community edition at `https://accounts.cloud.databricks.com/registration.html#signup/community`. This process is pretty simple and quick, and an account can be created in a matter of minutes. Once the necessary information is provided and submitted in the sign-up form, you will receive an email from Databricks to confirm your email, which looks something like Figure 2-22.

Welcome to Databricks Community Edition!

Databricks Community Edition provides you with access to a free micro-cluster as well as a cluster manager and a notebook environment - ideal for developers, data scientists, data engineers and other IT professionals to get started with Spark.

We need you to verify your email address by clicking on this link. You will then be redirected to Databricks Community Edition!

Get started by visiting: https://accounts.cloud.databricks.com/signup/validate?emailToken= 8bd0dc3b61aef61054250663a000478b&ce=true

If you have any questions, please contact feedback@databricks.com.

- The Databricks Team

Figure 2-22. *Databricks email to confirm your email address*

By clicking the link in the previous email, you will be taken to the Databricks sign-in form, as shown in Figure 2-23.

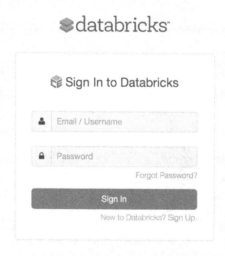

Figure 2-23. *Databricks sign-in page*

After a successful sign-in using the email and password that you provided during the sign-up step, you will see the Databricks welcome page, as shown in Figure 2-24.

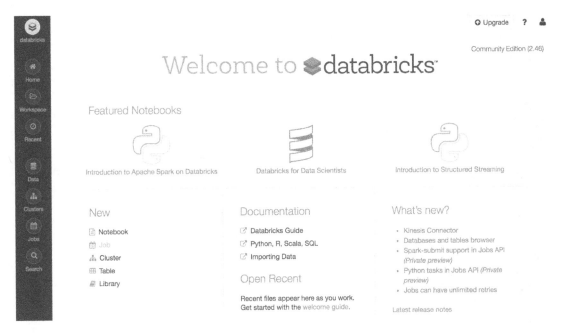

Figure 2-24. *Databricks welcome page*

Over time, the welcome page may evolve, so it may not look exactly like Figure 2-24. Feel free to explore by going into those featured notebooks at the top.

The goal of this section is to create a notebook in Databricks so you can learn the commands that were covered in the previous section. To this, you need to do the following:

1.   Create a cluster.

2.   Create a folder.

3.   Create a notebook.

Creating a Cluster

One of the coolest features of the Databricks community edition (CE) is that it provides a single-node Spark cluster with 6GB of memory for free. At the time of writing this book, this single-node cluster is hosted on the AWS cloud. Each Databricks CE account can

33

create only one cluster at a time. A cluster will continue to stay up as long as it is being used. Databricks will automatically shut it down if it is idle for a certain amount of time (two hours). This means you can either shut down the cluster yourself or let Databricks do it on your behalf.

To create a cluster, click the Clusters icon in the vertical navigation bar on the left side of the page. The Clusters page looks like Figure 2-25.

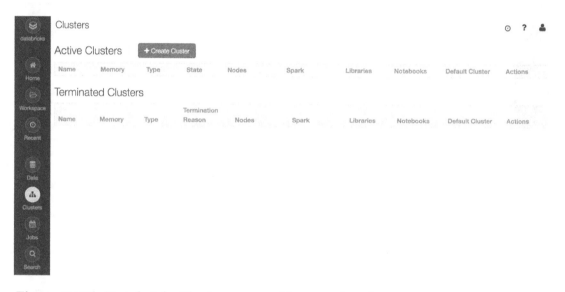

Figure 2-25. *Databricks Clusters page with no active clusters*

Now click the Create Cluster button to bring up the New Cluster form, as shown in Figure 2-26.

Figure 2-26. *Create Cluster form*

The only required field on this form is the cluster name. Table 2-4 briefly describes all the fields.

Table 2-4. *Fields on the Databricks New Cluster Form*

Name	Description
Cluster Name	This is a unique name to identify your cluster. The name can have a space between each word. For example, it can be named "my spark cluster."
Databricks Runtime Version	Databricks supports many versions of Spark. For learning purposes, select the latest version, which was automatically filled in for you. Each version is tied to a specific AWS image.
Instance	For the CE edition, no other choices are available.
AWS – Availability Zone	This allows you to decide which AWS availability zone your single-node cluster will run in. The options may look different based on your location.
Spark – Spark Config	This allows you to specify any application-specific configurations that should be included to launch the Spark cluster. Examples of this include JVM configurations, the ability to turn on certain Spark features, and so on.

Once the Cluster Name field is filled in, click the Create Cluster button. Depending on the day, it can take from one minute to ten minutes to create your single-node Spark cluster. Once the Spark cluster was successfully created, a green dot appears next to your cluster name, as shown in Figure 2-27.

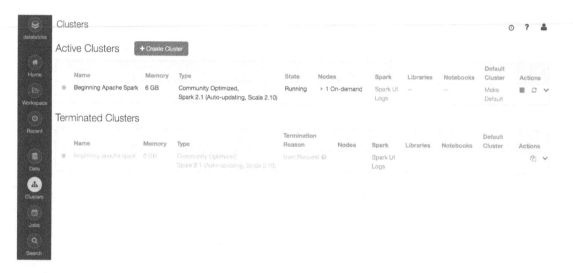

Figure 2-27. *After a cluster is created successfully*

Feel free to explore by clicking the name of your cluster or various links on this page. Notice if you try to create another Spark cluster by following the previous steps, Databricks will not allow you to do so while there is already a running cluster.

To stop an active Spark cluster, click the square in the Actions column.

For more information on creating and managing Spark clusters on Databricks, see `https://docs.databricks.com/user-guide/clusters/index.html`.

Let's move on to the next step, which is to create a folder.

Creating a Folder

Before going into how to create folder, it is worth taking a moment to describe the workspace concept in Databricks. The easiest way to think about a workspace is to treat it as the root folder on your computer, which means you can put files there or create folders to help you organize your files in a specific manner.

To create a folder, click the Workspace icon in the vertical navigation bar on the left side of the page. The Workspace column will slide out, as shown in Figure 2-28.

Figure 2-28. *Workspace column*

Now click the downward arrow in the upper right of the Workspace column, and a cascading drop-down menu will appear, as shown in Figure 2-29.

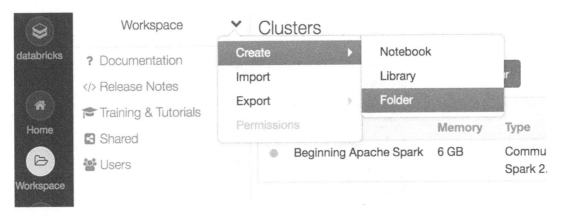

Figure 2-29. *Menu item for creating a folder*

Selecting the Folder menu item will bring up the New Folder Name dialog box, as shown in Figure 2-30.

Figure 2-30. *New Folder Name dialog box*

Now you can enter a folder name, such as **Chapter 2**, and click the Create Folder button to complete the process. The Chapter 2 folder should now appear in the Workspace column, as shown in Figure 2-31.

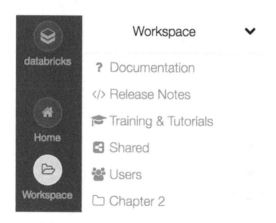

Figure 2-31. *Chapter 2 folder appears in the Workspace column*

Before moving on to create a notebook, it is worth mentioning there is an alternative way to create a folder, which is by placing the mouse pointer anywhere in the Workspace column and right-clicking; then the same menu options will appear.

For more details on using workspaces and creating folders, please check out https://docs.databricks.com/user-guide/workspace.html.

Creating a Notebook

Next you want to create a Scala notebook in the Chapter 2 folder. First select the Chapter 2 folder in the Workspace column. The Chapter 2 column slides out after the Workspace column, and it looks something like Figure 2-32.

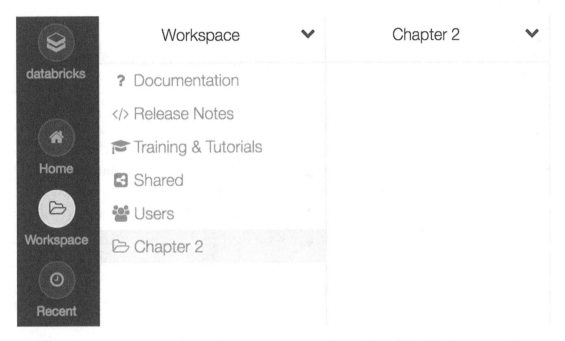

Figure 2-32. *The Chapter 2 column appears to the right of the Workspace column*

Now you can either click the downward arrow in the upper-right corner of the Chapter 2 column or right-click anywhere in the Chapter 2 column to bring up the menu, as shown in Figure 2-33.

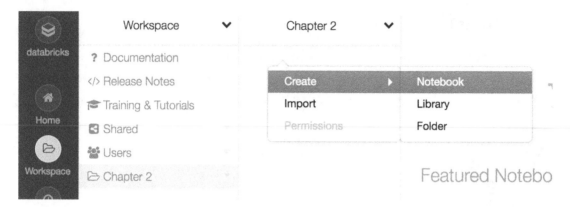

Figure 2-33. *Creating a notebook menu item*

Selecting the Notebook menu item will bring up the Create Notebook dialog box. Give your notebook a name and make sure to select the Scala option for the Language field. The value for the cluster should be filled in automatically because the Databricks CE edition can have only one cluster a time. Your dialog box should look something like Figure 2-34.

Create Notebook

Name	Scala and Spark Interactions
Language	Scala
Cluster	Beginning Apache Spark (6 GB, R)

Cancel   Create

Figure 2-34. *Create Notebook dialog box with the Scala language option selected*

Once the Create button is clicked, a new notebook is created, as shown in Figure 2-35.

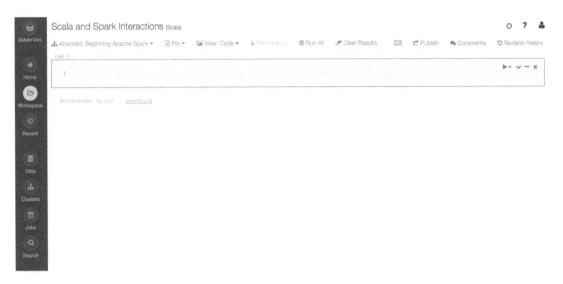

Figure 2-35. *New Scala notebook*

If you have never worked with IPython Notebook, the notebook concept may seem a bit strange at first. However, once you get used to it, you will love it.

A *notebook* is essentially an interactive computational environment (similar to the Spark shell but way better) in which you can execute Spark code, document your code with rich text using Markdown or HTML, and visualize the result of your data analysis with various types of charts and graphs.

The following section will cover only a few essential instructions to help you be productive at using Spark notebooks. For a comprehensive list of instructions on how to use and interact with Databricks notebooks, please see `https://docs.databricks.com/user-guide/notebooks/index.html`.

A Spark notebook contains a collection of cells, where each one contains a block of code either to execute or to mark up for documentation purposes.

> **Note**   A good practice of using a Spark notebook is to break your data processing logic into multiple logical groups so each group resides in one or more cells. This is similar to the practice of developing maintainable software applications.

You are going to divide your notebook into two parts. The first part will contain the code snippets you typed in the earlier "Basic Interactions with Scala" section, and the second part will contain the code snippets you typed in the earlier "Basic Interactions with Spark" section.

Let's start with adding a markdown statement into the first cell of the notebook by enter the following (see Figure 2-36):

```
%md #### Basic Interactions with Scala
```

Figure 2-36.   *Cell containing section header markup statement*

To execute that markup statement, first make sure the mouse cursor is in cell 1 and then hold down the Shift key and hit the Enter key. That is the shortcut for running code or markup statements in a cell. The result should look like Figure 2-37.

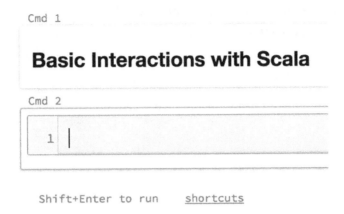

Figure 2-37. *The output of executing a markup statement in a cell*

Notice the Shift+Enter key combination not only executed what's in that cell but also created a new cell below it. Now let's type the "Hello World" example from earlier into the second cell and execute that cell. The output should look like Figure 2-38.

```
Cmd 1
```

Basic Interactions with Scala

```
Cmd 2

    1   println("Hello from Spark Scala shell")

Hello from Spark Scala shell
    Command took 0.10 seconds -- by hienluu@gmail.com at 6/4/2017, 10:01:19 AM on Beginning Apache Spark

Cmd 3

    1
```

Figure 2-38. *Output of executing the println statement*

Copy the remaining three code statements in the "Interactions with Scala" section into the notebook, as shown in Figure 2-39.

```
Cmd 3

1  val ages = Array(20, 50, 35, 41)
2  ages.foreach(println)

20
50
35
41
ages: Array[Int] = Array(20, 50, 35, 41)
Command took 0.81 seconds -- by hienluu@gmail.com at 6/4/2017, 10:04:57 AM on Beginning Apache Spark
```

```
Cmd 4

1  def isOddAge(age:Int) : Boolean = {
2    (age % 2) == 1
3  }

isOddAge: (age: Int)Boolean
Command took 0.13 seconds -- by hienluu@gmail.com at 6/4/2017, 10:05:41 AM on Beginning Apache Spark
```

```
Cmd 5

1  ages.filter(age => isOddAge(age)).foreach(println)

35
41
Command took 0.34 seconds -- by hienluu@gmail.com at 6/4/2017, 10:05:50 AM on Beginning Apache Spark
```

Figure 2-39. *The remaining code statements from the "Interactions with Scala" section*

Just like the Spark Scala shell, a Scala notebook is a full-blown Scala interactive environment where you can execute Scala code.

Now let's enter the second markup statement to denote the beginning of the second part of the notebook and then paste the remaining code snippets from the "Interactions with Spark" section. See Figure 2-40 for the output.

```
%md #### Basic Interactions with Spark
```

Figure 2-40. *Output of the code snippets from the "Interactions with Spark" section*

There are a few important notes to know when working with a Spark notebook. One of the convenient features in a Spark notebook is autosaving. The content of the notebook is automatically saved as you enter market statements or code snippets. In fact, the available menu items under the File menu item don't even have an option for saving a notebook.

Sometimes there is a need to create a new cell between two existing cells. One way to do this is to move the mouse cursor to the space between two existing cells; then click the plus icon that appears to create a new cell. See Figure 2-41 to see what the plus icon looks like.

```
Cmd 8

1   println("Spark version: " + spark.version)

Spark version: 2.1.1
Command took 0.09 seconds -- by hienluu@gmail.com at 6/4/2017, 10:34:48 AM on Beginning Apache Spark

Cmd 9                                                             (+)

1   spark.conf.getAll.foreach(println)
```

Figure 2-41. *Using a plus icon to insert a new cell between two existing cells*

Sometimes you will want to share your notebook with a co-worker who works in a remote office or with other collaborators to either show off your awesome Spark knowledge or get their feedback on your analysis of certain datasets. Databricks makes it easy to do that. Simply click the File menu item at the top of your Spark notebook and select the Publish submenu item, as shown in Figure 2-42.

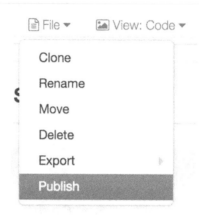

Figure 2-42. *Notebook publishing menu item*

Clicking the Publish submenu item will bring up the confirmation dialog box (Figure 2-43), and if you follow through with it, then the Notebook Published dialog box (Figure 2-44) provides a URL that you can send to anyone in the world. With that URL, your co-worker or collaborators will have access to the read-only view of your book plus the options of importing it into their Databricks accounts.

Publish Notebook

Do you want to publish this notebook publicly? This action will overwrite any previously-published version of this notebook. Anyone with the link can view it and link will remain valid for 6 months.

☐ Don't show me this again

Cancel   Publish

Figure 2-43. *Publishing confirmation dialog box*

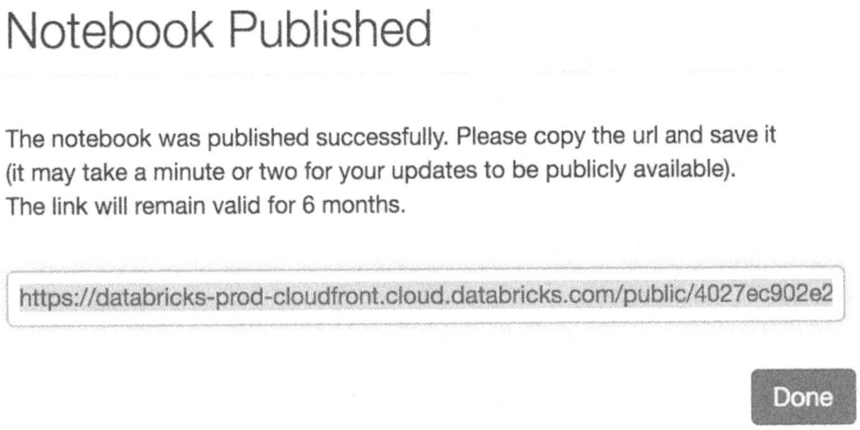

Notebook Published

The notebook was published successfully. Please copy the url and save it
(it may take a minute or two for your updates to be publicly available).
The link will remain valid for 6 months.

https://databricks-prod-cloudfront.cloud.databricks.com/public/4027ec902e2

Done

Figure 2-44. *Notebook published URL*

This section covered only the essential parts of using Databricks. There are other advanced features that make it really enticing to use Databricks as the platform of choice for performing interactive data analysis or building advanced data solutions.

The Databricks CE has made it much easier than ever before to learn Spark. I highly recommend giving Databricks a try in your journey of learning Spark.

Setting Up the Spark Source Code

This section is geared toward software developers or anyone who is interested in learning how Spark works at the code level. Since Apache Spark is an open source project, its source code is public and available for you to download, examine, and study how certain features were implemented. The Spark code was written in Scala by some of the smartest Scala programmers on the planet, so examining the Spark code is another way of improving your Scala programming skills and knowledge.

There are two ways to download the Apache Spark source code to your computer. The first way is to download it from the Spark download page (http://spark.apache.org/downloads.html), which is the same page you used earlier to download the Spark binary file. This time choose the Source Code package type, as shown in Figure 2-45.

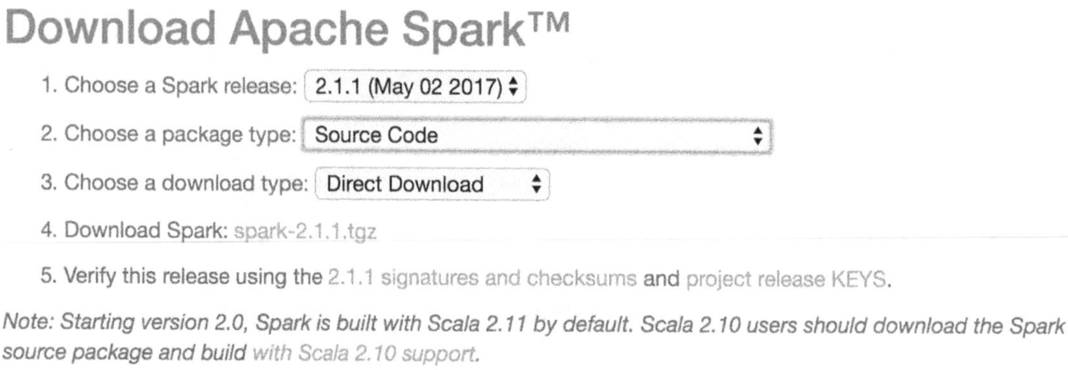

Download Apache Spark™

1. Choose a Spark release: `2.1.1 (May 02 2017) ⬍`

2. Choose a package type: `Source Code                               ⬍`

3. Choose a download type: `Direct Download   ⬍`

4. Download Spark: spark-2.1.1.tgz

5. Verify this release using the 2.1.1 signatures and checksums and project release KEYS.

Note: Starting version 2.0, Spark is built with Scala 2.11 by default. Scala 2.10 users should download the Spark source package and build with Scala 2.10 support.

Figure 2-45. *Apache Spark source download option*

To complete the source code download process, click the link on line 4 to download the compressed source code file. The final step is to uncompress that file into your choice of directory.

The second way to download the Apache Spark source code is to use the `git clone` command. This requires an installation of `git` on your computer. You can download `git` from `https://git-scm.com/downloads`; the installation instructions are available at `https://git-scm.com/book/en/v2/Getting-Started-Installing-Git`. Once `git` is properly installed on your computer, issue the following command to clone the Apache Spark `git` repository on GitHub (`https://github.com/apache/spark`):

```
git clone git://github.com/apache/spark.git
```

There are roughly about 2,600 Scala files in Spark, so it will take a minute or two to download all those files.

Once the Apache Spark source code is downloaded on your computer, check `http://spark.apache.org/developer-tools.html` for the details about how to import them into your favorite IDE.

Summary

In this chapter, you learned the following:

- There are a few tools to use to learn Spark. You can either use the locally installed Spark or use a Databricks CE account. These tools make it easy for anyone to learn Spark.

- The Spark shell is a powerful and interactive environment to learn Spark or to analyze data interactively. There are two types of Spark shell: the Spark Scala shell and the Spark Python shell.

- The Spark shell provides a set of commands to help its users become productive.

- Databricks is a fully managed data platform designed to make big data simple and to empower anyone to easily build and deploy advanced analytics solutions. The interactive workspace helps you organize notebooks into folders. Each notebook contains a combination of markup statements and Spark code snippets. Sharing a notebook with others requires only a few mouse clicks.

- For software developers who are really interested in learning about the internals of Spark, downloading and examining the Apache Spark source code is a great way to satisfy that curiosity.

CHAPTER 3

Resilient Distributed Datasets

This chapter covers the oldest foundational concept in Spark called *resilient distributed datasets* (RDDs). To truly understand how Spark works, you must understand the essence of RDDs. They provide an extremely solid foundation that other abstractions are built upon. The ideas behind RDDs are pretty unique in the distributed data processing framework landscape, and they were introduced in a timely manner to solve the pressing needs of dealing with the complexity and efficiency of iterative and interactive data processing use cases. Starting with Spark 2.0, Spark users will have fewer needs for directly interacting with RDD, but having a strong mental model of how RDD works is essential. In a nutshell, Spark revolves around the concept of RDDs.

Introduction to RDDs

RDDs represent both the idea of how a large dataset is represented in Spark and the abstraction for working with it. This section will cover the former part, and the following sections will cover the latter part.

According to the seminal paper on Spark,[1] RDDs are immutable, fault-tolerant, parallel data structures that let users explicitly persist intermediate results in memory, control their partitioning to optimize data placement, and manipulate them using a rich set of operators. Let's dissect this description to truly understand the ideas behind the RDD concept.

---

[1]"Resilient Distributed Datasets: A Fault-Tolerant Abstraction for In-Memory Cluster Computing"

© Hien Luu 2018
H. Luu, *Beginning Apache Spark 2*, https://doi.org/10.1007/978-1-4842-3579-9_3

Immutable

RDDs are designed to be immutable, which means you can't specifically modify a particular row in the dataset represented by that RDD. You can call one of the available RDD operations to manipulate the rows in the RDD into the way you want, but that operation will return a new RDD. The basic RDD will stay unchanged, and the new RDD will contain the data in the way that you want. The immutability of RDDs essentially requires an RDD to carry its lineage information that Spark leverages to efficiently provide the fault tolerance capability.

Fault Tolerant

The ability to process multiple datasets in parallel usually requires a cluster of machines to host and execute the computational logic. If one or more of those machines dies or becomes extremely slow because of unexpected circumstances, then how will that affect the overall data processing of those datasets? The good news is that Spark automatically takes care of handling the failure on behalf of its users by rebuilding the failed portion using the lineage information, which will be discussed later in this chapter.

Parallel Data Structures

Imagine the use case where someone gives you a large log file that is 1TB size and you are asked to find out how many log statements contain the word *exception* in it. A slow solution would be to iterate through that log file from the beginning to the end and execute the logic of determining whether a particular log statement contains the word *exception*. A faster solution would be to divide that 1TB file into several chunks and execute the aforementioned logic on each chunk in a parallelized manner to speed up the overall processing time. Each chunk contains a collection of rows.

The collection of rows is essentially the data structure that holds a set of rows and provides the ability to iterate through each row. Each chunk contains a collection of rows, and all the chunks are being processed in parallel. This is where the phrase *parallel data structures* comes from.

In-Memory Computing

The idea of speeding up the computation of large datasets that reside on disks in a parallelized manner using a cluster of machines was introduced by a MapReduce paper[2] from Google. This idea was implemented and is made available in the Hadoop open source project. Building on that solid foundation, RDD pushes the speed boundary by introducing a novel idea, which is the ability to do distributed in-memory computation.

It is always fascinating to examine the stories that led up the creation of an innovative idea. In the world of big data processing, once you are able to extract insights from large datasets in a reliable manner using a set of rudimentary techniques, then you want to use more sophisticated techniques as well to reduce the amount of time it takes to do that. This is where distributed in-memory computation helps. The sophisticated technique I am referring to is using machine learning to perform various predictions or to extract patterns out of large datasets. Machine learning algorithms are iterative in nature, meaning they need to go through many iterations to arrive at an optimal state. This is where distributed in-memory computation can help in reducing the completion time from days to hours. Another use case that can hugely benefit from distributed in-memory computation is interactive data mining, where multiple ad hoc queries are performed on the same subset of data. If that subset of data is persisted in memory, those queries will take seconds and not minutes to complete.

Data Partitioning and Placement

The information about how the rows in a dataset are partitioned into chunks and about their physical location is considered to be the dataset metadata. This information helps Spark perform optimizations while executing the computational logic.

For example, while joining two datasets, the data partition information is useful to determine whether it is necessary to move the rows from various chunks of the two datasets to the same location to perform the join. Moving data across machines is an expensive operation, and therefore minimizing it would dramatically reduce the overall processing time.

Data placement information helps to reinforce the data locality concept, which means bringing the computation to where the data lives. Knowing where the chunks

---

[2]"MapReduce: Simplified Data Processing on Large Clusters". https://static. googleusercontent.com/media/research.google.com/en//archive/mapreduce-osdi04.pdf

are located on a cluster, Spark can use those machines to host and execute the computational logic on those chunks, and therefore the time to read the rows from those chunks would be much less than reading them from a different node on the cluster.

Rich Set of Operations

RDDs provide a rich set of commonly needed data processing operations. They include the ability to perform data transformation, filtering, grouping, joining, aggregation, sorting, and counting. These operations will be covered in more detail in the second half of this chapter.

One thing to note about these operations is that they operate at the coarse-grained level, meaning the same operation is applied to many rows, not to any specific row.

In summary, an RDD is represented as an abstraction and is defined by the following five pieces of information:

- A set of partitions, which are the chunks that make up the entire dataset

- A set of dependencies on parent RDDs

- A function for computing all the rows in the data set

- Metadata about the partitioning scheme (optional)

- Where the data lives on the cluster (optional); if the data lives on HDFS, then it would be where the block locations are located

The Spark runtime uses these five pieces of information to schedule and execute the user data processing logic that is expressed via the RDD operations, which are described in the following section.

The first three pieces of information make up the lineage information, which Spark uses for two purposes. The first one is determining the order of execution of RDDs, and the second one is for failure recovery purposes.

RDD Operations

This section will go into detail about the commonly used RDD operations and their behavior. Before going into the details, it is imperative to internalize a few core concepts about them.

The RDD operations operate at a coarse-grained level, which was described earlier. Each row in a dataset is represented as a Java object, and the structure of this Java object is opaque to Spark. The user of RDD has complete control over how to manipulate this

Java object. This flexibility comes with a lot of responsibilities, meaning some of the commonly needed operations such as the computing average will have to be hand-crafted. Higher-level abstractions such as the Spark SQL component will provide this functionality out of the box.

The RDD operations are classified into two types: transformations and actions. Table 3-1 describes the main differences between them.

Table 3-1. *Main Differences Between Transformations and Actions*

Type	Evaluation	Returned Value
Transformation	Lazy	Another RDD
Action	Eager	Some result or write result to disk

Transformation operations are lazily evaluated, meaning Spark will delay the evaluations of the invoked operations until an action is taken. In other words, the transformation operations merely record the specified transformation logic and will apply them at a later point. On the other hand, invoking an action operation will trigger the evaluation of all the transformations that preceded it, and it will either return some result to the driver or write data to a storage system, such as HDFS or the local file system.

The lazy evaluation design makes sense in the world of big data. It is not desirable to immediately trigger an evaluation of every single filtering operation when a dataset is large in size. The typical end goal of a data processing task is to write the result out to some external storage system or to see how many records there are. This is when it makes sense to evaluate all the previously specified computational logic. One important optimization technique behind the lazy evaluation concept is the ability to collapse or combine similar transformations into a single operation during execution time.

In short, RDDs are immutable, RDD transformations are lazily evaluated, and RDD actions are eagerly evaluated and trigger the computation of your data processing logic.

Creating RDDs

Before invoking any transformation or action operations, you must have an RDD in hand. There are three ways to create an RDD.

The first way to create an RDD is to parallelize an object collection, meaning converting it to a distributed dataset that can be operated in parallel. This is a great way to get started in learning Spark because it is simple and doesn't require any data files. This approach is often used to quickly try a feature or do some experimenting in Spark. The way to parallelize an object collection is to call the `parallelize` method of the SparkContext class. See Listing 3-1 for an example.

Listing 3-1. Creating an RDD from an Object Collection

```
val stringList = Array("Spark is awesome","Spark is cool")
val stringRDD = spark.sparkContext.parallelize(stringList)
```

The `stringRDD` variable represents an RDD that you can apply transformation or action operations to.

The second way to create an RDD is to read a dataset from a storage system, which can be a local computer file system, HDFS, Cassandra, Amazon S3, and so on. Listing 3-2 shows an example of reading a text file called `data.txt` from the local computer file system in the `/tmp` directory.

Listing 3-2. Creating an RDD from a File Data Source

```
val fileRDD = spark.sparkContext.textFile("/tmp/data.txt")
```

The first argument of the `textFile` method is an URI that points to a path or a file on the local machine or to a remote storage system. When it starts with an `hdfs://` prefix, it points to a path or a file that resides on HDFS, and when it starts with an `s3n://` prefix, then it points to a path or a file that resides on AWS S3. If a URI points to a directory, then the `textFile` method will read all the files in that directory.

The `textFile` method assumes each file is a text file and each line is delimited by a new line. The `textFile` method returns an RDD that represents all the lines in all the files. One important to note for Spark beginners is that the `textFile` method is lazily evaluated, which means if you made the mistake of specifying a wrong file or path or misspelling a directory name, then this problem would not surface until one of the actions is taken.

The third way to create an RDD is by invoking one of the transformation operations on an existing RDD. Once you start becoming competent with Spark, you will do this all the time without thinking twice about it.

Transformations

Table 3-2 describes commonly used transformations. For a complete list of transformations, refer to the RDD API documentation at `https://spark.apache.org/docs/latest/api/scala/index.html#org.apache.spark.rdd`. Remember, these transformations operate on the dataset being associated with an RDD instance and return a new RDD.

By going through the following examples, ideally you get a sense of how easy it is to manipulate small and large datasets using the functional APIs provided by RDD.

Table 3-2. *Common Transformations*

Name	Description
map(func)	This applies the provided function to each row as iterating through the rows in the dataset. The returned RDD will contain whatever the provided func returns.
flatMap(func)	Similar to map(func), the func should return a collection rather than a single element, and this method will flatten out the returned collection. This allows an input item to map to zero or more output items.
filter(func)	Only the elements that the func function returns true will be collected in the returned RDD. In other words, collect only the rows that meet the condition defined in the given func function.
mapPartitions(func)	Similar to map(func), but this applies at the partition (chunk) level. This requires the func function to take the input as an iterator to iterate through each row in the partition.

(*continued*)

Table 3-2. (*continued*)

Name	Description
mapParitionsWithIndex(func)	This is similar to mapPartitions, but an additional partition index number is provided to the func function.
union(otherRDD)	This transformation does what it sounds like. It combines the rows in the source RDD with otherRDD.
intersection(otherRDD)	Only the rows that exist in both the source RDD and otherRDD are returned.
substract(otherRDD)	This subtracts the rows in otherRDD from the source RDD.
distinct([numTasks])	This removes duplicate rows from the source RDD.
sample(withReplace, fraction, seed)	This is usually used to reduce a large dataset to a smaller one by randomly selecting a fraction of rows using the given seed and with or without replacements.

Note   The func argument in each of the transformations listed in Table 3-2 represents either an anonymous function or a fully defined function definition.

Transformation Examples

The following examples build on the stringRDD created in the "Creating RDDs" section.

map(func)

The most fundamental, versatile, and commonly used transformation is the map operation. It is used to transform some aspect of the data per row to something else. Listing 3-3 shows a simple example to convert each line to uppercase.

Listing 3-3. Using a Map Transformation to Convert All Characters in the String to Uppercase

```
val allCapsRDD = stringRDD.map(line => line.toUpperCase)
allCapsRDD.collect().foreach(println)
```

The second statement will collect all the rows in `allCapsRDD` and transfer them to the driver side, then they will be printed out one per line. Listing 3-4 displays the output.

Listing 3-4. Output After the Converting All the Strings to Uppercase

```
SPARK IS COOL
SPARK IS AWESOME
```

Sometimes the transformation logic is complex and requires calling other APIs. In that case, it is best to define a function to encapsulate that complexity. See Listing 3-5 for an example of defining a function and using it in the map transformation.

Listing 3-5. Defining a Function and Using It in the Map Transformation

```
def toUpperCase(line:String) : String = {  line.toUpperCase }
stringRDD.map(l => toUpperCase(l)).collect.foreach(println)
```

The output of the second line should be identical to the output in Listing 3-4. By abstracting the complex logic in a function, it will be easier to test that logic in an independent manner as well as improve the readability and maintainability of the data processing logic.

Another common usage of the map transformation is to convert data in text format to a Scala object via a case class. The will improve the readability and maintainability of the data processing logic because the logic can refer to the actual parameter name. See Listing 3-6 for an example.

Listing 3-6. Using a map Transformation to Convert Text Data into Scala Contact Objects

```
case class Contact(id:Long, name:String, email:String)
val contactData = Array("1#John Doe#jdoe@domain.com","2#Mary
Jane#mjane@domain.com")
val contactDataRDD = spark.sparkContext.parallelize(contactData)
val contactRDD = contactDataRDD.map(l => {
        val contactArray = l.split("#")
        Contact(contactArray(0).toLong, contactArray(1), contactArray(2))
})
contactRDD.collect.foreach(println)
```

The output should look something like Listing 3-7.

Listing 3-7. Output of the Contact Data from Contact Objects

```
Contact(1,John Doe,jdoe@domain.com)
Contact(2,Mary Jane,mjane@domain.com)
```

Note   In the context of data processing in Spark using Scala APIs, the `case` class is often used as a light-weight and immutable data object.

One last note about the `map` transformation is that the input type and the return type of func don't have to be of the same type. To illustrate this behavior, Listing 3-8 uses a map transformation to transform a collection of strings to a collection of integers. The `stringRDD` is `RDD[String]`, and the `stringLenRDD` is `RDD[Int]`.

Listing 3-8. Transforming from a Collection of Strings to a Collection of Integers

```
val stringLenRDD = stringRDD.map(l => l.length)
stringLenRDD.collect.foreach(println)
```

flatMap(func)

The second most commonly used transformation is `flatMap`. Let's say you want to transform the `stringRDD` from a collection of strings to a collection of words. The `flatMap` transformation is perfect for this use case. See Listing 3-9 for an example.

Listing 3-9. Using the flatMap Transformation to Transform Lines into Words

```
val wordRDD = stringRDD.flatMap(line => line.split(" "))
wordRDD.collect().foreach(println)
```

The output will look something like Listing 3-10.

Listing 3-10. Output of the flatMap Transformation Operation

```
Spark
is
awesome
Spark
is
cool
```

It is extremely important to have a clear understanding of the behavior differences between the map and flatMap transformations. See Listing 3-11 for an example and then closely examine the output in Listing 3-12 and Listing 3-13 to see the output differences.

Listing 3-11. The Behavior of map vs. flatMap

```
stringRDD.map(line => line.split(" ")).collect
stringRDD.flatMap(line => line.split(" ")).collect
```

Listing 3-12. The Output of the map Transformation

```
Array[Array[String]] = Array(Array(Spark, is, awesome), Array(Spark, is, cool))
```

Listing 3-13. The Output of the flatMap Transformation

```
Array[String] = Array(Spark, is, awesome, Spark, is, cool)
```

The logic inside both the map and flatMap methods is identical, but their output is very different. When a line of words is split by a space, its output contains an array of words, and that's why there are two arrays in Listing 3-12. flatMap transformation flattens the array, and therefore its output contains only the single array of words.

flatMap is a powerful and useful transformation to know, so make sure to grok it.

filter(func)

Another commonly used transformation is the filter transformation. It does what its name sounds like, which is to filter a dataset down to the rows that meet the conditions defined inside the given func.

A simple example is to find out how many lines in the stringRDD contain the word *awesome*. Another example is to filter a 1TB log file down to only the lines that contain the word *Exception*. See Listing 3-14 for an example.

Listing 3-14. Filtering for Lines That Contain the Word Awesome

```
val awesomeLineRDD = stringRDD.filter(line => line.contains("awesome"))
awesomeLineRDD.collect
```

There should be only one line in the output, as shown in Listing 3-15.

Listing 3-15. Output After the Filtering

```
Array(Spark is awesome)
```

In the simple example, the anonymous function has only one Boolean predicate. The filtering logic can be as complex as it needs to be, just as long as the given func returns a Boolean value.

mapPartitions(func)/mapPartitionsWithIndex(index, func)

Both mapPartitions and mapPartitionsWithIndex are useful transformations for situations where there is a need to perform some expensive and required setups before the transformation of each row starts. Instead of performing this expensive operation per row, you can reduce it to just the number of partitions. An example of an expensive setup could be creating a database connection or creating an HttpClient or JSON parser. In general, the number of partitions in an RDD is way smaller than the number of rows in a dataset; therefore, reducing the number of expensive setup operations to just the number of partitions is preferred. The mapPartition transformation calls the provided func once per partition. If an RDD has ten partitions, then the given func will be called exactly ten times. Each time it is called, the mapPartition transformation passes an iterator to the given func for it to loop through each of the rows in that particular partition.

The method signature of the given func must be func(Iterator[T]) => Iterator[U]), which means it takes an iterator of type T and returns an iterator of type U, where type U and type T don't necessarily have to the same.

One small difference between the mapPartitionWithIndex and mapPartition transformations is that the partition number is available to the former transformation.

In short, the mapPartitions and mapPartitionsWithIndex transformations are used to optimize the performance of your data processing logic by reducing the number of times the expensive setup step is called.

Listing 3-16 first creates an RDD with two partitions and then creates a random generator per partitions before iterating through each row. Finally, as it iterates through the row, it adds a random number to each row in each partition in the RDD. Listing 3-17 shows the output after collecting. Your output maybe different because of the random number generator.

Listing 3-16. Performing a Setup Before Performing a Transformation on Each Row

```
import scala.util.Random
val sampleList = Array("One", "Two", "Three", "Four","Five")
val sampleRDD = spark.sparkContext.parallelize(sampleList, 2)
val result = sampleRDD.mapPartitions((itr:Iterator[String]) => {
              val rand = new Random(System.currentTimeMillis +
              Random.nextInt)
              itr.map(l => l + ":" + rand.nextInt)
          }

result.collect()
```

Listing 3-17. Output After Collecting

```
Array[String] = Array(One : -570064612, Two : -171309453,
Three : -1918855253, Four : 1535308064, Five : 1033042948)
```

If the processing logic inside the mapPartitions and mapPartitionsWitIndex transformations is complex and becoming difficult to read, it is better to abstract that logic into a function. That approach not only improves the readability but makes it easier to test that logic.

See Listing 3-18 for an example of defining a function and how it is used; Listing 3-19 shows the output.

Listing 3-18. Creating a Function to Encapsulate the Logic of Adding Random Numbers to Each Row

```
import scala.util.Random
def addRandomNumber(rows:Iterator[String]) = {
  val rand = new Random(System.currentTimeMillis + Random.nextInt)
  rows.map(l => l + " : " + rand.nextInt)
}
```

You can call the function defined in Listing 3-18 inside the `mapPartitions` transformation.

Listing 3-19. Using the addRandomNumber Function in the mapPartitions Transformation

```
val result = sampleRDD.mapPartitions((rows:Iterator[String]) =>
addRandomNumber(rows))
```

A silly example of using the `mapPartitionsWithIndex` transformation is to see which numbers belong to each partition. See Listing 3-20 for how to do that.

Listing 3-20. Using the mapPartitionsWithIndex Transformation

```
val numberRDD = spark.sparkContext.parallelize(List(1,2,3,4,5,6,7,8,9,10), 2)
numberRDD.mapPartitionsWithIndex((idx:Int, itr:Iterator[Int]) => {
        itr.map(n => (idx, n) )
    }).collect()
```

Listing 3-21 shows the output where each row is a tuple; the first element is the partition number, and the second element is the original integer value.

Listing 3-21. Output of the mapPartitionsWithIndex Transformation

```
Array[(Int, Int)] = Array((0,1), (0,2), (0,3), (0,4), (0,5), (1,6), (1,7),
(1,8), (1,9), (1,10))
```

Based on the output in Listing 3-21, you know that the partition number starts with 0 rather than 1. By rearranging the numbers in the format in Listing 3-21, you can easily determine how many integers each partition has. This knowledge is useful to determine whether it is necessary to repartition the numbers so they are evenly distributed across the partitions. This will help speed up the data processing logic.

The next three transformations belong to a category called *set operations*. They are `union`, `intersection`, and `subtract`.

union(otherRDD)

Unlike previous transformations that take a function as an argument, a union transformation takes another RDD as an argument, and it will return an RDD that combines the rows from both RDDs. This is useful for situations when there is a need to append some rows to an existing RDD. This transformation does not remove duplicate rows of the resulting RDD.

See Listing 3-22 for how to combine rows from two RDDs.

Listing 3-22. Combining Rows from Two RDDs

```
val rdd1 = spark.sparkContext.parallelize(Array(1,2,3,4,5))
val rdd2 = spark.sparkContext.parallelize(Array(1,6,7,8))
val rdd3 = rdd1.union(rdd2)
rdd3.collect()
```

See Listing 3-23 for the output from the union transformation.

Listing 3-23. Output of the union Transformation

```
Array[Int] = Array(1, 2, 3, 4, 5, 1, 6, 7, 8)
```

intersection(otherRDD)

If there were two RDDs and there is a need to find out which rows exist in both of them, then this is the right transformation to use. The way this transformation figures out which rows exist in both RDDs is by comparing their hash codes. This transformation guarantees the returned RDD will not contain any duplicate rows. Unlike the map and filter transformations, the implementation of this transformation moves rows with the same hash code to the same executor to perform the intersection. See Listing 3-24 for an example of using the intersection transformation.

Listing 3-24. Performing an Intersection of Two RDDs

```
val rdd1 = spark.sparkContext.parallelize(Array("One", "Two", "Three"))
val rdd2 = spark.sparkContext.parallelize(Array("two","One","threed","One"))
val rdd3 = rdd1.intersection(rdd2)
rdd3.collect()
```

As expected, the output in Listing 3-25 shows the only value that appears in the output is One.

Listing 3-25. Output of an Intersection Transformation

```
Array[Int] = Array(One)
```

Note   If you are curious about the implementation of the intersection transformation, take a look at that function in the RDD.scala file at https://github.com/apache/spark. You will see that it uses a cogroup with a null value.

---

substract(otherRDD)

A good use case for this transformation is when there is a need to compute the statistics of word usage in a certain book or a set of speeches. A typical first task in this process is to remove the *stop words*, which refers to a set of commonly used words in a language. In the English language, examples of stop words are *is*, *it*, *the*, and *and*. So, if you have one RDD that contains all the words in a book and another RDD that contains just the list of stop words, then subtracting the first one from the second one will yield another RDD that contains only nonstop words. See Listing 3-26 for an example of using the subtract transformation.

Listing 3-26. Removing Stop Words Using the subtract Transformation

```
val words = spark.sparkContext.parallelize(List("The amazing thing about
spark is that it is very simple to learn")).flatMap(l => l.split(" ")).
map(w => w.toLowerCase)

val stopWords = spark.sparkContext.parallelize(List("the it is to that")).
flatMap(l => l.split(" "))
val realWords = words.substract(stopWords)
realWords.collect()
```

The output in Listing 3-27 should not contain any of the stop words.

Listing 3-27. Output of the subtract Transformation

```
Array[String] = Array(simple, learn, amazing, spark, about, very, thing)
```

distinct()

The distinct transformation represents another flavor of transformation where it doesn't take any function or another RDD as an input parameter. Instead, it is a directive to the source RDD to remove any duplicate rows. The question is, how does it determine whether two rows are the same? A common approach is to transpose the content of each row into a numeric value by computing the hash code of the content. That is exactly what Spark does. To remove duplicate rows in an RDD, it simply computes the hash code of each row and compares them to determine whether two rows are identical.

See Listing 3-28 for an example of the distinct transformation.

Listing 3-28. Removing Duplicates Using the distinct Transformation

```
val duplicateValueRDD = spark.sparkContext.parallelize(List("one", 1,
"two", 2, "three", "one", "two", 1, 2)
duplicateValueRDD.distinct().collect
```

As expected, the output contains only unique rows. See Listing 3-29 for the output.

Listing 3-29. Output of the distinct Transformation

```
Array[Any] = Array(1, 2, two, one, three)
```

sample(withReplacement, fraction, seed)

Sampling is a common technique used in statistical analysis or machine learning to either reduce a large dataset to a more manageable size or to split the input dataset into a training set and a validation set when training a machine learning model. This transformation performs the sampling of the rows in the source RDD based on the following three inputs: with replacement, fraction, and seed values. The withReplacement parameter determines whether an already sampled row will be placed back into RDD for the next sampling. If the withReplacement parameter value is true, it means a particular row may appear multiple times in the output. The given fraction value must be between 0 and 1, and it is not guaranteed that the returned RDD will have the exact fraction number of rows of the original RDD. The optional seed parameter is used to seed the random generator, and it has a default value if one is not provided.

The example in Listing 3-30 first creates an RDD with ten numbers, which are placed in two partitions; then it will try to sample the `withReplacement` value as true and the fraction as 0.3.

Listing 3-30. Sampling with Replacement

```
val numbers = spark.sparkContext.parallelize(List(1,2,3,4,5,6,7,8,9,10), 2)
numbers.sample(true, 0.3).collect
```

If you run the second statement multiple times, you will see a value may appear multiple times in the output and the number of elements may be less than or more than fraction 0.3. See Listing 3-31 for a few sample outputs.

Listing 3-31. Output of Sampling

```
Array[Int] = Array(1, 7, 7, 8)
Array[Int] = Array(1, 6, 6, 7, 8, 9, 10)
```

Note   To visually understand how RDD transformations and actions work, check out the visual diagrams provided by Jeff Thompson at `http://training.databricks.com/visualapi.pdf`.

Actions

The data processing logic in a typical Spark application will contain one or more actions, which tell Spark to start executing all the transformation logic that led up to a particular action. Since an action is what triggers the execution of the transformation logic in an application, the absence of actions in a Spark application would mean that the application does absolutely nothing. In exploratory data analysis, it is fairly common either to want to know the size of the input dataset or to see what the first few rows look like. Spark provides a set of diverse actions to help with these use cases. One way to distinguish whether an RDD API is an action or a transformation is that an action will either write the content of an RDD out to a storage system or return all or a subset of the content to the user, but it doesn't return an RDD. Table 3-3 lists the commonly used actions.

Table 3-3. *Common Actions*

Name	Description
collect()	Collects all the rows in the dataset from executors. All the rows will be sent from executors to the driver program. The collect action is usually used after the dataset is filtered down to a small dataset.
count()	Returns the number of rows in the dataset.
first()	Returns the first row in the dataset to the driver program.
take(n)	Returns the first n rows in the dataset to the driver program. first() is equivalent to take(1).
reduce(func)	Performs an aggregation on the rows in the dataset using the provided func. The provided func should follow the commutative and associative rule for the result to be correctly computed in parallel.
takeSample(withReplacement, n, [seed])	Randomly samples up to n rows with either a replacement or not and returns them to the driver program.
takeOrdered(n, [ordering])	Returns the first n rows in the dataset to the driver program and orders them by either natural ordering or custom ordering.
top(n, [ordering])	Returns the top n elements in the dataset.
saveAsTextFile(path)	Writes all the rows in the dataset as a text file into the provided directory. Each row will be converted to a string using the toString() method.

Action Examples

The following section will provide more details and working examples of the previous actions.

collect()

This is a fairly easy-to-understand action because it does exactly what it sounds like. It collects all the rows from each of the partitions in an RDD and brings them over to the driver program. If your RDD contains 100 million rows, then it is not a good idea to invoke the `collect` action because the driver program most likely doesn't have sufficient memory to hold all those rows. As a result, the driver will most likely run into an out-of-memory error and your Spark application or shell will die. This action is typically used once the RDD is filtered down to a smaller size that can fit the memory size of the driver program. See Listing 3-32 for an example of using this action. Listing 3-33 shows the output.

Listing 3-32. Using the collect Action to See the Rows in the Small RDD

```
val numberRDD = spark.sparkContext.parallelize(List(1,2,3,4,5,6,7,8,9,10), 2)
numberRDD.collect()
```

Listing 3-33. The Output of the collect Action: An Array of Integers

```
Array[Int] = Array(1, 2, 3, 4, 5, 6, 7, 8, 9, 10)
```

count()

Similar to the `collect` action, this action does exactly what it sounds like. It returns the number of rows in an RDD by getting the count from all partitions and finally sums them up. See Listing 3-34 for an example of using the `count` action. Listing 3-35 shows the output.

Listing 3-34. Counting the Number of Rows in an RDD

```
val numberRDD = spark.sparkContext.parallelize(List(1,2,3,4,5,6,7,8,9,10), 2)
numberRDD.count()
```

Listing 3-35. Output of the count Action: A long

```
Long = 10
```

first()

This action returns the first row in an RDD. Now you may be wondering, what does the first row mean? Is there any ordering involved? It turns out it literally means the first row in the first partition. However, be careful about calling this action if your RDD is empty. In that case, this action will throw an exception. See Listing 3-36 for an example of using this action. Listing 3-37 shows the output.

Listing 3-36. Getting the First Row in an RDD

```
val numberRDD = spark.sparkContext.parallelize(List(1,2,3,4,5,6,7,8,9,10), 2)
numberRDD.first()
```

Listing 3-37. The Output of the first Action

```
Int = 1
```

take(n)

This action returns the first n rows in the RDD by collecting rows from the first partition and then moves to the next partition until the number of rows matches n or the last partition is reached. If n is larger than the number of rows in the dataset, then it will return all the rows. take(1) is equivalent to the first() action. See Listing 3-38 for an example of using this action. Listing 3-39 shows the output.

Listing 3-38. Getting the First Row in an RDD

```
val numberRDD = spark.sparkContext.parallelize(List(1,2,3,4,5,6,7,8,9,10), 2)
numberRDD.take(6)
```

Listing 3-39. The Output of the take(6) Action

```
Array[Int] = Array(1, 2, 3, 4, 5, 6)
```

reduce(func)

Compared to other actions, this one is pretty different. It reduces all the rows in the dataset to a single value using the provided function. A common use case is to perform a sum of all the integers in the dataset. There are two rules that the provided functions must follow. The first one is it must be a binary operator, meaning it must take two arguments of the same type, and it produces an output of the same type. The second one is it must follow the commutative and associative properties in order for the result to be computed correctly in a parallel manner. See the following note for more details about the commutative and associative properties.

If you haven't worked with Scala collection APIs much, then it can be kind of confusing to understand what's going on. Let's say you have an RDD of integers like Listing 3-40.

Listing 3-40. Defining an RDD of Integers

```
val numberRDD = spark.sparkContext.parallelize(List(1,2,3,4,5,6,7,8,9,10), 2)
```

The provided function to the reduce action will need to have a function signature like in Listing 3-41.

Listing 3-41. Defining a function to perform addition

```
def add(v1:Int, v2:Int) : Int = {
    println(s"v1: $v1, v2: $v2 => (${v1 + v2})")
    v1 + v2
}
```

Now let's call the reduce action on the numberRDD. See Listing 3-42.

Listing 3-42. Using the Function add as an Argument for the reduce Action

```
numberRDD.reduce(add)
```

You should see output similar to Listing 3-43.

Listing 3-43. The Output from Calling the reduce Action

```
v1: 1, v2: 2 => (3)
v1: 6, v2: 7 => (13)
v1: 3, v2: 3 => (6)
v1: 13, v2: 8 => (21)
v1: 6, v2: 4 => (10)
v1: 10, v2: 5 => (15)
v1: 21, v2: 9 => (30)
v1: 30, v2: 10 => (40)
v1: 15, v2: 40 => (55)
res62: Int = 55
```

As expected, the sum of the integers from 1 to 10 is 55. Now if you closely inspect the first line in the output, you will see that the inputs are basically the first two values of 1 and 2. On the third line, the first value is the sum of 1 and 2, and the second value is 3.

Basically, at the beginning of each partition it takes the first two numbers and passes them into the provided function. For the remaining numbers in the partition, it takes the output of the function and passes it in as the first argument, and the value of the second argument is the next number in the partition.

Note   In mathematics, the commutative property of a binary operation implies that changing the order of the operands has no impact on the result. On the other hand, the associative property says that changing how the operands are grouped has no impact on the result. Examples of binary operations that obey both the commutative and associative properties are addition and multiplication.

---

takeSample(withReplacement, n, [seed])

The behavior of this action is similar to the behavior of the `sample` transformation. The main difference is this action returns an array of sampled rows to the driver program. The same caution for the `collect` action is applicable here in terms of the large number of returned rows.

takeOrdered(n, [ordering])

This action returns n rows in a certain order. The default ordering for this action is the natural ordering. If the rows are integers, then the default ordering is ascending. If you need to return n rows with the values in descending order, then you specify the reverse ordering. See Listing 3-44 for an example of using this action with both ascending and descending order. Listing 3-45 shows the output.

Listing 3-44. Examples of the takeOrdered Action with Ascending and Descending Order

```
val numberRDD = spark.sparkContext.parallelize(List(1,2,3,4,5,6,7,8,9,10), 2)
numberRDD.takeOrdered(4)
numberRDD.takeOrdered(4)(Ordering[Int].reverse)
```

Listing 3-45. Output for the takeOrdered Action with Ascending and Descending Order

```
Array[Int] = Array(1, 2, 3, 4)
Array[Int] = Array(10, 9, 8, 7)
```

top(n, [ordering])

A good use case for using this action is for figure out the top *k* (largest) rows in an RDD as defined by the implicit ordering. This action does the opposite of the takeOrdered action. See Listing 3-46 for an example of using this action. Listing 3-47 shows the output.

Listing 3-46. Using the top Action

```
val numberRDD = spark.sparkContext.parallelize(List(1,2,3,4,5,6,7,8,9,10), 2)
numberRDD.top(4)
```

Listing 3-47. Output of Using the top Action

```
Array[Int] = Array(10, 9, 8, 7)
```

saveAsTextFile(path)

Unlike previous actions, this one does not return anything to the driver program. Instead, it will write out each row in the RDD as a string to the specified path. If an RDD has five partitions, the saveAsTextFile action will write out the rows in each partition in its own file; therefore, there will be five part files in the specified path. Notice that this action takes a path name rather than a file name, and it will fail if the specified path already exists. The intention for this behavior is to prevent the accidental overwriting of existing data.

Working with Key/Value Pair RDD

Up until now, you've worked with RDDs where each row represents a single value, such as an integer or a string. There are many use cases where there is a need to perform grouping by a certain key or aggregate or join two RDDs. For example, if you have a dataset that contains the population at the city level and you want to roll up at the state level, then you need to group those rows by state and sum the population of all the cities in each state. Spark provides a specific RDD type called a *key/value pair* RDD for these use cases. To qualify as a key/value pair RDD, each row must consist of a tuple where the first element represents the key and the second element represents the value. The type of both key and value can be a simple type such as an integer or string or can be a complex type such as an object or a collection of values or another tuple.

The pair RDD comes with a set of APIs to allow you to perform general operations around the key such as grouping, aggregation, and joining. The following sections cover how to create key/value pair RDDs and use the associated transformations and actions.

Creating Key/Value Pair RDD

In Scala, the simplest way to create a pair RDD is to arrange the data of each row into two parts: key and value. Then use the built-in Scala class called Tuple2, which is a shorthand version of using parentheses. See Listing 3-48 for an example of creating a pair RDD.

Listing 3-48. Creating a Pair RDD

```
val rdd = sc.parallelize(List("Spark","is","an", "amazing", "piece",
"of","technology"))
val pairRDD = rdd.map(w => (w.length,w))
pairRDD.collect().foreach(println)
```

Listing 3-48 creates a tuple for each row, where the key is the length and the value is the word. They are wrapped inside a pair of parentheses. Once each row is arranged in such a manner, then you can easily discover words with the same length by grouping by key. See Listing 3-49 for the output of calling the collect action on pairRDD.

Listing 3-49. Output of Pair RDD

```
(5,Spark)
(2,is)
(2,an)
(7,amazing)
(5,piece)
(2,of)
(10,technology)
```

The key and value in a pair RDD can be a scalar value or a complex value, which can be an object, collection of objects, or another tuple. So, it is quite flexible.

Note   When using a custom object as the key in the pair RDD, the class of that object must have both custom equals() and hashCode() methods defined.

Key/Value Pair RDD Transformations

In addition to the transformations listed in Table 3-4, a key/value pair RDD has additional transformations that are designed to operate on keys.

Table 3-4. *Common Transformations for Pair RDD*

Name	Description
groupByKey([numTasks])	Groups all the values of the same key together. For a dataset of (K,V) pairs, the returned RDD has the type (K, Iterable<V>).
reduceByKey(func, [numTasks])	First performs the grouping of values with the same key and then applies the specified func to return the list of values down to a single value. For a dataset of (K,V) pairs, the returned RDD has the type of (K, V).
sortByKey([ascending], [numTasks])	Sorts the rows according to the keys. By default, the keys are sorted in ascending order.
join(otherRDD, [numTasks])	Joins the rows in both RDDs by matching their keys. Each row of the returned RDD contains a tuple where the first element is the key and the second element is another tuple containing the values from both RDDs.

Some of the transformations listed in Table 3-4 have an optional numTasks parameter, which is used to control the degree of parallelism when Spark performs the transformation on the parent RDD. By default, the degree of parallelism is the number of partitions of the parent RDD. During the tuning process, if there is a belief the transformation will be completed sooner by increasing the degree of parallelism, then you can specify a value for the numTasks that is larger than the number of partitions of the parent RDD.

The following section provides an example of using the pair RDD transformations listed in Table 3-4.

groupByKey([numTasks])

This transformation does exactly what it sounds like. It will group all the rows with the same key into a single row. Essentially the number of rows in the returned RDD will be the same as the number of unique keys in the parent RDD. Each row in the returned RDD contains a unique key and a list of values of that same key. See Listing 3-50 for an example of using this transformation; Listing 3-51 shows the output.

Listing 3-50. Using the groupByKey Transformation to Group Words by Their Length

```
val rdd = sc.parallelize(List("Spark","is","an", "amazing", "piece",
"of","technology"))
val pairRDD = rdd.map(w => (w.length,w))
val wordByLenRDD = pairRDD.groupByKey()
wordByLenRDD.collect().foreach(println)
```

Listing 3-51. Output of the groupByKey Transformation After Grouping Words by Their Length

```
(10,CompactBuffer(technology))
(2,CompactBuffer(is, an, of))
(5,CompactBuffer(Spark, piece))
(7,CompactBuffer(amazing))
```

Oftentimes there is a need to perform some processing on the list of values of each key after the groupByKey transformation is performed. If that processing is done using a binary operation that complies with the commutative and associated properties, then it is best to use the reduceByKey transformation to speed up the processing logic. You can find more details about this in the following section.

reduceByKey(func, [numTasks])

This transformation is often used to reduce all the values of the same key to a single value. The process is carried out in two steps, as depicted in Figure 3-1. The first one is to group the values of the same key together, and the second step is to apply the given reduce function to the list of values of each key. The implementation of this transformation contains a built-in optimization to perform this two-step process at two levels. The first level is at each individual partition, and the second level is across all the partitions. By applying this transformation at each individual partition first, it therefore collapses all the rows with the same key in the same partition to a single row, and as a result, the amount of data that needs to be moved across many partitions is dramatically reduced. See Listing 3-52 for an example of using this transformation; Listing 3-53 shows the output.

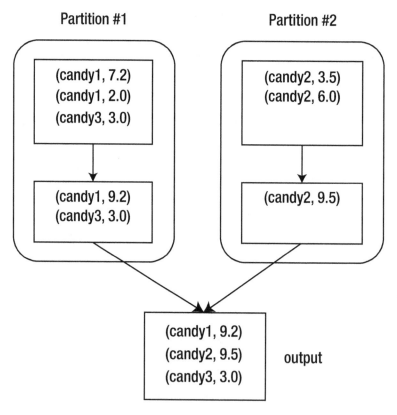

Figure 3-1. *The two-step process in the reduceByKey transformation*

Listing 3-52. Using the reduceByKey Transformation to Tally the Price

```
val candyTx = sc.parallelize(List(("candy1", 5.2), ("candy2", 3.5),
                                                    ("candy1", 2.0),
                                                    ("candy2", 6.0),
                                                    ("candy3", 3.0))
val summaryTx = candyTx.reduceByKey((total, value) => total + value)
summaryTx.collect()
```

Listing 3-53. Output of reduceByKey After Tallying the Price

```
(candy1,7.2)
(candy2,9.5)
(candy3,3.0)
```

sortByKey([ascending],[numTasks])

This transformation is simple to understand. It sorts the rows according the key, and there is an option to specify whether the result should be in ascending (default) or descending order. Building on the example in Listing 3-52, the key and value are swapped so you can sort the rows based on the transaction amount. See Listing 3-54 for an example of sorting by the transaction amount; Listing 3-55 shows the output.

Listing 3-54. Using the sortByKey Transformation to Sort by Price

```
val summaryByPrice = summaryTx.map(t => (t._2, t._1)).sortByKey()
summaryByPrice.collect
```

Listing 3-55. Output of Using the sortByKey Transformation to Sort Based on Price

```
Array[(Double, String)] = Array((3.0,candy3), (7.2,candy1), (9.5,candy2))
```

If you want to sort the price in descending order, then you just need to set the value of the first parameter to false. See Listing 3-56 for an example of sorting in descending order, and see Listing 3-57 for the output.

Listing 3-56. Using the sortByKey transformation Based on Price in Descending Order

```
val summaryByPrice = summaryTx.map(t => (t._2, t._1)).sortByKey(false)
summaryByPrice.collect
```

Listing 3-57. Output of Using the sortByKey Transformation to Sort Based on Price in Descending Order

```
(9.5,candy2)
(7.2,candy1)
(3.0,candy3)
```

join(otherRDD)

Performing any meaningful data analysis usually involves joining two or more datasets. The join transformation is used to combine the information of two datasets to enable rich data analysis or to extract insights. For example, if one dataset contains the transaction information and it has a member ID and details of the transaction and another dataset contains the member information, by joining these two datasets you can answer questions such as, what is the breakdown of the transactions by the age group, and which age group made the largest number of transactions?

By joining the dataset of type (K,V) and dataset (K,W), the result of the joined dataset is (K,(V,W)). There are several variations of joining two datasets, like left and right outer joins. For more details on the behavior of these types of join, please refer to https://en.wikipedia.org/wiki/Join_(SQL).

The example in Listing 3-58 has two datasets that are already set up as key/value pair RDDs. The first one contains the member transaction. The second contains information about each member ID and a group each member belongs to.

Listing 3-58. Join of Member Transaction Dataset and Member Group Dataset

```
val memberTx = sc.parallelize(List((110, 50.35), (127, 305.2), (126, 211.0),
                                  (105, 6.0),(165, 31.0), (110, 40.11)))
val memberInfo = sc.parallelize(List((110, "a"), (127, "b"), (126, "b"),
(105, "a"),(165, "c")))
val memberTxInfo = memberTx.join(memberInfo)
memberTxInfo.collect().foreach(println)
```

The join in Listing 3-58 is the inner join type, where the output contains only the rows with matching keys from both datasets. See Listing 3-59 for the output.

Listing 3-59. Output of the Join Transformation

```
(105,(6.0,a))
(165,(31.0,c))
(110,(50.35,a))
(110,(40.11,a))
(126,(211.0,b))
(127,(305.2,b))
```

Key/Value Pair RDD Actions

In addition to the actions listed in Table 3-5, pair RDD has a small set of actions. This section provides some details and working examples of these actions. These actions will bring the result back to the driver side, so be careful about the amount of data that will be brought back.

Table 3-5. *Actions for Pair RDD*

Name	Description
countByKey()	Returns a map where each entry contains the key and a count of values
collectAsMap()	Similar behavior as the collect action; return type is a map
lookup(key)	Performs a look by key and returns all values that have the same specified key

The following section provides an example for each of the actions listed in Table 3-5.

countByKey()

For a given pair RDD, this action ignores the value of each row and reports only the number of values with the same key for each key to the driver. See Listing 3-60 for an example and Listing 3-61 for the output. Notice the returned data is a Scala map data structure.

Listing 3-60. Using countByKey to count the number of elements for each key

```
val candyTx = sc.parallelize(List(("candy1", 5.2), ("candy2", 3.5),
("candy1", 2.0), ("candy3", 6.0)))
candyTx.countByKey()
```

Listing 3-61. Using countByKey

```
scala.collection.Map[String,Long] = Map(candy1 -> 2, candy2 -> 1, candy3 -> 1)
```

collectAsMap()

Similar to the `collect` action, this one brings the entire dataset to the driver side as a map, where each entry represents a row. See Listing 3-62 for the example and Listing 3-63 for the output.

Listing 3-62. Using the collectAsMap Action

```
val candyTx = sc.parallelize(List(("candy1", 5.2), ("candy2", 3.5),
("candy1", 2.0), ("candy3", 6.0)))
candyTx.collectAsMap()
```

Listing 3-63. Output of the collectAsMap Action

```
scala.collection.Map[String,Double] = Map(candy2 -> 3.5, candy1 -> 2.0,
candy3 -> 6.0)
```

Notice if the dataset contains multiple rows with the same key, it will be collapsed into a single entry in the map. There are four rows in the candyTx pair RDD; however, there are only three rows in the output. Two candy1 rows are collapsed into a single row.

lookup(key)

This action can be used as a quick way to verify whether a particular key exists in the RDD. See Listing 3-64 for an example and Listing 3-65 for the output. If there is more than one row with the same key, then the value of all those rows will be returned.

Listing 3-64. Using the lookup Action

```
val candyTx = sc.parallelize(List(("candy1", 5.2), ("candy2", 3.5),
("candy1", 2.0), ("candy3", 6.0)))
candyTx.lookup("candy1")
candyTx.lookup("candy2")
candyTx.lookup("candy5")
```

Listing 3-65. Output of the lookup Examples in Listing 3-64

```
Seq[Double] = WrappedArray(5.2, 2.0)
Seq[Double] = WrappedArray(3.5)
Seq[Double] = WrappedArray()
```

Understand Data Shuffling

Certain key/value transformations and actions require moving data from multiple partitions to other partitions, meaning across executors and machines. This process is known as the *shuffle*, which is quite important to be familiar with because it is an expensive operation. During the shuffling process, the data needs to be serialized, written to disk, transferred over the network, and finally deserialized. It is not possible to completely avoid the shuffling, but there are techniques or best practices to minimize the need to shuffle the data. Shuffling data will add latency to the completion of the data processing in your Spark jobs.

Let's take the reduceByKey transformation as an example to understand the shuffle. This transformation needs to read data from all partitions to find all the values for all keys in the RDD, and for each key it brings all the values from different partitions together to compute the final value. To prepare for the shuffle, each partition prepares the data by sorting them based on the targeted partition and then writing them to a single file. On the targeted partition, it will read the relevant blocks of this file based on its partition index.

In general, any transformation or action that performs some sort of grouping, aggregating, or joining by key will need to perform data shuffling. Here is a subset of the transformations that fall into this category: groupByKey, reduceByKey, aggregateByKey, and join.

Having Fun with RDD Persistence

One of the distinguishing features of Spark from other data processing engines or frameworks is the ability to persist the data of an RDD in memory across all the executors in a cluster. Once the data of an RDD is persisted in memory, then any future computations on that data will be really fast, often more than ten times the data that is not in memory. There are two typical use cases that can tremendously benefit from the data persisted in memory. The first one is data exploration or interactive analysis. Let's say there is a large service log file that is several hundred gigabytes, and there is a need to perform analysis on various types of exceptions. The first step is to filter this log file down to only the lines that contain the key word *Exception* and then cache that dataset in memory. Subsequent exploratory and interactive analysis of various types of exceptions can be done on that dataset in memory, and they will be very fast. The second use case is the iterative algorithms. Machine learning algorithms are often iterative in nature, meaning they will run through many iterations to optimize the loss function. In this process, they might use one or more datasets that don't change with each iteration; therefore, if those datasets are persisted, then that will help speeding up the time it takes for the algorithms to complete.

Persisting an RDD is extremely simple to do by calling the transformation persist() or cache(). Since they are transformations, only once a subsequent action is taken will the RDD be persisted in memory. By default, Spark will persist the dataset in memory. One question to ask is what happens if there isn't sufficient memory in all the executors in your Spark applications to persist an RDD in memory. For instance, let's say a Spark application has ten executors and each one has 6GB of RAM. If the size of an RDD you would like to persist in memory is 70GB, then that wouldn't fit into 60GB of RAM. This is where the storage-level concept comes in. There are two options that you can specify when persisting the data of an RDD in memory: location and serialization. The location option determines whether the data of an RDD should be stored in memory or on disk or a combination of the two. The serialization option determines whether the data in the RDD should be stored as a serialized object or not. These two options represent the different types of trade-offs you are making: CPU time and memory usage. See Table 3-6 for the details of the two aforementioned options.

Table 3-6. *Storage Options for Persisting RDD*

Option	Memory Space	CPU Time	In Memory	On Disk
MEMORY_ONLY	High	Low	Yes	No
MEMORY_AND_DISK	High	Medium	Some	Some
MEMORY_ONLY_SER	Low	High	Yes	No
MEMORY_AND_DISK_SER	Low	High	Some	Some
DISK_ONLY	Low	High	No	Yes

If the data of an RDD is no longer needed to be persisted in memory, then you can use the `unpersist()` function to remove it from memory to make room for other RDDs. A Spark cluster usually has a limited amount of memory; if you keep persisting RDDs, Spark will use the LRU eviction policy to automatically evict the RDDs that have not been recently accessed.

Summary

You learned the following in this chapter:

- In Spark, RDD is the foundational abstraction in terms of concepts and programming model. Other programming abstractions are built on top of RDD.

- RDD provides a rich set of operations to make it easy to perform data analysis in Spark. Operations are classified into two types: transformation and action. Transformations are designed to be lazy evaluated to provide opportunities for Spark to perform optimizations. Actions are eager evaluated, and they trigger the computation of all the transformation logic that preceded the call to an action.

- Pair RDD provides the additional capabilities of grouping, aggregation, and joining of datasets based on key.

- The data shuffle is an expensive but necessary data movement process, so it is important for Spark developers to be familiar with it. The goal is to not eliminate the shuffle process but to minimize the number of times the shuffling needs to happen in your Spark application.

- RDD persistence is a great way to speed the computation logic in your Spark jobs. Understanding the various storage levels will give you the confidence to pick the right one that is appropriate for your use case and to make the right trade-off in terms of CPU time and space efficiency.

RDD EXERCISES

The following exercises are based on the `movies.tsv` and `movie-ratings.tsv` files in the `chapter3/data/movies` directory. The columns in these files are delimited by a tab.

Each line in the `movies.tsv` file represents an actor who played in a movie. If a movie has ten actors in it, then there will be ten rows for that particular movie.

1. Compute the number of movies produced in each year. The output should have two columns: year and count. The output should be ordered by the count in descending order.

2. Compute the number of movies each actor was in. The output should have two columns: actor and count. The output should be ordered by the count in descending order.

3. Compute the highest-rated movie per year and include all the actors in that movie. The output should have only one movie per year, and it should contain four columns: year, movie title, rating, and a semicolon-separated list of actor names. This question will require joining the `movies.tsv` and `movie-ratings.tsv` files. There are two approaches to this problem. The first one is to figure out the highest-rated movie per year first and then join with the list of actors. The second one is to perform the join first and then figure out the highest-rated movies per year along with a list of actors. The result of each approach is different than the other one. Why do you think that is?

4. Determine which pair of actors worked together most. Working together is defined as appearing in the same movie. The output should have three columns: actor 1, actor 2, and count. The output should be sorted by the count in descending order. The solution to this question will require a self-join.

CHAPTER 4

Spark SQL (Foundations)

As Spark evolves as a unified data processing engine with more features in each new release, its programming abstraction also evolves. The RDD was the initial core programming abstraction when Spark was introduced to the world in 2012. In Spark 1.6, a new programming abstraction, called Structured APIs, was introduced. This is the preferred way of performing data processing for the majority of use cases. The Structured APIs were designed to enhance developers' productivity with easy-to-use, intuitive, and expressive APIs. In this new way of doing data processing, the data needs to be organized into a structured format, and the data computation logic needs to follow a certain structure. Armed with these two pieces of information, Spark can perform optimizations to speed up data processing applications.

Figure 4-1 shows how the Spark SQL component is built on top of the good old reliable Spark Core component. This layered architecture means any improvements in the Spark Core component will be automatically available to the Spark SQL component.

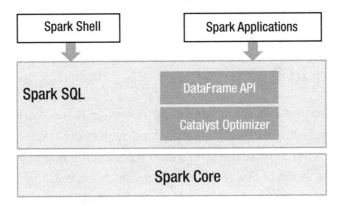

Figure 4-1. *Spark SQL components*

© Hien Luu 2018
H. Luu, *Beginning Apache Spark 2*, https://doi.org/10.1007/978-1-4842-3579-9_4

This chapter covers the Spark SQL module, which enables you to write less code to get things done, and underneath the covers it intelligently performs optimizations. The Spark SQL module consists of two main parts. The first one is the representation of the Structure APIs, called DataFrames and Datasets, that define the high-level APIs for working with structured data. The DataFrame concept was inspired by the Python pandas DataFrame; the main difference is that a DataFrame in Spark can handle a large volume of data that is spread across many machines. The second part of the Spark SQL module is the Catalyst optimizer, which does all the hard work behind the scenes to make your life easier and to speed up your data processing logic. One of the cool features the Spark SQL module offers is the ability to execute SQL queries to perform data processing. By virtue of this capability, Spark is able to gain a new group of users called *business analysts*, who are familiar with the SQL language because it is one of the main tools they use on a regular basis.

One main concept that differentiates structured data from unstructured data is a *schema*, which defines the structure of the data in the form of column names and associated data types. The schema concept is an integral part of the Spark Structured APIs.

Structured data is often captured in a certain format. Some of the formats are text based, and some of them are binary based. Common formats for text data are CSV, XML, and JSON, and common formats for binary data are Avro, Parquet, and ORC. Out of the box, the Spark SQL module makes it easy to read data and write data from and to any of these formats. One unanticipated benefit comes out of this versatility is that Spark can be used as a data format conversion tool.

Introduction to DataFrames

A *DataFrame* is an immutable, distributed collection of data that is organized into rows, where each one consists a set of columns and each column has a name and an associated type. In other words, this distributed collection of data has a structure defined by a schema. If you are familiar with the table concept in a relational database management system (RDBMS), then you will realize that a DataFrame is essentially equivalent. Each row in the DataFrame is represented by a generic Row object. Unlike the RDD APIs, the DataFrame APIs offer a set of domain-specific operations that are relational and have rich semantics. The details of the APIs will be covered in the following sections. Like the RDD APIs, the DataFrame APIs are classified into two buckets: transformations and actions. The evaluation semantics are identical in RDDs. Transformations are lazily evaluated, and actions are eagerly evaluated.

DataFrames can be created by reading data from the many structured data sources mentioned previously as well as by reading data from tables in Hive and databases. In addition, the Spark SQL module makes it easy to convert an RDD to a DataFrame by providing the schema information about the data in the RDD. The DataFrame APIs are available in Scala, Java, Python, and R.

Creating DataFrames

There are many ways to create a DataFrame; one common thing among them is the need to provide a schema, either implicitly or explicitly.

Creating DataFrames from RDDs

Let's start with creating a DataFrame from an RDD. Listing 4-1 first creates an RDD with two columns of the integer type, and then it calls the toDF implicit function to convert an RDD to a DataFrame using the specified column names. The column types are inferred from the data in the RDD. Listing 4-2 shows two of the commonly used functions in a DataFrame, printSchema and show. Function printSchema prints out the column names and their associated type to the console. Function show prints the data in a DataFrame out in a tabular format. By default, it displays 20 rows. To change the default number of rows to display, you can pass in a number to the show function. See Listing 4-3 for an example of specifying a number of rows to display.

Listing 4-1. Creating a DataFrame from an RDD of Numbers

```scala
import scala.util.Random
val rdd = spark.sparkContext.parallelize(1 to 10).map(x => (x,
Random.nextInt(100)* x))
val kvDF = rdd.toDF("key","value")
```

Listing 4-2. Printing the Schema and Showing the Data of a DataFrame

```
kvDF.printSchema
|-- key: integer (nullable = false)
|-- value: integer (nullable = false)

kvDF.show
+---+-----+
|key|value|
+---+-----+
|  1|   58|
|  2|   18|
|  3|  237|
|  4|   32|
|  5|   80|
|  6|  210|
|  7|  567|
|  8|  360|
|  9|  288|
| 10|  260|
+---+-----+
```

Listing 4-3. Calling the Function show to Display Five Rows in Tabular Format

```
kvDF.show(5)
+---+-----+
|key|value|
+---+-----+
|  1|   59|
|  2|   60|
|  3|   66|
|  4|  280|
|  5|   40|
+---+-----+
```

Note   The actual numbers in the value column may look different for you because they are generated randomly by calling the Random.nextInt() function.

Another way to create a DataFrame is by specifying an RDD with a schema that is created programmatically. Listing 4-4 first creates an RDD using an array of Row objects, where each Row object contains three columns; then it creates a schema programmatically. Finally, it provides the RDD and schema to the function createDataFrame to convert to a DataFrame. Listing 4-5 shows the schema and the data in the peopleDF DataFrame.

Listing 4-4. Creating a DataFrame from an RDD with a Schema Created Programmatically

```
import org.apache.spark.sql.Row
import org.apache.spark.sql.types._

val peopleRDD = spark.sparkContext.parallelize(Array(Row(1L, "John
Doe",  30L),
                                        Row(2L, "Mary Jane", 25L)))

val schema = StructType(Array(
        StructField("id", LongType, true),
        StructField("name", StringType, true),
        StructField("age", LongType, true)
))

val peopleDF = spark.createDataFrame(peopleRDD, schema)
```

Listing 4-5. Displaying the Schema of peopleDF and Its Data

```
peopleDF.printSchema
 |-- id: long (nullable = true)
 |-- name: string (nullable = true)
 |-- age: long (nullable = true)

peopleDF.show
+--+-----------+---+
|id|       name|age|
+--+-----------+---+
| 1|   John Doe| 30|
| 2|  Mary Jane| 25|
+--+-----------+---+
```

The ability to programmatically create a schema gives Spark applications the flexibility to adjust the schema based on some external configuration.

Each StructField object has three pieces of information: name, type, and whether the value is nullable.

The type of each column in a DataFrame is mapped to an internal Spark type, which can be a simple scalar type or a complex type. Table 4-1 describes the available internal Spark data types and associated Scala types.

Table 4-1. *Spark Scala Types*

Data Type	Scala Type
BooleanType	Boolean
ByteType	Byte
ShortType	Short
IntegerType	Int
LongType	Long
FloatType	Float
DoubleType	Double
DecimalType	java.math.BigDecial
StringType	String
BinaryType	Array[Byte]
TimestampType	java.sql.Timestamp
DateType	java.sql.Date
ArrayType	scala.collection.Seq
MapType	scala.collection.Map
StructType	org.apache.spark.sql.Row

Creating DataFrames from a Range of Numbers

Spark 2.0 introduced a new entry point for Spark applications. It is represented by a class called SparkSession, which has a convenient function called range that can easily create a DataFrame with a single column with the name id and the type

LongType. This function has a few variations that can take additional parameters to specify the start and end of a range as well as the steps of the range. Listing 4-6 provides examples of using this function to create a DataFrame.

Listing 4-6. Using the SparkSession.range Function to Create a DataFrame

```
val df1 = spark.range(5).toDF("num").show
+---+
|num|
+---+
|  0|
|  1|
|  2|
|  3|
|  4|
+---+

spark.range(5,10).toDF("num").show
+---+
|num|
+---+
|  5|
|  6|
|  7|
|  8|
|  9|
+---+

spark.range(5,15,2).toDF("num").show
+---+
|num|
+---+
|  5|
|  7|
|  9|
| 11|
| 13|
+---+
```

The previous version of the range function takes three parameters. The first one represents the starting value, the second one represents the end value (exclusive), and the last one represents the step size. Notice the range function can create only a single-column DataFrame. Do you have any ideas about how to create a DataFrame with more than one column?

One option to create a multicolumn DataFrame is to use Spark's implicits that convert a collection of tuples inside a Scala Seq collection. See Listing 4-7 for examples of using Spark's toDF implicit.

Listing 4-7. Converting a Collection Tuple to a DataFrame Using Spark's toDF Implicit

```
val movies = Seq(("Damon, Matt", "The Bourne Ultimatum", 2007L),
                 ("Damon, Matt", "Good Will Hunting", 1997L))

val moviesDF = movies.toDF("actor", "title", "year")


moviesDF.printSchema
|-- actor: string (nullable = true)
|-- title: string (nullable = true)
|-- year: long (nullable = false)

moviesDF.show
+-----------+--------------------+----+
|      actor|               title|year|
+-----------+--------------------+----+
|Damon, Matt|The Bourne Ultimatum|2007|
|Damon, Matt|   Good Will Hunting|1997|
+-----------+--------------------+----+
```

These fun ways of creating DataFrames make it easy to learn and to work with the DataFrame APIs without needing to load the data from some external files. However, when you start doing serious data analysis with large datasets, then it is imperative to know how to load data from external data sources, which will be covered next.

Creating DataFrames from Data Sources

Out of the box, Spark SQL supports six built-in data sources, where each data source is mapped to a data format. The data source layer in the Spark SQL module is designed to be extensible, so custom data sources can be easily integrated into the DataFrame APIs. There are hundreds of custom data sources written by the Spark community, and it is not too difficult to implement them.

The two main classes in Spark SQL for reading and writing data are `DataFrameReader` and `DataFrameWriter`, respectively. This section will cover the details of working with the APIs in the `DataFrameReader` class and the various available options when reading data from a specific data source.

An instance of the `DataFrameReader` class is available as the `read` variable of the `SparkSession` class. Listing 4-8 provides an example of referring to this variable.

Listing 4-8. Using read Variable from SparkSession

```
spark.read
```

The common pattern for interacting with `DataFrameReader` is described in Listing 4-9.

Listing 4-9. Common Pattern for Interacting with DataFrameReader

```
spark.read.format(...).option("key", value").schema(...).load()
```

Table 4-2 describes the three main pieces of information that are used when reading data: format, option, and schema. More specific details about these three pieces of information will be provided in upcoming sections.

Table 4-2. *Three Main Pieces of Information for DataFrameReader*

Name	Optional	Comments
`format`	No	This can be one of the built-in data sources or a custom format. For a built-in format, you can use a short name (`json`, `parquet`, `jdbc`, `orc`, `csv`, `text`). For a custom data source, you need to provide a fully qualified name. See Listing 4-10 for details and examples.
`option`	Yes	DataFrameReader has a set of default options for each data source format. You can override those default values by providing a value to the `option` function.
`schema`	Yes	Some data sources have the schema embedded inside the data files, i.e., Parquet and ORC. In those cases, the schema is automatically inferred. For other cases, you may need to provide a schema.

Listing 4-10. Specifying the Data Source Format

```
spark.read.json("<path>")
spark.read.format("json")

spark.read.parquet("<path>")
spark.read.format("parquet")

spark.read.jdbc
spark.read.format("jdbc")

spark.read.orc("<path>")
spark.read.format("orc")

spark.read.csv("<path>")
spark.read.format("csv")

spark.read.text("<path>")
spark.read.format("text")

// custom data source - fully qualifed package name
spark.read.format("org.example.mysource")
```

Table 4-3 describes Spark's six built-in data sources and provides comments for each of them.

Table 4-3. Spark's Built-in Data Sources

Name	Data Format	Comments
Text file	Text	No structure.
CSV	Text	Comma-separated values. This can be used to specify another delimiter. The column name can be referred from the header.
JSON	Text	Popular semistructured format. The column name and data type are inferred automatically.
Parquet	Binary	(Default format.) Popular binary format in the Hadoop community.
ORC	Binary	Another popular binary format in the Hadoop community.
JDBC	Binary	A common format for reading and writing to the RDBMS.

Creating DataFrames by Reading Text Files

Text files contain unstructured data. As it is read into Spark, each line becomes a row in the DataFrame. There are lots of free books available for download in plain-text format at www.gutenberg.org/. For plain-text files, one common way to parse the words of each line is by splitting it with a space as a delimiter. This is similar to how a typical word count example works. See Listing 4-11 for an example of reading a text file.

Listing 4-11. Reading the README.md File As a Text File from a Spark Shell

```
val textFile = spark.read.text("README.md")

textFile.printSchema
|-- value: string (nullable = true)

// show 5 lines and don't truncate
textFile.show(5, false)
```

```
+-------------------------------------------------------------------------+
|value                                                                    |
+-------------------------------------------------------------------------+
|# Apache Spark                                                           |
|                                                                         |
|Spark is a fast and general cluster computing system for Big Data. It provides |
|high-level APIs in Scala, Java, Python, and R, and an optimized engine that    |
|supports general computation graphs for data analysis. It also supports a      |
+-------------------------------------------------------------------------+
```

If a text file contains a delimiter that you can use to parse the columns in each line, then it is better to read it using the CSV format, which will be covered in the following section.

Creating DataFrames by Reading CSV Files

One of the popular text file formats is CSV, which stands for *comma-separated values*. Popular tools such as Microsoft Excel can easily import and export data in CSV format. The CSV parser in Spark is designed to be flexible such that it can parse a text file using a user-provided delimiter. The comma delimiter just happens to be the default one. This means you can use the CSV format to read tab-separated value text files or other text files with an arbitrary delimiter.

Some CSV files have a header, and some don't. Since a column value may contain a comma, it is a good practice to escape it using a special character. Table 4-4 describes commonly used options when working with the CSV format. For a complete list of options, please see the CSVOptions class at Spark GitHub (https://github.com/apache/spark).

Table 4-4. *CSV Common Options*

Key	Values	Default	Description
sep	Single character	,	This is a single-character value used as a delimiter for each column.
header	true, false	false	If the value is true, it means the first line in the file represents the column names.
escape	Any character	\	This is the character to use to escape the character in the column value that is the same as sep.
inferSchema	true, false	false	This specifies whether Spark should try to infer the column type based on column value.

Specifying the header and inferSchema options as true won't require you to specify a schema. Otherwise, you need to define a schema by hand or programmatically create it and pass it into the schema function. If the inferSchema option is false and no schema is provided, Spark will assume the data type of all the columns to be the string type.

The data file you are using as an example is called movies.csv in the folder data/ chapter4. This file contains a header for each column: actor, title, year. Listing 4-12 provides a few examples of reading a CSV file.

Listing 4-12. Reading CSV Files with Various Options

```
val movies = spark.read.option("header","true").csv("<path>/book/chapter4/
data/movies/movies.csv")


movies.printSchema
 |-- actor: string (nullable = true)
 |-- title: string (nullable = true)
 |-- year: string (nullable = true)

// now try to infer the schema
val movies2 = spark.read.option("header","true").
option("inferSchema","true")
    .csv("<path>/book/chapter4/data/movies/movies.csv")
```

```
movies2.printSchema
 |-- actor: string (nullable = true)
 |-- title: string (nullable = true)
 |-- year: integer (nullable = true)

// now try to manually provide a schema
import org.apache.spark.sql.types._
val movieSchema = StructType(Array(StructField("actor_name", StringType, true),
                            StructField("movie_title", StringType, true),
                            StructField("produced_year", LongType, true)))
val movies3 = spark.read.option("header","true").schema(movieSchema)
                        .csv("<path>/book/chapter4/data/movies/
                        movies.csv")

movies3.printSchema
 |-- actor_name: string (nullable = true)
 |-- movie_title: string (nullable = true)
 |-- produced_year: long (nullable = true)

movies3.show(5)

+-----------------+--------------+--------------+
|       actor_name|   movie_title| produced_year|
+-----------------+--------------+--------------+
|McClure, Marc (I)| Freaky Friday|          2003|
|McClure, Marc (I)|  Coach Carter|          2005|
|McClure, Marc (I)|    Superman II|         1980|
|McClure, Marc (I)|     Apollo 13|          1995|
|McClure, Marc (I)|      Superman|          1978|
+-----------------+--------------+--------------+
```

The first example reads the file movies.csv by specifying the first line as the header. Spark was able to recognize the column names. However, since you didn't specify the inferSchema option, all the columns have the type as string. The second example added the inferSchema option, and Spark was able to identify the column type. The third example provides a schema with column names different than what is in the header, so Spark uses the column names from the schema.

Now let's try to read in a text file with a delimiter that is different, not a comma. Instead, it is a tab. In this case, you specify a value for the sep option that Spark will use. See Listing 4-13 for an example of reading a file called movies.tsv in the folder data/ chapter4.

Listing 4-13. Reading a TSV File with the CSV Format

```
val movies4 = spark.read.option("header","true").option("sep", "\t")
    .schema(movieSchema).csv("<path>/book/chapter4/data/movies/movies.tsv")

movies.printSchema
|-- actor_name: string (nullable = true)
|-- movie_title: string (nullable = true)
|-- produced_year: long (nullable = true)
```

As you can see, it is quite easy to work with text files that have comma-separated values as well as other-separated values.

Creating DataFrames by Reading JSON Files

JSON is a well-known format in the JavaScript community. It is considered to be a semistructured format because each object (aka row) has a structure and each column has a name. In the web application development space, JSON is a widely used data format for transferring data between the back-end server and the browser side. One of the strengths of JSON is that it provides a flexible format that can model any use case; it can also support a nested structure. JSON has one disadvantage that is related to verbosity. The column names are repeated in each row in the data file (imagine your data file has 1 million rows).

Spark makes it easy to read data in a JSON file. However, there is one thing that you need to pay attention to. A JSON object can be expressed on a single line or across multiple lines, and this is something you need to let Spark know. Given that a JSON data file contains only column names and no data type, how is Spark able to come up with a schema? Spark tries its best to infer the schema by parsing a set of sample records. The number of records to sample is determined by the samplingRatio option, which has a default value of 1.0. Therefore, it is quite expensive to read a large JSON file. In this case, you can lower the samplingRatio value to speed up the data loading process. Table 4-5 describes the common options for the JSON format.

Table 4-5. *JSON Common Options*

Key	Values	Default	Description
allowComments	true, false	false	Ignores comments in the JSON file
multiLine	true, false	false	Treats the entire file as a large JSON object that spans many lines
samplingRatio	0.3	1.0	Specifies the sampling size to read to infer the schema

Listing 4-14 shows two examples of reading JSON files. The first one simply reads a JSON file without overriding any option value. Notice Spark automatically detects the column name and data type based on the information in the JSON file. The second example specifies a schema.

Listing 4-14. Various Examples of Reading a JSON File

```
val movies5 = spark.read.json("<path>/book/chapter4/data/movies/movies.json")

movies.printSchema
 |-- actor_name: string (nullable = true)
 |-- movie_title: string (nullable = true)
 |-- produced_year: long (nullable = true)

// specify a schema to override the Spark's inferring schema.
// producted_year is specified as integer type
import org.apache.spark.sql.types._
val movieSchema2 = StructType(Array(StructField("actor_name", StringType, true),
                        StructField("movie_title", StringType, true),
                        StructField("produced_year", IntegerType, true)))

val movies6 = spark.read.option("inferSchema","true").schema(movieSchema2)
                    .json("<path>/book/chapter4/data/movies/
                    movies.json")

movies6.printSchema
 |-- actor_name: string (nullable = true)
 |-- movie_title: string (nullable = true)
 |-- produced_year: integer (nullable = true)
```

What happens when a column data type specified in the schema doesn't match up with the value in the JSON file? By default, when Spark encounters a corrupted record or runs into a parsing error, it will set the value of all the columns in that row to null. Instead of getting null values, you can tell Spark to fail fast. Listing 4-15 tells Spark's parsing logic to fail fast by specifying the mode option as failFast.

Listing 4-15. Parsing Error and How to Tell Spark to Fail Fast

```
// set data type for actor_name as BooleanType
import org.apache.spark.sql.types._
val badMovieSchema = StructType(Array(StructField("actor_name",
BooleanType, true),
                                    StructField("movie_title",
                                    StringType, true),
                                    StructField("produced_year",
                                    IntegerType, true)))

val movies7 = spark.read.schema(badMovieSchema)
                            .json("<path>/book/chapter4/data/movies/
                            movies.json")
movies7.printSchema
 |-- actor_name: boolean (nullable = true)
 |-- movie_title: string (nullable = true)
 |-- produced_year: integer (nullable = true)

movies7.show(5)
+----------+-----------+-------------+
|actor_name|movie_title|produced_year|
+----------+-----------+-------------+
|      null|       null|         null|
|      null|       null|         null|
|      null|       null|         null|
|      null|       null|         null|
|      null|       null|         null|
+----------+-----------+-------------+
```

```
// tell Spark to fail fast when facing a parsing error
val movies8 = spark.read.option("mode","failFast").schema(badMovieSchema)
                        .json("<path>/book/chapter4/data/movies/
                        movies.json")
```

```
movies8.printSchema
 |-- actor_name: boolean (nullable = true)
 |-- movie_title: string (nullable = true)
 |-- produced_year: integer (nullable = true)
```

```
// Spark will throw a RuntimeException when executing an action
movies8.show(5)
ERROR Executor: Exception in task 0.0 in stage 3.0 (TID 3)
java.lang.RuntimeException: Failed to parse a value for data type
BooleanType (current token: VALUE_STRING).
```

Creating DataFrames by Reading Parquet Files

Parquet is one of the most popular open source columnar storage formats in the Hadoop ecosystem, and it was created at Twitter. Its popularity is because it is a self-describing data format and it stores data in a highly compact structure by leveraging compressions. The columnar storage format is designed to work well with a data analytics workload where only a small subset of the columns are used during the data analysis. Parquet stores the data of each column in a separate file; therefore, columns that are not needed in a data analysis wouldn't have to be unnecessarily read in. It is quite flexible when it comes to supporting a complex data type with a nested structure. Text file formats such as CVS and JSON are good for small files, and they are human-readable. For working with large datasets that are stored in long-term storage, Parquet is a much better file format to use to reduce storage costs and to speed up the reading step. If you take a peek at the movies.parquet file in the chapter4/data/movies folder, you will see that its size is about one-sixth the size of movies.csv.

Spark works extremely well with the Parquet file format, and in fact Parquet is the default file format for reading and writing data in Spark. Since Parquet files are self-contained, meaning the schema is stored inside the Parquet data file, it is easy to work with Parquet in Spark. Listing 4-16 shows an example of reading a Parquet file. Notice that you don't need to provide a schema or ask Spark to infer the schema. Spark can retrieve the schema from the Parquet file.

One of the cool optimizations that Spark does when reading data from Parquet is that it does decompression and decoding in column batches.

Listing 4-16. Reading a Parquet File in Spark

```
// Parquet is the default format, so we don't need to specify the format
when reading
val movies9 = spark.read.load("<path>/book/chapter4/data/movies/movies.
parquet")
movies9.printSchema
 |-- actor_name: string (nullable = true)
 |-- movie_title: string (nullable = true)
 |-- produced_year: long (nullable = true)

// If we want to be more explicit, we can specify the path to the parquet
function
val movies10 = spark.read.parquet("<path>/book/chapter4/data/movies/movies.
parquet")
movies10.printSchema
 |-- actor_name: string (nullable = true)
 |-- movie_title: string (nullable = true)
 |-- produced_year: long (nullable = true)
```

Creating DataFrames by Reading ORC Files

Optimized Row Columnar (ORC) is another popular open source self-describing columnar storage format in the Hadoop ecosystem. It was created by a company called Cloudera as part of the initiative to massively speed up Hive. It is quite similar to Parquet in terms of efficiency and speed and was designed for analytics workloads. Working with ORC files is just as easy as working with Parquet files. Listing 4-17 shows an example of creating a DataFrame from reading from an ORC file.

Listing 4-17. Reading an ORC File in Spark

```
val movies11 = spark.read.orc("<path>/book/chapter4/data/movies/movies.orc")
movies11.printSchema
 |-- actor_name: string (nullable = true)
 |-- movie_title: string (nullable = true)
 |-- produced_year: long (nullable = true)
```

```
movies11.show(5)
+------------------------+------------------+-------------+
|            actor_name|      movie_title| produced_year|
+------------------------+------------------+-------------+
|       McClure, Marc (I)|      Coach Carter|         2005|
|       McClure, Marc (I)|      Superman II|         1980|
|       McClure, Marc (I)|        Apollo 13|         1995|
|       McClure, Marc (I)|         Superman|         1978|
|       McClure, Marc (I)| Back to the Future|         1985|
+------------------------+------------------+-------------+
```

Creating DataFrames from JDBC

JDBC is a standard application API for reading data from and writing data to a relational database management system. Spark has support for JDBC data sources, which means you can use Spark to read data from and write data to any of the existing RDBMSs such as MySQL, PostgreSQL, Oracle, SQLite, and so on. There are a few important pieces of information you need to provide when working with a JDBC data source: a JDBC driver for your RDBMS, a connection URL, authentication information, and a table name.

For Spark to connect to an RDBMS, it must have access to the JDBC driver JAR file at runtime. Therefore, you need to add the location of a JDBC driver to the Spark classpath. Listing 4-18 shows how to connect to MySQL from the Spark shell.

Listing 4-18. Specifying a JDBC Driver When Starting a Spark Shell

```
./bin/spark-shell ../jdbc/mysql-connector-java-5.1.45/mysql-connector-
java-5.1.45-bin.jar  --jars ../jdbc/mysql-connector-java-5.1.45/mysql-
connector-java-5.1.45-bin.jar
```

Once the Spark shell is successfully started, you can quickly verify to see whether Spark can connect to the RDBMS by using the java.sql.DriverManager class, as shown in Listing 4-19. This example is trying to test a connection to MySQL. The URL format will be a bit different if your RDBMS is not MySQL, so consult the documentation of the JDBC driver you are using.

Listing 4-19. Testing the Connection to MySQL in the Spark Shell

```
import java.sql.DriverManager
val connectionURL = "jdbc:mysql://localhost:3306/<table>?user=<username>
&password=<password>"
val connection = DriverManager.getConnection(connectionURL)
connection.isClosed()
connection close()
```

If you didn't get any exception about the connection, then the Spark shell was able to successfully connect to your RDBMS.

Table 4-6 describes the main options that you need to specify when using a JDBC data source. For a complete list of options, please consult https://spark.apache.org/docs/latest/sql-programming-guide.html#jdbc-to-other-databases.

Table 4-6. *Main Options for a JDBC Data Source*

Key	Description
url	The JDBC URL for Spark to connect to. At the minimum, it should contain the host, port, and database name. For MySQL, it may look something like this: jdbc:mysql://localhost:3306/sakila.
dbtable	The name of a database table for Spark to read data from or write data to.
driver	The class name of the JDBC driver that Spark will instantiate to connect to the previous URL. Consult the JDBC driver documentation that you are using. For the MySQL Connector/J driver, the class name is com.mysql.jdbc.Driver.

Listing 4-20 shows an example of reading data from a table called `film` of the `sakila` database on a MySQL server that runs on localhost at port 3306.

Listing 4-20. Reading Data from a Table in MySQL Server

```
val mysqlURL= "jdbc:mysql://localhost:3306/sakila"
val filmDF = spark.read.format("jdbc").option("driver", "com.mysql.jdbc.
Driver")
                                      .option("url", mysqlURL)
                                      .option("dbtable", "film")
                                      .option("user", "<username>")
                                      .option("password","<password>")
                                      .load()

filmDF.printSchema
 |-- film_id: integer (nullable = false)
 |-- title: string (nullable = false)
 |-- description: string (nullable = true)
 |-- release_year: date (nullable = true)
 |-- language_id: integer (nullable = false)
 |-- original_language_id: integer (nullable = true)
 |-- rental_duration: integer (nullable = false)
 |-- rental_rate: decimal(4,2) (nullable = false)
 |-- length: integer (nullable = true)
 |-- replacement_cost: decimal(5,2) (nullable = false)
 |-- rating: string (nullable = true)
 |-- special_features: string (nullable = true)
 |-- last_update: timestamp (nullable = false)

filmDF.select("film_id","title").show(5)

+-------+-----------------+
|film_id|            title|
+-------+-----------------+
|      1| ACADEMY DINOSAUR|
|      2|   ACE GOLDFINGER|
|      3| ADAPTATION HOLES|
|      4| AFFAIR PREJUDICE|
|      5|       AFRICAN EGG|
+-------+-----------------+
```

When working with a JDBC data source, Spark pushes the filter conditions all the way down to the RDBMS as much as possible. By doing this, much of the data will be filtered out at the RDBMS level, and therefore this will not only speed up the data filtering logic but dramatically reduce the amount of data Spark needs to read. This optimization technique is known as *predicate pushdown*, and Spark will often do this when it knows a data source can support the filtering capability. Parquet is another data source that has this capability. The "Catalyst Optimizer" section in chapter 5 will provide an example of what this looks like.

Working with Structured Operations

Now that you know how to create DataFrames, the next part is to learn how to manipulate or transform them using the provided structured operations. Unlike the RDD operations, the structured operations are designed to be more relational, meaning these operations mirror the kind of expressions you can do with SQL, such as projection, filtering, transforming, joining, and so on. Similar to RDD operations, the structured operations are divided into two categories: transformation and action. The semantics of the structured transformations and actions are identical to the ones in RDDs. In other words, structured transformations are lazily evaluated, and structured actions are eagerly evaluated.

Structured operations are sometimes described as a *domain-specific language* (DSL) for distributed data manipulation. A DSL is a computer language specialized for a particular application domain. In this case, the application domain is the distributed data manipulation. If you have ever worked with SQL, then it is fairly easy to learn the structured operations.

Table 4-7 describes the commonly used DataFrame structured transformations. As a reminder, DataFrames are immutable, and their transformation operations always return a new DataFrame.

Table 4-7. *Commonly Used DataFrame Structured Transformations*

Operation	Description
select	This selects one or more columns from an existing set of columns in the DataFrame. A more technical term for select is projection. During the projection process, columns can be transformed and manipulated.
selectExpr	This supports powerful SQL expressions in transforming columns while performing projection.
filter where	Both filter and where have the same semantics. where is more relational than filter, and it is similar to the where condition in SQL. They are both used for filtering rows based on the given Boolean conditions.
distinct dropDuplicates	This removes duplicate rows from the DataFrame.
sort orderBy	This sorts the DataFrame by the provided columns.
limit	This returns a new DataFrame by taking the first n rows.
union	This combines two DataFrames and return them as a new DataFrame.
withColumn	This is used to add a new column or replace an existing column in the DataFrame.
withColumnRenamed	This renames an existing column. If a given column name doesn't exist in the schema, then it is a no-op.
drop	This drops one or more columns from a DataFrame. This operation does nothing if a specified given column name doesn't exist.
sample	This randomly selects a set of rows based on the given fraction parameter, an optional seed value, and an optional replacement option.
randomSplit	This splits the DataFrames into one or more DataFrames based on the given weights. It is commonly used to split the master data set into training and test data sets in the machine learning model training process.
join	This joins two DataFrames. Spark supports many types of joins. You can find more details in Chapter 5.

(continued)

Table 4-7. (*continued*)

Operation	Description
groupBy	This groups a DataFrame by one or more columns. A common pattern is to perform some kind of aggregation after the groupBy operation. You can find more details in Chapter 5.
describe	This computes the common statistics about numeric and string columns in the DataFrame. Available statistics are count, mean, stddev, min, max, and arbitrary approximate percentiles.

Working with Columns

Most of the DataFrame structured operations in Table 4-7 will require you to specify one or more columns. For some of them, the columns are specified in the form of a string, and for some the columns need to be specified as instances of the Column class. It is completely fair to question why there are two options and when to use what. To answer those questions, you need to understand the functionality the Column class provides. At a high level, the functionalities that the Column class provides can be broken down into the following categories:

- Mathematical operations such as addition, multiplication, and so on

- Logical comparisons between a column value or a literal such as equality, greater than, less than, and so on

- String pattern matching such as like, starting with, ending with, and so on

For a complete list of available functions in the Column class, please refer to the Scala documentation at https://spark.apache.org/docs/latest/api/scala/index.html#org.apache.spark.sql.Column.

With an understanding of the functionality that the Column class provides, you can conclude that whenever there is a need to specify some kind of column expression, then it is necessary to specify the column as an instance of the Column class rather than a string. The upcoming examples will make this clear.

There are different ways of referring to a column, which has created confusion in the Spark user community. A common question is when to use which one, and the answer is it depends. Table 4-8 describes the available options.

Table 4-8. *Different Ways of Referring to a Column*

Way	Example	Description
" "	"columName"	This refers to a column as a string type.
col	col("columnName")	The col function returns an instance of the Column class.
column	column("columnName")	Similar to col, this function returns an instance of the Column class.
$	$"columnName"	This is a syntactic sugar way of constructing a Column class in Scala.
' (tick mark)	'columnName	This is a syntactic sugar way of constructing a Column class in Scala by leveraging the Scala symbolic literals feature.

The col and column functions are synonymous, and both are available in the Scala and Python Spark APIs. If you often switch between the Spark Scala and Python APIs, then it makes sense to use the col function so there is a consistency in your code. If you mostly or exclusively use the Spark Scala APIs, then my recommendation is to use ' (tick mark) because there is only a single character to type. The DataFrame class has its own col function, which is used to disambiguate between columns with the same name from two or more DataFrames when performing a join. Listing 4-21 provides examples of different ways to refer to a column.

Listing 4-21. Different Ways of Referring to a Column

```
import org.apache.spark.sql.functions._

val kvDF = Seq((1,2),(2,3)).toDF("key","value")

// to display column names in a DataFrame, we can call the columns function
kvDF.columns
Array[String] = Array(key, value)

kvDF.select("key")
kvDF.select(col("key"))
```

```
kvDF.select(column("key"))
kvDF.select($"key")
kvDF.select('key)

// using the col function of DataFrame
kvDF.select(kvDF.col("key"))

kvDF.select('key, 'key > 1).show
+---+----------+
|key| (key > 1)|
+---+----------+
|  1|     false|
|  2|      true|
+---+----------+
```

The previous example illustrates a column expression, and therefore it is required to specify a column as an instance of the Column class. If the column was specified as a string, then it would result in a type mismatch error. More examples of column expressions will be shown in the following examples of using various DataFrame structure operations.

Working with Structured Transformations

This section provides examples of working with the structured transformations listed in Table 4-7. All the examples will consistently use ' as a way to refer to columns in a DataFrame. To reduce redundancy, most of the examples will refer to the same movies DataFrame that was created from reading from a Parquet file, illustrated in Listing 4-22.

Listing 4-22. Creating the movies DataFrame from a Parquet File

```
val movies = spark.read.parquet("<path>/chapter4/data/movies/movies.parquet")
```

select(columns)

This transformation is commonly used to perform projection, meaning selecting all or a subset of columns from a DataFrame. During the selection, each column can be transformed via a column expression. There are two variations of this transformation.

113

One takes the column as a string, and the other takes columns as the Column class. This transformation does not permit you to mix the column type when using one of these two variations. See Listing 4-23 for an example of the two variations.

Listing 4-23. Two Variations of the select Transformation

```
movies.select("movie_title","produced_year").show(5)
+-------------------+--------------+
|        movie_title| produced_year|
+-------------------+--------------+
|       Coach Carter|          2005|
|        Superman II|          1980|
|          Apollo 13|          1995|
|           Superman|          1978|
| Back to the Future|          1985|
+-------------------+--------------+

// using a column expression to transform year to decade
movies.select('movie_title,('produced_year - ('produced_year % 10)).
as("produced_decade")).show(5)

+-------------------+----------------+
|        movie_title| produced_decade|
+-------------------+----------------+
|       Coach Carter|            2000|
|        Superman II|            1980|
|          Apollo 13|            1990|
|           Superman|            1970|
| Back to the Future|            1980|
+-------------------+----------------+
```

The second example requires two column expressions: modulo and subtraction. Both them are implemented by the modulo (%) and subtraction (-) functions in the Column class (see the Scala documentation mentioned earlier). By default, Spark uses the column expression as the name of the result column. To make it more readable, the as function is commonly used to rename it to a more human-readable column name. As an astute reader, you can probably figure out the select transformation can be used to add one or more columns to a DataFrame.

selectExpr(expressions)

This transformation is a variant of the select transformation. The one big difference is that it accepts one or more SQL expressions, rather than columns. However, both are essentially performing the same projection task. SQL expressions are powerful and flexible constructs to allow you to express column transformation logic in a natural way, just like the way you think. You can express SQL expressions in a string format, and Spark will parse them into a logical tree so they will be evaluated in the right order. Let's say you want to create a new DataFrame that has all the columns in the movies DataFrame and introduce a new column to represent the decade a movie was produced in; then you would do something like in Listing 4-24.

Listing 4-24. Adding the decade Column to the movies DataFrame Using a SQL Expression

```
movies.selectExpr("*","(produced_year - (produced_year % 10)) as decade").
show(5)
```

```
+----------------+-------------------+-------------+------+
|      actor_name|        movie_title|produced_year|decade|
+----------------+-------------------+-------------+------+
|McClure, Marc (I)|        Coach Carter|         2005|  2000|
|McClure, Marc (I)|        Superman II|         1980|  1980|
|McClure, Marc (I)|          Apollo 13|         1995|  1990|
|McClure, Marc (I)|           Superman|         1978|  1970|
|McClure, Marc (I)| Back to the Future|         1985|  1980|
+----------------+-------------------+-------------+------+
```

The combination of SQL expressions and built-in functions makes it easy to perform certain data analysis that otherwise would take multiple steps. Listing 4-25 shows how easy it is to determine the number of unique movie titles and unique actors in the movies dataset in a single statement. The count function performs an aggregation over the entire DataFrame.

Listing 4-25. Using a SQL Expression and Built-in Functions

```
movies.selectExpr("count(distinct(movie_title)) as
movies","count(distinct(actor_name)) as actors").show
+-------+-------+
| movies| actors|
+-------+-------+
|   1409|   6527|
+-------+-------+
```

filler(condition), where(condition)

This transformation is a fairly straightforward one to understand. It is used to filter out the rows that don't meet the given condition, in other words, when the condition evaluates to false. A different way of looking at the behavior of the filter transformation is that it returns only the rows that meet the specified condition. The given condition can simple or as complex as it needs to be. Using this transformation will require knowing how to leverage a few logical comparison functions in the Column class, like equality, less than, greater than, and inequality. Both the filter and where transformations have the same behavior, so pick the one you are most comfortable with. The latter one is just a bit more relational than the former. See Listing 4-26 for a few examples of performing filtering.

Listing 4-26. Filter Rows with Logical Comparison Functions in the Column Class

```
movies.filter('produced_year < 2000)
movies.where('produced_year > 2000)

movies.filter('produced_year >= 2000)
movies.where('produced_year >= 2000)
```

```
// equality comparison require 3 equal signs
movies.filter('produced_year === 2000).show(5)
```

```
+-----------------+--------------------+-------------+
|       actor_name|         movie_title|produced_year|
+-----------------+--------------------+-------------+
| Cooper, Chris (I)|    Me, Myself & Irene|         2000|
| Cooper, Chris (I)|          The Patriot|         2000|
|   Jolie, Angelina| Gone in Sixty Sec...|         2000|
|    Yip, Françoise|      Romeo Must Die|         2000|
|   Danner, Blythe|     Meet the Parents|         2000|
+-----------------+--------------------+-------------+
```

```
// inequality comparison uses an interesting looking operator =!=
movies.select("movie_title","produced_year").filter('produced_year =!=
2000).show(5)
```

```
+------------------+-------------+
|       movie_title|produced_year|
+------------------+-------------+
|      Coach Carter|         2005|
|       Superman II|         1980|
|         Apollo 13|         1995|
|          Superman|         1978|
| Back to the Future|         1985|
+------------------+-------------+
```

```
// to combine one or more comparison expressions, we will use either the OR
and AND expression operator
movies.filter('produced_year >= 2000 && length('movie_title) < 5).show(5)
```

```
+----------------+------------+-------------+
|      actor_name| movie_title|produced_year|
+----------------+------------+-------------+
| Jolie, Angelina|        Salt|         2010|
|   Cueto, Esteban|         xXx|         2002|
|    Butters, Mike|         Saw|         2004|
|    Franko, Victor|          21|         2008|
|    Ogbonna, Chuk|        Salt|         2010|
+----------------+------------+-------------+
```

```
// the other way of accomplishing the same result is by calling the filter
function two times
movies.filter('produced_year >= 2000).filter(length('movie_title) < 5).show(5)
```

distinct, dropDuplicates

These two transformations have identical behavior. However, dropDuplicates allows
you to control which columns should be used in deduplication logic. If none is specified,
the deduplication logic will use all the columns in the DataFrame. Listing 4-27 shows
different ways of counting how many movies are in the movies data set.

Listing 4-27. Using distinct and dropDuplicates to Achieve the Same Goal

```
movies.select("movie_title").distinct.selectExpr("count(movie_title) as
movies").show
movies.dropDuplicates("movie_title").selectExpr("count(movie_title) as
movies").show

+------+
|movies|
+------+
|  1409|
+------+
```

In terms of performance, there is no difference between these two approaches
because Spark will transform them into the same logical plan.

sort(columns), orderBy(columns)

Both of these transformations have the same semantics. The orderBy transformation is
more relational than the other one. By default, the sorting is in ascending order, and it is
fairly easy to change it to descending. When specifying more than one column, it is possible
to have a different order for each of the columns. See Listing 4-28 for some examples.

Listing 4-28. Sorting the DataFrame in Ascending and Descending Order

```
val movieTitles = movies.dropDuplicates("movie_title")
                    .selectExpr("movie_title", "length(movie_title) as
                    title_length", , "produced_year")
```

```
movieTitles.sort('title_length).show(5)
+-----------+------------+-------------+
|movie_title| title_length| produced_year|
+-----------+------------+-------------+
|         RV|           2|         2006|
|         12|           2|         2007|
|         Up|           2|         2009|
|         X2|           2|         2003|
|         21|           2|         2008|
+-----------+------------+-------------+


// sorting in descending order
movieTitles.orderBy('title_length.desc).show(5)
+--------------------+------------+-------------+
|         movie_title| title_length| produced_year|
+--------------------+------------+-------------+
| Borat: Cultural L...|          83|         2006|
| The Chronicles of...|          62|         2005|
| Hannah Montana & ...|          57|         2008|
| The Chronicles of...|          56|         2010|
| Istoriya pro Rich...|          56|         1997|
+--------------------+------------+-------------+


// sorting by two columns in different orders
movieTitles.orderBy('title_length.desc, 'produced_year).show(5)
+--------------------+------------+-------------+
|         movie_title| title_length| produced_year|
+--------------------+------------+-------------+
| Borat: Cultural L...|          83|         2006|
| The Chronicles of...|          62|         2005|
| Hannah Montana & ...|          57|         2008|
| Istoriya pro Rich...|          56|         1997|
| The Chronicles of...|          56|         2010|
+--------------------+------------+-------------+
```

119

In the previous example, notice the title of the last two movies are at the same length, but their years are ordered in the correct ascending order.

limit(n)

This transformation returns a new DataFrame by taking the first n rows. This transformation is commonly used after the sorting is done to figure out the top n or bottom n rows based on the sorting order. Listing 4-29 shows an example of using the `limit` transformation to figure out the top ten actors with the longest names.

Listing 4-29. Using the limit Transformation to Figure Out the Top Ten Actors with the Longest Names

```
// first create a DataFrame with their name and associated length
val actorNameDF = movies.select("actor_name").distinct.selectExpr
("*", "length(actor_name) as length")

// order names by length and retrieve the top 10
actorNameDF.orderBy('length.desc).limit(10).show
+----------------------------+-------+
|                 actor_name| length|
+----------------------------+-------+
| Driscoll, Timothy 'TJ' James|     28|
| Badalamenti II, Peter Donald|     28|
|   Shepard, Maridean Mansfield|     27|
|   Martino, Nicholas Alexander|     27|
|   Marshall-Fricker, Charlotte|     27|
|    Phillips, Christopher (III)|     27|
|   Pahlavi, Shah Mohammad Reza|     27|
|    Juan, The Bishop Don Magic|     26|
|    Van de Kamp Buchanan, Ryan|     26|
|    Lough Haggquist, Catherine|     26|
+----------------------------+-------+
```

union(otherDataFrame)

You learned earlier that DataFrames are immutable. So if there is a need to add more rows to an existing DataFrame, then the union transformation is useful for that purpose as well as for combining rows from two DataFrames. This transformation requires both DataFrames to have the same schema, meaning both column names and their order must exactly match. Let say one of the movies in the DataFrame is missing an actor and you want to fix that issue. See Listing 4-30 for how to do that using the union transformation.

Listing 4-30. Adding a Missing Actor to the movies DataFrame

```
// we want to add a missing actor to movie with title as "12"
val shortNameMovieDF = movies.where('movie_title === "12")
shortNameMovieDF.show
+--------------------+------------+--------------+
|         actor_name| movie_title| produced_year |
+--------------------+------------+--------------+
|     Efremov, Mikhail|          12|          2007|
|     Stoyanov, Yuriy|          12|          2007|
|      Gazarov, Sergey|          12|          2007|
| Verzhbitskiy, Viktor|          12|          2007|
+--------------------+------------+--------------+

// create a DataFrame with one row
import org.apache.spark.sql.Row
val forgottenActor = Seq(Row("Brychta, Edita", "12", 2007L))
val forgottenActorRDD = spark.sparkContext.parallelize(forgottenActor)
val forgottenActorDF = spark.createDataFrame(forgottenActorRDD,
shortNameMovieDF.schema)
```

```
// now adding the missing action
val completeShortNameMovieDF = shortNameMovieDF.union(forgottenActorDF)
completeShortNameMovieDF.union(forgottenActorDF).show
+--------------------+------------+--------------+
|          actor_name| movie_title| produced_year|
+--------------------+------------+--------------+
|    Efremov, Mikhail|          12|          2007|
|    Stoyanov, Yuriy |          12|          2007|
|    Gazarov, Sergey |          12|          2007|
| Verzhbitskiy, Viktor|         12|          2007|
|      Brychta, Edita|          12|          2007|
+--------------------+------------+--------------+
```

withColumn(colName, column)

This transformation is used to add a new column to a DataFrame. It requires two input parameters: a column name and a value in the form of a column expression. You can accomplish pretty much the same goal by using the selectExpr transformation. However, if the given column name matches one of the existing ones, then that column is replaced with the given column expression. Listing 4-31 provides examples of adding a new column as well as replacing an existing one.

Listing 4-31. Adding a Column As Well As Replacing a Column Using the withColumn Transformation

```
// adding a new column based on a certain column expression
movies.withColumn("decade", ('produced_year - 'produced_year % 10)).show(5)
+------------------+-------------------+--------------+-------+
|        actor_name|        movie_title| produced_year| decade|
+------------------+-------------------+--------------+-------+
| McClure, Marc (I)|       Coach Carter|          2005|   2000|
| McClure, Marc (I)|       Superman II |          1980|   1980|
| McClure, Marc (I)|         Apollo 13 |          1995|   1990|
| McClure, Marc (I)|           Superman|          1978|   1970|
| McClure, Marc (I)| Back to the Future|          1985|   1980|
+------------------+-------------------+--------------+-------+
```

```
// now replace the produced_year with new values
movies.withColumn("produced_year", ('produced_year - 'produced_year % 10)).
show(5)
```

```
+-----------------+------------------+-------------+
|       actor_name|       movie_title|produced_year|
+-----------------+------------------+-------------+
| McClure, Marc (I)|      Coach Carter|         2000|
| McClure, Marc (I)|       Superman II|         1980|
| McClure, Marc (I)|         Apollo 13|         1990|
| McClure, Marc (I)|          Superman|         1970|
| McClure, Marc (I)| Back to the Future|         1980|
+-----------------+------------------+-------------+
```

withColumnRenamed(existingColName, newColName)

This transformation is strictly about renaming an existing column name in a DataFrame. It is fair to ask why in the world Spark provides this transformation. As it is turns out, this transformation is useful in the following situations:

- To rename a cryptic column name to a more human-friendly name. The cryptic column name can come from an existing schema that you don't have control of, such as when the column you need in a Parquet file was produced by your company's partner.

- Before joining two DataFrames that happen to have one or more same column name. This transformation can be used to rename one or more columns in one of the two DataFrames so you can refer to them easily after the join.

Notice that if the provided existingColName doesn't exist in the schema, Spark doesn't throw an error, and it will silently do nothing. Listing 4-32 renames some of the column names in the movies DataFrame to short names. By the way, this is something that can be accomplished by using the select or selectExpr transformation. I will leave that as an exercise for you.

Listing 4-32. Using the withColumnRenamed Transformation to Rename Some of the Column Names

```
movies.withColumnRenamed("actor_name", "actor")
     .withColumnRenamed("movie_title", "title")
     .withColumnRenamed("produced_year", "year").show(5)
+------------------+-------------------+-----+
|             actor|              title| year|
+------------------+-------------------+-----+
| McClure, Marc (I)|       Coach Carter| 2005|
| McClure, Marc (I)|       Superman II | 1980|
| McClure, Marc (I)|          Apollo 13| 1995|
| McClure, Marc (I)|           Superman| 1978|
| McClure, Marc (I)|  Back to the Future| 1985|
+------------------+-------------------+-----+
```

drop(columnName1, columnName2)

This transformation simply drops the specified columns from the DataFrame. You can specify one or more column names to drop, but only the ones that exist in the schema will be dropped and the ones that don't will be silently ignored. You can use the select transformation to drop columns by projecting only the columns that you want to keep. In the case that a DataFrame has 100 columns and you want to drop a few, then this transformation is more convenient to use than the select transformation. Listing 4-33 provides examples of dropping columns.

Listing 4-33. Dropping Two Columns: One Exists and the Other One Doesn't

```
movies.drop("actor_name", "me").printSchema
 |-- movie_title: string (nullable = true)
 |-- produced_year: long (nullable = true)
```

As you can see from the previous example, the second column, me, doesn't exist in the schema, so the drop transformation simply ignores it.

sample(fraction), sample(fraction, seed), sample(fraction, seed, withReplacement)

This transformation returns a randomly selected set of rows from the DataFrame. The number of the returned rows will be approximately equal to the specified fraction, which represents a percentage, and the value has to be between 0 and 1. The seed is used to seed the random number generator, which is used to generate a row number to include in the result. If a seed is not specified, then a randomly generated value is used. The withReplacement option is used to determine whether a randomly selected row will be placed back into the selection pool. In other words, when withReplacement is true, a particular selected row has the potential to be selected more than once. So, when would you need to use this transformation? It is useful in the case where the original dataset is large and there is a need to reduce it to a smaller size so you can quickly iterate on the data analysis logic. Listing 4-34 provides examples using the sample transformation.

Listing 4-34. Different Ways of Using the sample Transformation

```
// sample with no replacement and a fraction
movies.sample(false, 0.0003).show(3)
+--------------------+--------------------+-------------+
|          actor_name|         movie_title| produced_year|
+--------------------+--------------------+-------------+
|     Lewis, Clea (I)| Ice Age: The Melt...|         2006|
|      Lohan, Lindsay|   Herbie Fully Loaded|         2005|
| Tagawa, Cary-Hiro...|     Licence to Kill|         1989|
+--------------------+--------------------+-------------+

// sample with replacement, a fraction and a seed
movies.sample(true, 0.0003, 123456).show(3)
+--------------------+--------------+-------------+
|          actor_name|   movie_title| produced_year|
+--------------------+--------------+-------------+
| Panzarella, Russ (V)| Public Enemies|         2009|
|         Reed, Tanoai|     Daredevil|         2003|
|        Moyo, Masasa|   Spider-Man 3|         2007|
+--------------------+--------------+-------------+
```

As you can see, the returned movies are pretty random.

randomSplit(weights)

This transformation is commonly used during the process of preparing the data to train machine learning models. Unlike the previous transformations, this one returns one or more DataFrames. The number of DataFrames it returns is based on the number of weights you specify. If the provided set of weights don't add up to 1, then they will be normalized accordingly to add up to 1. Listing 4-35 provides an example of splitting the movies DataFrames into three smaller ones.

Listing 4-35. Using randomSplit to split the movies DataFrames into Three Parts

```
// the weights need to be an Array
val smallerMovieDFs = movies.randomSplit(Array(0.6, 0.3, 0.1))

// let's see if the counts are added up to the count of movies DataFrame
movies.count
Long = 31393

smallerMovieDFs(0).count
Long = 18881

smallerMovieDFs(0).count + smallerMovieDFs(1).count + smallerMovieDFs(2).count
Long = 31393
```

Working with Missing or Bad Data

In reality, the data you often work with is not as clean as you would like. Maybe it's because the data evolves over time, and therefore some columns have values and some don't. It is important to deal with this kind of issue at the beginning of your data manipulation logic to prevent any unpleasant surprises that will cause your long-running data processing job to stop working.

The Spark community recognizes that the need to deal with missing data is a fact of life; therefore, Spark provides a dedicated class called DataFrameNaFunctions to help in dealing with this inconvenient issue. An instance of DataFrameNaFunctions is available as the an member variable inside the DataFrame class. There are three common ways of dealing with missing or bad data. The first way is to drop the rows that have missing values in a one or more columns. The second way is to fill those missing values with user-provided values. The third way is to replace the bad data with something that you know how to deal with.

Let's start with dropping rows with missing data. You can tell Spark to drop rows where any column or only the specific columns have missing values. Listing 4-36 shows a few different ways of dropping rows with missing data.

Listing 4-36. Dropping Rows with Missing Data

```
// first create a DataFrame with missing values in one or more columns
import org.apache.spark.sql.Row

val badMovies = Seq(Row(null, null, null),
                    Row(null, null, 2018L),
                    Row("John Doe", "Awesome Movie", null),
                    Row(null, "Awesome Movie", 2018L),
                    Row("Mary Jane", null, 2018L))
val badMoviesRDD = spark.sparkContext.parallelize(badMovies)
val badMoviesDF = spark.createDataFrame(badMoviesRDD, movies.schema)
badMoviesDF.show
+----------+--------------+--------------+
|actor_name|   movie_title| produced_year|
+----------+--------------+--------------+
|      null|          null|          null|
|      null|          null|          2018|
|  John Doe| Awesome Movie|          null|
|      null| Awesome Movie|          2018|
| Mary Jane|          null|          2018|
+----------+--------------+--------------+
```

```
// dropping rows that have missing data in any column
// both of the lines below will achieve the same purpose
badMoviesDF.na.drop().show
badMoviesDF.na.drop("any").show
+----------+------------+--------------+
|actor_name| movie_title| produced_year|
+----------+------------+--------------+
+----------+------------+--------------+

// drop rows that have missing data in every single column
badMoviesDF.na.drop("all").show
+----------+--------------+--------------+
|actor_name|   movie_title| produced_year|
+----------+--------------+--------------+
|      null|          null|          2018|
|  John Doe| Awesome Movie|          null|
|      null| Awesome Movie|          2018|
| Mary Jane|          null|          2018|
+----------+--------------+--------------+

// drops rows when column actor_name has missing data
badMoviesDF.na.drop(Array("actor_name")).show
+----------+--------------+--------------+
|actor_name|   movie_title| produced_year|
+----------+--------------+--------------+
|  John Doe| Awesome Movie|          null|
| Mary Jane|          null|          2018|
+----------+--------------+--------------+
```

describe(columnNames)

Sometimes it is useful to have a general sense of the basic statistics of the data you are working with. The basic statistics this transformation can compute for string and numeric columns are count, mean, standard deviation, minimum, and maximum. You can pick and choose which string or numeric columns to compute the statistics for. See Listing 4-37 for an example.

Listing 4-37. Use the describe Transformation to Show Statistics for the produced_year Column

```
movies.describe("produced_year").show
+-------+-------------------+
|summary|      produced_year|
+-------+-------------------+
|  count|              31392|
|   mean| 2002.7964449541284|
| stddev|  6.377236851493877|
|    min|               1961|
|    max|               2012|
+-------+-------------------+
```

Working with Structured Actions

This section covers the structured actions. They have the same eager evaluated semantics as the RDD actions, so they trigger the computation of all the transformations that lead up to a particular action. Table 4-9 describes the structured actions.

Table 4-9. *Commonly Used Structured Actions*

Operation	Description
show() show(numRows) show(truncate) show(numRows, truncate)	Displays a number of rows in a tabular format. If numRows is not specified, it will show the top 20 rows. The truncate option controls whether to truncate the string column if it is longer than 20 characters.
head() first() head(n) take(n)	Returns the first row. If n is specified, then it will return the first n rows. first is an alias for head. take(n) is an alias for first(n).
takeAsList(n)	Returns the first n rows as a Java list. Be careful not to take too many rows; otherwise, it may cause an out-of-memory error on the application's driver process.
collect collectAsList	Returns all the rows as an array or Java list. Apply the same caution as the one described in the takeAsList action.
count	Returns the number of rows in a DataFrame.

Most of these are self-explanatory. The show action was used in many examples earlier in the chapter. One interesting action is called describe, which is described next.

Introduction to Datasets

At one point in the history of Spark, there was a lot of confusion about the differences between the DataFrame and Dataset APIs. Given these options, it is fair to ask what are the differences between them, what are the advantages and disadvantages of each option, and when to use which one. Recognizing this huge confusion in the Spark user community, Spark designers decided to unify the DataFrame APIs with the Dataset APIs in Spark 2.0 to have one fewer abstraction for users to learn and remember. Starting with the Spark 2.0 release, there is only one high-level abstraction called a Dataset, which has two flavors: a strongly typed API and an untyped API. The term *DataFrame* didn't go away; instead, it has been redefined as an alias for a collection of generic objects in a Dataset. From the code perspective, what I am saying is a DataFrame is essentially a type alias for Dataset[Row], where a Row is a generic untyped JVM object. A Dataset is defined as a collection of strongly typed JVM objects, represented by either a case class in Scala or a class in Java. Table 4-10 describes the Dataset API flavors that are available in each of the programming languages that Spark supports.

The Python and R languages have no compile-time type safety; therefore, only the untyped Dataset APIs (aka DataFrame) are supported.

Table 4-10. *Dataset Flavors*

Language	Flavor
Scala	Dataset[T] and DataFrame
Java	Dataset[T]
Python	DataFrame
R	DataFrame

Consider the Dataset as a younger brother of the DataFrame; however, it is more about type safety and is object-oriented. A Dataset is a strongly typed, immutable collection of data. Similar to a DataFrame, the data in a Dataset is mapped to a defined schema. However, there are a few important differences between a DataFrame and a Dataset.

- Each row in a Dataset is represented by a user-defined object so that you can refer to an individual column as a member variable of that object. This provides you with compile-type safety.

- A Dataset has helpers called *encoders*, which are smart and efficient encoding utilities that convert data inside each user-defined object into a compact binary format. This translates into a reduction of memory usage if and when a Dataset is cached in memory as well as a reduction in the number of bytes that Spark needs to transfer over a network during the shuffling process.

In terms of limitations, the Dataset APIs are available in only strongly typed languages such as Scala and Java. At this point, a question should pop into your mind regarding when to use the DataFrame APIs and the Dataset APIs. The Dataset APIs are good for production jobs that need to run on a regular basis and are written and maintained by data engineers. For most interactive and explorative analysis use cases, using the DataFrame APIs would be sufficient.

Note A case class in the Scala language is like a JavaBean class in the Java language; however, it has a few built-in interesting properties. An instance of a case class is immutable, and therefore it is commonly used to model domain-specific objects. In addition, it is easy to reason about the internal states of the instances of a case class because they are immutable. The toString and equals methods are automatically generated to make it easier to print out the content of the case class and to compare different case class instances. Scala case classes work well with the pattern matching feature in Scala language.

Creating Datasets

There are a few ways to create a Dataset, but the first thing you need to do is to define a domain-specific object to represent each row. The first way is to transform a DataFrame to a Dataset using the as(Symbol) function of the DataFrame class. The second way is to use the SparkSession.createDataset() function to create a Dataset from a local collection objects. The third way is to use the toDS implicit conversion utility. Listing 4-38 provides examples of creating Datasets using the different ways described earlier.

Listing 4-38. Different Ways of Creating Datasets

```
// define Movie case class
case class Movie(actor_name:String, movie_title:String, produced_year:Long)

// convert DataFrame to strongly typed Dataset
val moviesDS = movies.as[Movie]

// create a Dataset using SparkSession.createDataset() and the toDS
implicit function
val localMovies = Seq(Movie("John Doe", "Awesome Movie", 2018L),
                             Movie("Mary Jane", "Awesome Movie", 2018L))

val localMoviesDS1 = spark.createDataset(localMovies)
val localMoviesDS2 = localMovies.toDS()
localMoviesDS1.show
```

```
+----------+-------------+-------------+
|actor_name|  movie_title| produced_year|
+----------+-------------+-------------+
|  John Doe| Awesome Movie|         2018|
| Mary Jane| Awesome Movie|         2018|
+----------+-------------+-------------+
```

Out of the three ways of creating Datasets, the first way is the most popular one. During the process of transforming a DataFrame to a Dataset using a Scala case class, Spark will perform a validation to ensure the member variable names in the Scala case class matches up with the column names in the schema of the DataFrame. If there is a mismatch, Spark will let you know.

Working with Datasets

Now that you have a Dataset, you can manipulate it using the transformations and actions described earlier. Previously you referred to the columns in the DataFrame using one of the options described earlier. With a Dataset, each row is represented by a strongly typed object; therefore, you can just refer to the columns using the member variable names, which will give you type safety as well as compile-time validation. If there is a misspelling in the name, the compiler will flag them immediately during the development phase. See Listing 4-39 for examples of manipulating a Dataset.

Listing 4-39. Manipulating a Dataset in a Type-Safe Manner

```
// filter movies that were produced in 2010 using
moviesDS.filter(movie => movie.produced_year == 2010).show(5)
+-------------------+--------------------+-------------+
|         actor_name|         movie_title| produced_year|
+-------------------+--------------------+-------------+
|  Cooper, Chris (I)|            The Town|         2010|
|    Jolie, Angelina|                Salt|         2010|
|    Jolie, Angelina|         The Tourist|         2010|
|     Danner, Blythe|      Little Fockers|         2010|
| Byrne, Michael (I)| Harry Potter and ...|         2010|
+-------------------+--------------------+-------------+
```

```
// displaying the title of the first movie in the moviesDS
moviesDS.first.movie_title
String = Coach Carter
```

```
// try with misspelling the movie_title and get compilation error
moviesDS.first.movie_tile
error: value movie_tile is not a member of Movie
```

```
// perform projection using map transformation
val titleYearDS = moviesDS.map(m => ( m.movie_title, m.produced_year))
titleYearDS.printSchema
 |-- _1: string (nullable = true)
 |-- _2: long (nullable = false)
```

```
// demonstrating a type-safe transformation that fails at compile time,
performing subtraction on a column with string type
```

```
// a problem is not detected for DataFrame until runtime
movies.select('movie_title - 'movie_title)
```

```
// a problem is detected at compile time
moviesDS.map(m => m.movie_title - m.movie_title)
error: value - is not a member of String
```

```
// take action returns rows as Movie objects to the driver
moviesDS.take(5)
Array[Movie] = Array(Movie(McClure, Marc (I),Coach Carter,2005),
Movie(McClure, Marc (I),Superman II,1980), Movie(McClure, Marc (I),Apollo
13,1995))
```

For those who use the Scala programming language on a regular basis, working with the strongly typed Dataset APIs will feel natural and give you impression that those objects in the Dataset reside locally.

When you use the strongly typed Dataset APIs, Spark implicitly converts each Row instance to the domain-specific object that you provide. This conversion has some cost in terms of performance; however, it provides more flexibility.

One general guideline to help with deciding when to use a DataSet over a DataFrame is the desire to have a higher degree of type safety at compile time.

Using SQL in Spark SQL

In the big data era, SQL has been described as the lingua franca for big data analysis. One of the coolest features Spark provides is the ability to use SQL to perform distributed data manipulation or analysis at scale. Data analysts who are proficient at SQL can now be productive at using Spark to perform data analysis on large datasets. One important note to remember is SQL in Spark is designed to be used for online analytic processing (OLAP) use cases and not online transaction processing (OLTP) use cases. In other words, it is not applicable for low-latency use cases.

SQL has evolved and improved over time. Spark implements a subset of the ANSI SQL:2003 revision, which most popular RDBMS servers support. Being compliant with this particular revision means the Spark SQL data processing engine can be evaluated by an existing and widely used industry-standard decision support benchmark called TPC-DS.

As a testament of the power of the Spark SQL engine, in late 2016, Facebook started migrating some of its largest Apache Hive workloads to Spark to take advantage of the power of the Spark SQL engine. See this post for more details: `https://code.facebook.com/posts/1671373793181703/apache-spark-scale-a-60-tb-production-use-case/`.

Note   Structured Query Language (SQL) is a domain-specific language, and it is widely used to perform data analysis and manipulation of structured data organized in a table format. The concepts in SQL are based on relational algebra; however, it is an easy language to learn. One key difference between SQL and other programming languages such as Scala or Python is that SQL is a declarative programming language, which means you express what want to do with the data and let the SQL execution engine figure out the necessary optimizations to speed up execution time. If you are new to SQL, there is a free course at `https://www.datacamp.com/courses/intro-to-sql-for-data-science`.

Running SQL in Spark

Spark provides a few different ways to run SQL in Spark.

- Spark SQL CLI (./bin/spark-sql)

- JDBC/ODBC server

- Programmatically in Spark applications

This first two options provide an integration with Apache Hive to leverage the Hive metastore, which is a repository that contains the metadata and schema information about the various system and user-defined tables. This section will cover only the last option.

DataFrames and Datasets are essentially like tables in a database. Before you can issue SQL queries to manipulate them, you need to register them as temporary views. Each view has a name, and that is what is used as the table name in the select clause. Spark provides two levels of scoping for the temporary views. One is at the Spark session level. When a DataFrame is registered at this level, only the queries that are issued in the same session can refer to that DataFrame. The session-scoped level will disappear when a Spark session is closed. The second scoping level is at the global level, which means these views are available to SQL statements in all Spark sessions. All the registered views are maintained in the Spark metadata catalog that can be accessed through SparkSession. See Listing 4-40 for example of registering views and using the Spark catalog to inspect the metadata of those views.

Listing 4-40. Registering the movies DataFrame as a Temporary View and Inspecting the Spark Metadata Catalog

```
// display tables in the catalog, expecting an empty list
spark.catalog.listTables.show
+-----+---------+------------+----------+------------+
| name| database| description| tableType| isTemporary|
+-----+---------+------------+----------+------------+
+-----+---------+------------+----------+------------+

// now register movies DataFrame as a temporary view
movies.createOrReplaceTempView("movies")
```

```
// should see the movies view in the catalog
spark.catalog.listTables.show
```

name	database	description	tableType	isTemporary
movies	null	null	TEMPORARY	true

```
// show the list of columns of movies view in catalog
spark.catalog.listColumns("movies").show
```

name	description	dataType	nullable	isPartition	isBucket
actor_name	null	string	true	false	false
movie_title	null	string	true	false	false
produced_year	null	bigint	true	false	false

```
// register movies as global temporary view called movies_g
movies.createOrReplaceGlobalTempView("movies_g")
```

The previous example gives you a couple of views to select from. The programmatic way of issuing SQL queries is to use the sql function of the SparkSession class. Inside the SQL statement, you have access to all SQL expressions and built-in functions. Once the SparkSession.sql function executes the given SQL query, it will return a DataFrame. The ability to issue SQL statements and use DataFrame transformations and actions provides you with a lot of flexibility in how you choose to perform distributed data processing in Spark. Listing 4-41 provides examples of issuing simple and complex SQL statements.

Listing 4-41. Programmatically Executing SQL Statements in Spark

```
// simple example of executing a SQL statement without a registered view
val infoDF = spark.sql("select current_date() as today , 1 + 100 as value")
infoDF.show
```

today	value
2017-12-27	101

```
// select from a view
spark.sql("select * from movies where actor_name like '%Jolie%' and
produced_year > 2009").show
+---------------+---------------+-------------+
|     actor_name|    movie_title| produced_year|
+---------------+---------------+-------------+
|Jolie, Angelina|           Salt|         2010|
|Jolie, Angelina| Kung Fu Panda 2|         2011|
|Jolie, Angelina|     The Tourist|         2010|
+---------------+---------------+-------------+

// mixing SQL statement and DataFrame transformation
spark.sql("select actor_name, count(*) as count from movies group by actor_name")
        .where('count > 30)
        .orderBy('count.desc)
        .show
+------------------+------+
|        actor_name| count|
+------------------+------+
|   Tatasciore, Fred|    38|
|      Welker, Frank|    38|
| Jackson, Samuel L.|    32|
|      Harnell, Jess|    31|
+------------------+------+

// using a subquery to figure out the number movies were produced in each year.
// leverage """ to format multi-line SQL statement

spark.sql("""select produced_year, count(*) as count
                from (select distinct movie_title, produced_year from
                movies)
                group by produced_year""")
        .orderBy('count.desc).show(5)
```

```
+-------------+------+
|produced_year| count|
+-------------+------+
|         2006|    86|
|         2004|    86|
|         2011|    86|
|         2005|    85|
|         2008|    82|
+-------------+------+
```

```
// select from a global view requires prefixing the view name with key word
'global_temp'
spark.sql("select count(*) from global_temp.movies_g").show
+-----+
|count|
+-----+
|31393|
+-----+
```

Instead of reading the data file through DataFrameReader and then registering the newly created DataFrame as a temporary view, it is possible to issue a SQL query directly from a file. See Listing 4-42 for an example.

Listing 4-42. Issuing a SQL Query Directly from a File

```
spark.sql("SELECT * FROM parquet.`<path>/chapter4/data/movies/movies.
parquet`").show(5)
```

Writing Data Out to Storage Systems

At this point, you know how to read data from various file formats or from a database server using DataFrameReader, and you know how use SQL or transformations and actions of structured APIs to manipulate the data. At some point, you will need to write the data in a DataFrame out to an external storage system, i.e., a local file system, HDFS, or Amazon S3. In a typical ETL data processing job, the results will most likely be written out to some storage system.

In Spark SQL, the DataFrameWriter class is responsible for the logic and complexity of writing out the data in a DataFrame to an external storage system. An instance of the DataFrameWriter class is available to you as the write variable in the DataFrame class. The pattern for interacting with DataFrameWriter is somewhat similar to the interacting pattern of DataFrameReader. From a Spark shell or in a Spark application, you refer to it as in Listing 4-43.

Listing 4-43. Using the write Variable from the DataFrame Class

```
movies.write
```

Listing 4-44 describes the common pattern for interacting with DataFrameWriter.

Listing 4-44. Common Interacting Pattern with DataFrameWriter

```
movies.write.format(...).mode(...).option(...).partitionBy(...).bucketBy(...)
.sortBy(...).save(path)
```

Similar to DataFrameReader, the default format is Parquet; therefore, it is not necessary to specify a format when writing the data out in Parquet format. The partitionBy, bucketBy, and sortBy functions are used to control the directory structure of the output files in the file-based data sources. By structuring the directory layout based on the read patterns, it will dramatically reduce the amount of data that needs to be read for analysis. You'll learn more about this later in the chapter. The input to the save function is a directory name, not a file name.

One of the important options in the DataFrameWriter class is the save mode, which controls how Spark will handle the situation when the specified output folder already exists. Table 4-11 lists the various supported save modes.

Table 4-11. *Save Modes*

Mode	Description
append	This appends the DataFrame data to the list of files that already exist at the specified destination location.
overwrite	This completely overwrites any data files that already exist at the specified destination location with the data in the DataFrame.
error errorIfExists default	This is the default mode. If the specified destination location exists, then DataFrameWriter will throw an error.
ignore	If the specified destination location exists, then simply do nothing. In other words, silently don't write out the data in the DataFrame.

Listing 4-45 shows a few examples of using various combinations of formats and modes.

Listing 4-45. Using DataFrameWriter to Write Data to File-Based Sources

```
// write data out as CVS format, but using a '#' as delimiter
movies.write.format("csv").option("sep", "#").save("/tmp/output/csv")

// write data out using overwrite save mode
movies.write.format("csv").mode("overwrite").option("sep", "#").save
("/tmp/output/csv")
```

The number of files written out to the output directory corresponds to the number of partitions a DataFrame has. Listing 4-46 shows how to find out the number of partitions a DataFrame has.

Listing 4-46. Displaying the Number of Partitions a DataFrame Has

```
movies.rdd.getNumPartitions
Int = 1
```

In some cases, the content of a DataFrame is not large, and there is a need to write to a single file. A small trick to achieve this goal is to reduce the number of partitions in your DataFrame to one and then write it out. Listing 4-47 shows an example of how to do that.

Listing 4-47. Reducing the Number of Partitions in a DataFrame to 1

```
val singlePartitionDF = movies.coalesce(1)
```

The idea of writing data out using partitioning and bucketing is borrowed from the Apache Hive user community. As a general rule of thumb, the partition by column should have low cardinality. In the movies DataFrame, the produced_year column is a good candidate for the partition by column. Let's say you are going to write out the movies DataFrame with partitioning by the produced_year column. DataFrameWriter will write out all the movies with the same produced_year into a single directory. The number of directories in the output folder will correspond to the number of years in the movies DataFrame. See Listing 4-48 for an example of using the partitionBy function.

Listing 4-48. Writing the movies DataFrame Using the Parquet Format and Partition by the produced_year Column

```
movies.write.partitionBy("produced_year").save("/tmp/output/movies")

// the /tmp/output/movies directory will contain the following subdirectories
produced_year=1961 to produced_year=2012
```

The directory names generated by the partitionBy option seems strange because each directory name consists of the partitioning column name and the associated value. These two pieces of information are used at data reading time to choose which directory to read based on the data access pattern, and therefore it ends up reading much less data than otherwise.

The Trio: DataFrames, Datasets, and SQL

Now you know there are three different ways of manipulating structured data in the Spark SQL module. Table 4-12 shows where each option falls in the syntax and analysis spectrum.

The main point here is the earlier you can catch the errors, the more productive you will be and the more stable your data processing applications will be.

Table 4-12. *Syntax and Analysis Errors Spectrum*

	SQL	DataFrame	Dataset
System errors	Runtime	Compile time	Compile time
Analysis errors	Runtime	Runtime	Compile time

DataFrame Persistence

DataFrames can be persisted/cached in memory just like how it is done with RDDs. The same familiar persistence APIs (persist and unpersist) are available in the DataFrame class. However, there is one big difference when caching a DataFrame. Spark SQL knows the schema of the data inside a DataFrame, so it organizes the data in a columnar format as well as applies any applicable compressions to minimize space usage. The net result is it will require much less space to store a DataFrame in memory than storing an RDD when both are backed by the same data file. All the different storage options described in Table 3-5 are applicable for persisting a DataFrame. Listing 4-49 demonstrates persisting a DataFrame with a human-readable name so it is easy to identify in the Spark UI.

Listing 4-49. Persisting a DataFrame with a Human-Readable Name

```
val numDF = spark.range(1000).toDF("id")


// register as a view
numDF.createOrReplaceTempView("num_df")

// use Spark catalog to cache the numDF using name "num_df"
spark.catalog.cacheTable("num_df")

// force the persistence to happen by taking the count action
numDF.count
```

At this point, point your browser to the Spark UI (`http://localhost:4040` when running the Spark shell) and click the Storage tab. See Figure 4-2 for an example.

RDD Name	Storage Level	Cached Partitions	Fraction Cached	Size in Memory	Size on Disk
In-memory table num_df	Memory Deserialized 1x Replicated	8	100%	3.1 KB	0.0 B

Figure 4-2. *Storage tab*

Summary

In this chapter, you learned the following:

- The Spark SQL module provides a new and powerful abstraction for structured distributed data manipulation. Structured data has a defined schema, which consists of column names and a column data type.

- The main programming abstraction in Spark SQL is the Dataset, and it has two flavors of APIs: a strongly typed API and an untyped API. For strongly typed APIs, each row is represented by a domain-specified object. For untyped APIs, each row is represented by a Row object. A DataFrame is now just an alias of Dataset[Row]. The strongly typed APIs give you static typing and compile-time checking; therefore, they are available only in the strongly typed languages (Scala and Java).

- Spark SQL supports a variety of popular data sources, and the DataFrameReader class is responsible for creating DataFrames by reading data from any of these data sources.

- Similar to RDD, a Dataset has two types of structured operations. They are transformation and actions. The former is lazy evaluated, and the latter is eagerly evaluated.

- Spark SQL supports the ability to use SQL for queries against large sets. This opens up Spark to data analysts and nonprogrammers.

- Writing out data from either a Dataset or DataFrame is done via a class called DataFrameWriter.

SPARK SQL EXERCISES

The following questions are identical to the ones in Chapter 3. Here you should use the Spark SQL Structured APIs or SQL to solve these problems.

1. Compute the number of movies produced in each year. The output should have two columns: year and count. The output should be ordered by the count in descending order.

2. Compute the number of movies each actor was in. The output should have two columns: actor and count. The output should be ordered by the count in descending order.

3. Compute the highest-rated movie per year and include all the actors in that movie. The output should have only one movie per year, and it should contain four columns: year, movie title, rating, and a semicolon-separated list of actor names. This question will require joining the movies.tsv and movie-ratings.tsv files. There are two approaches to this problem. The first one is to figure out the highest-rated movie per year first and then join with the list of actors. The second one is to perform the join first and then figure out the highest-rated movies per year along with a list of actors. The result of each approach is different than the other one. Why do you think that is?

4. Determine which pair of actors worked together most. Working together is defined as appearing in the same movie. The output should have three columns: actor 1, actor 2, and count. The output should be sorted by the count in descending order. The solution to this question will require a self-join.

CHAPTER 5

Spark SQL (Advanced)

Chapter 4 introduced the foundational elements of the Spark SQL module including the core abstraction, structured operations for manipulating structured data, and the support for reading data from and writing data to a variety of data sources. Building on top of that foundation, this chapter covers some of the advanced capabilities of the Spark SQL module as well as takes a peek behind the curtain to explain the optimization and execution efficiency that the Catalyst optimizer and Tungsten engine provide. To help you perform complex analytics, Spark SQL provides a set of powerful and flexible aggregation capabilities, the ability to join multiple datasets, a large set of built-in and high-performant functions, and a set of advanced analytic functions. This chapter covers each of these topics in detail.

Aggregations

Performing any interesting analytics on big data usually involves some kind of aggregation to summarize the data in order to extract patterns or insights or to generate summary reports. Aggregations usually require some form of grouping either on the entire dataset or on one or more columns, and then they apply aggregation functions such as summing, counting, or averaging to each group. Spark provides many commonly used aggregation functions as well as the ability to aggregate the values into a collection, which then can be further analyzed. The grouping of rows can be done at different levels, and Spark supports the following levels:

- Treat a DataFrame as one group.

- Divide a DataFrame into multiple groups by using one or more columns and perform one or more aggregations on each of those groups.

- Divide a DataFrame into multiple windows and perform moving average, cumulative sum, or ranking. If a window is based on time, the aggregations can be done with tumbling or sliding windows.

© Hien Luu 2018
H. Luu, *Beginning Apache Spark 2*, https://doi.org/10.1007/978-1-4842-3579-9_5

Aggregation Functions

In Spark, all aggregations are done via functions. The aggregation functions are designed to perform aggregation on a set of rows, whether that set of rows consists of all the rows or a subgroup of rows in a DataFrame. The documentation of the complete list of aggregation functions for Scala language is available at `http://spark.apache.org/docs/latest/api/scala/index.html#org.apache.spark.sql.functions$`. For the Spark Python APIs, sometimes there are gaps in terms of the availability of some functions.

Common Aggregation Functions

This section describes a set of commonly used aggregation functions and provides examples of working with them. Table 5-1 describes the aggregation functions. For a complete list, please see the URL mentioned earlier.

Table 5-1. *Commonly Used Aggregation Functions*

Operation	Description
count(col)	Returns the number of items per group.
countDistinct(col)	Returns the unique number of items per group.
approx_count_distinct(col)	Returns the approximate number of unique items per group.
min(col)	Returns the minimum value of the given column per group.
max(col)	Returns the maximum value of the given column per group.
sum(col)	Returns the sum of the values in the given column per group.
sumDistinct(col)	Returns the sum of the distinct values of the given column per group.
avg(col)	Returns the average of the values of the given column per group.
skewness(col)	Returns the skewness of the distribution of the values of the given column per group.
kurtosis(col)	Returns the kurtosis of the distribution of the values of the given column per group.

(*continued*)

Table 5-1. (*continued*)

Operation	Description
variance(col)	Returns the unbiased variance of the values of the given column per group.
stddev(col)	Returns the standard deviation of the values of the given column per group.
collect_list(col)	Returns a collection of values of the given column per group. The returned collection may contain duplicate values.
collect_set(col)	Returns a collection of unique values per group.

To demonstrate the usage of these functions, we are going to use the flight summary dataset, which is derived from the data files available on the Kaggle site (https://www.kaggle.com/usdot/flight-delays/data). This dataset contains the 2015 U.S. domestic flight delays and cancellations. Listing 5-1 contains the code for creating a DataFrame from reading this dataset.

Listing 5-1. Creating a DataFrame by Reading a Flight Summary Dataset

```
val flight_summary = spark.read.format("csv")
                              .option("header", "true")
                              .option("inferSchema","true")
                              .load("<path>/chapter5/data/flights/
                              flight-summary.csv")
// use count action to find out number of rows in this data set
flight_summary.count()
Long = 4693
```

Remember that the count() function of the DataFrame is an action, so it immediately returns a value. All the functions listed in Table 5-1 are lazily evaluated functions.

The following is the schema of the flight_summary dataset:

```
|-- origin_code: string (nullable = true)
|-- origin_airport: string (nullable = true)
|-- origin_city: string (nullable = true)
```

```
|-- origin_state: string (nullable = true)
|-- dest_code: string (nullable = true)
|-- dest_airport: string (nullable = true)
|-- dest_city: string (nullable = true)
|-- dest_state: string (nullable = true)
|-- count: integer (nullable = true)
```

Each row represents the flights from origin_airport to dest_airport. The count column contains the number of flights.

All the following examples are performing aggregation at the entire DataFrame level. Examples of performing aggregations at the subgroup level are given later in this chapter.

count(col)

Counting is a commonly used aggregation to find out the number of items in a group. Listing 5-2 computes the count for both the origin_airport and dest_airport columns, and as expected, the count is the same. To improve the readability of the result column, you can use the as function to give it a friendlier column name. Notice that you need to call the show action to see the result.

Listing 5-2. Computing the Count for Different Columns in the flight_summary DataFrame

```
flight_summary.select(count("origin_airport"), count("dest_airport").
as("dest_count")).show
+---------------------+-----------+
| count(origin_airport)| dest_count|
+---------------------+-----------+
|                 4693|       4693|
+---------------------+-----------+
```

When counting the number of items in a column, the count(col) function doesn't include the null value in the count. To include the null value, the column name should be replaced with *. Listing 5-3 demonstrates this behavior by creating a small DataFrame with a null value in a few columns.

Listing 5-3. Counting Items with a Null Value

```
import org.apache.spark.sql.Row
case class Movie(actor_name:String, movie_title:String, produced_year:Long)
val badMoviesDF = Seq( Movie(null, null, 2018L),
                       Movie("John Doe", "Awesome Movie", 2018L),
                       Movie(null, "Awesome Movie", 2018L),
                       Movie("Mary Jane", "Awesome Movie", 2018L)).toDF

badMoviesDF.show
```

```
+----------+-------------+-------------+
|actor_name|  movie_title| produced_year|
+----------+-------------+-------------+
|      null|         null|         2018|
|  John Doe| Awesome Movie|        2018|
|      null| Awesome Movie|        2018|
| Mary Jane| Awesome Movie|        2018|
+----------+-------------+-------------+
```

```
// now performing the count aggregation on different columns
badMoviesDF.select(count("actor_name"), count("movie_title"),
count("produced_year"), count("*")).show
+-----------------+------------------+--------------------+---------+
| count(actor_name)| count(movie_title)| count(produced_year)| count(1)|
+-----------------+------------------+--------------------+---------+
|                2|                 3|                   4|        4|
+-----------------+------------------+--------------------+---------+
```

The above output table confirms that the count(col) function doesn't include null in the final count.

countDistinct(col)

This function does what it sounds like. It counts only the unique items per group. The output in Listing 5-4 shows the difference in the count result between the countDistinct function and the count function. As it turns out, there are 322 unique airports in the flight_summary dataset.

Listing 5-4. Counting Unique Items in a Group

```
flight_summary.select(countDistinct("origin_airport"), countDistinct("dest_
airport"), count("*")).show
+-------------------------------+------------------------------+---------+
| count(DISTINCT origin_airport)| count(DISTINCT dest_airport)| count(1)|
+-------------------------------+------------------------------+---------+
|                           322|                          322|    4693|
+-------------------------------+------------------------------+---------+
```

approx_count_distinct (col, max_estimated_error=0.05)

Counting the exact number of unique items in each group in a large dataset is an expensive and time-consuming operation. In some use cases, it is sufficient to have an approximate unique count. One of those use cases is in the online advertising business where there are hundreds of millions of ad impressions per hour and there is a need to generate a report to show the number of unique visitors per certain type of member segment. Approximating a count of distinct items is a well-known problem in the computer science field, and it is also known as the *cardinality estimation problem*. Luckily, there is already a well-known algorithm called HyperLogLog (https://en.wikipedia.org/wiki/HyperLogLog) that you can use to solve this problem, and Spark has implemented a version of this algorithm inside the approx_count_distinct function. Since the unique count is an approximation, there will be a certain amount of error. This function allows you to specify a value for an acceptable estimation error for this use case. Listing 5-5 demonstrates the usage and behavior of the approx_count_distinct function. As you dial down the estimation error, it will take longer and longer for this function to complete and return the result.

Listing 5-5. Counting Unique Items in a Group

```
// let's do the counting on the "count" colum of flight_summary DataFrame.
// the default estimation error is 0.05 (5%)
flight_summary.select(count("count"),countDistinct("count"), approx_count_
distinct("count", 0.05)).show
```

```
+--------------+---------------------+----------------------------+
| count(count) | count(DISTINCT count)| approx_count_distinct(count)|
+--------------+---------------------+----------------------------+
|         4693|                 2033|                        2252|
+--------------+---------------------+----------------------------+
```

```
// to get a sense how much approx_count_distinct function is faster than
countDistinct function,
// trying calling them separately
flight_summary.select(countDistinct("count")).show

// specify 1% estimation error
flight_summary.select(approx_count_distinct("count", 0.01)).show
```

On my Mac laptop, the approx_count_distinct function took about 0.1 second, and the countDistinct function took 0.6 second. The larger the approximation estimation error, the less time the approx_count_distinct function takes to complete.

min(col), max(col)

The minimum value and maximum value of the items in a group are the two ends of a spectrum. These two functions are fairly easy to understand and work with. Listing 5-6 extracts these two values from the count column.

Listing 5-6. Getting the Minimum and Maximum Values of the count Column

```
flight_summary.select(min("count"), max("count")).show
```

```
+-----------+-----------+
| min(count)| max(count)|
+-----------+-----------+
|          1|      13744|
+-----------+-----------+
```

```
// looks like there is one very busy airport with 13744 incoming flights
from another airport. It will be interesting to find which airport.
```

sum(col)

This function computes the sum of the values in a numeric column. Listing 5-7 performs the sum of all the flights in the flight_summary dataset.

Listing 5-7. Using the sum Function to Sum Up the count Values

```
flight_summary.select(sum("count")).show

+-----------+
| sum(count)|
+-----------+
|    5332914|
+-----------+
```

sumDistinct(col)

This function does what it sounds like. It sums up only the distinct values of a numeric column. The sum of the distinct counts in the flight_summary DataFrame should be less than the total sum displayed in Listing 5-7. See Listing 5-8 for computing the sum of the distinct values.

Listing 5-8. Using the sumDistinct Function to Sum Up the Distinct count Values

```
flight_summary.select(sumDistinct("count")).show
+--------------------+
| sum(DISTINCT count)|
+--------------------+
|             3612257|
+--------------------+
```

avg(col)

This function calculates the average value of a numeric column. This convenient function simply takes the total and divides it by the number of items. Let's see whether Listing 5-8 can validate the hypothesis.

Listing 5-9. Computing the Average Value of the count Column Using Two Different Ways

```
flight_summary.select(avg("count"), (sum("count") / count("count"))).show
```

```
+------------------+---------------------------+
|       avg(count)| (sum(count) / count(count))|
+------------------+---------------------------+
| 1136.3549968037503|          1136.3549968037503|
+------------------+---------------------------+
```

skewness(col), kurtosis(col)

In the field of statistics, the distribution of the values in a dataset tells a lot of stories behind the dataset. *Skewness* is a measure of the symmetry of the value distribution in a dataset. In a normal distribution or bell-shaped distribution, the skew value is 0. Positive skew indicates the tail on the right side is longer or fatter than the left side. Negative skew indicates the opposite, where the tail of the left side is longer or fatter than the right side. The tail of both sides is even when the skew is 0.

Kurtosis is a measure of the shape of the distribution curve, whether the curve is normal, flat, or pointy. Positive kurtosis indicates the curve is slender and pointy, and negative kurtosis indicates the curve is fat and flat. Listing 5-10 calculates the skewness and kurtosis for the count distribution in the flight_summary dataset.

Listing 5-10. Computing the Skewness and Kurtosis of the column Count

```
flight_summary.select(skewness("count"), kurtosis("count")).show
+------------------+------------------+
|   skewness(count)|    kurtosis(count)|
+------------------+------------------+
| 2.682183800064101| 10.51726963017102|
+------------------+------------------+
```

The result seems to suggest the distribution of the counts is not symmetric and the right tail is longer or fatter than the left tail. The kurtosis value suggests that the distribution curve is pointy.

variance(col), stddev(col)

In statistics, variance and standard deviation are used to measure the dispersion, or the spread, of the data. In other words, they are used to tell the average distance of the values from the mean. When the variance value is low, it means the values are close to the mean. Variance and standard deviation are related; the latter is the square root of the former.

The `variance` and `stddev` functions are used to calculate the variance and standard deviation, respectively. Spark provides two different implementations of these functions; one uses sampling to speed up the calculation, and the other uses the entire population. Listing 5-11 shows the variance and standard deviation of the `count` column in the `flight_summary` DataFrame.

Listing 5-11. Computing the Variance and Standard Deviation Using the variance and sttdev Functions

```
// use the two variations of variance and standard deviation
flight_summary.select(variance("count"), var_pop("count"), stddev("count"),
stddev_pop("count")).show
```

```
+----------------+------------------+------------------+----------------+
|  var_samp(count)|    var_pop(count)|stddev_samp(count)|stddev_pop(count)|
+----------------+------------------+------------------+----------------+
|1879037.7571558713|1878637.3655604832|  1370.779981308405| 1370.633928355957|
+----------------+------------------+------------------+----------------+
```

It looks like the `count` values are pretty spread out in the `flight_summary` DataFrame.

Aggregation with Grouping

This section covers aggregation with grouping of one or more columns. The aggregations are usually performed on datasets that contain one or more categorical columns, which have low cardinality. Examples of categorical values are gender, age, city name, or country name. The aggregations will be done through the functions that are similar to the ones mentioned earlier. However, instead of performing aggregation on the global group in a DataFrame, they will perform the aggregation on each of the subgroups inside a DataFrame.

Performing aggregation with grouping is a two-step process. The first step is to perform the grouping by using the groupBy(col1,col2,...) transformation, and that's where you specify which columns to group the rows by. Unlike other transformations that return a DataFrame, the groupBy transformation returns an instance of the RelationalGroupedDataset class, which you then can apply one or more aggregation functions to. Listing 5-12 demonstrates a simple grouping of using one column and one aggregation. Notice that the groupBy columns will automatically be included in the output.

Listing 5-12. Grouping by origin_airport and Performing a count Aggregation

```
flight_summary.groupBy("origin_airport").count().show(5, false)
+----------------------------------------------------+------+
|                     origin_airport                 | count|
+----------------------------------------------------+------+
|Melbourne International Airport                      |     1|
|San Diego International Airport (Lindbergh Field)    |    46|
|Eppley Airfield                                     |    21|
|Kahului Airport                                     |    18|
|Austin-Bergstrom International Airport               |    41|
+----------------------------------------------------+------+
```

The previous result table tells you that the flights going out of the Melbourne International Airport (Florida) are going to only one other airport. However, the flights going out of the Kahului Airport can land at one of the 18 other airports.

To make things a bit more interesting, let's trying grouping by two columns to calculate the same metric at the city level. Listing 5-13 shows how to do that.

Listing 5-13. Grouping by origin_state and origin_city and Performing a Count
Aggregation

```
flight_summary.groupBy('origin_state, 'origin_city).count
                .where('origin_state === "CA").orderBy('count.desc).show(5)
+-------------+-----------------+-------+
| origin_state|      origin_city| count|
+-------------+-----------------+-------+
|           CA|    San Francisco|     80|
|           CA|      Los Angeles|     80|
|           CA|        San Diego|     47|
|           CA|          Oakland|     35|
|           CA|       Sacramento|     27|
+-------------+-----------------+-------+
```

In addition to grouping by two columns, the previous statement filters the rows
to only the ones with a CA state. The orderBy transformation is used to make it easier
to identify which city has the most number of options in terms of destination airport.
It makes sense that both San Francisco and Los Angeles in California have the largest
number of destination airports that one can fly to.

The class RelationalGroupedDataset provides a standard set of aggregation
functions that you can apply to each subgroup. They are avg(cols), count(),
mean(cols), min(cols), max(cols), and sum(cols). Except for the count() function, all
the remaining ones operate on numeric columns.

Multiple Aggregations per Group

Sometimes there is a need to perform multiple aggregations per group at the same time.
For example, in addition to the count, you also would like to know the minimum and
maximum values. The RelationalGroupedDataset class provides a powerful function
called agg that takes one or more column expressions, which means you can use any of
the aggregation functions including the ones listed in Table 5-1. One cool thing is these
aggregation functions return an instance of the Column class so you can then apply any
of the column expressions using the provided functions. A common need is to rename
the column after the aggregation is done to make it shorter, more readable, and easier to
refer to. Listing 5-14 demonstrates how to do everything that was just described.

Listing 5-14. Multiple Aggregations After Grouping by origin_airport

```
import org.apache.spark.sql.functions._
flight_summary.groupBy("origin_airport")
                      .agg(
                              count("count").as("count"),
                              min("count"), max("count"),
                              sum("count")
                      ).show(5)
```

```
+--------------------+------+-----------+-----------+-----------+
|      origin_airport| count| min(count)| max(count)| sum(count)|
+--------------------+------+-----------+-----------+-----------+
|Melbourne Interna...|     1|       1332|       1332|       1332|
|San Diego Interna...|    46|          4|       6942|      70207|
|    Eppley Airfield|    21|          1|       2083|      16753|
|    Kahului Airport|    18|         67|       8313|      20627|
|Austin-Bergstrom ...|    41|          8|       4674|      42067|
+--------------------+------+-----------+-----------+-----------+
```

By default the aggregation column name is the aggregation expression, which makes the column name a bit long and not easy to refer to. A common pattern is to use the Column.as function to rename the column to something more suitable.

The versatile agg function provides an additional way to express the column expressions via a string-based key-value map. The key is the column name, and the value is an aggregation function, which can be avg, max, min, sum, or count. Listing 5-15 shows examples of this approach.

Listing 5-15. Specifying Multiple Aggregations Using a Key-Value Map

```
flight_summary.groupBy("origin_airport")
                      .agg(
                              "count" -> "count",
                              "count" -> "min",
                              "count" -> "max",
                              "count" -> "sum")
                      .show(5)
```

The result is the same as in Listing 5-14. Notice there isn't an easy way to rename the aggregation result column name. One advantage this approach has over the first one is the map can programmatically be generated. When writing production ETL jobs or performing exploratory analysis, the first approach is used more often than the second one.

Collection Group Values

The functions collect_list(col) and collect_set(col) are useful for collecting all the values of a particular group after the grouping is applied. Once the values of each group are collected into a collection, then there is freedom to operate on them in any way you choose. There is one small difference between the returned collection of these two functions, which is the uniqueness. The collection_list function returns a collection that may contain duplicate values, and the collection_set function returns a collection that contains only unique values. Listing 5-16 shows using the collection_list function to collect the destination cities that have more 5,500 flights coming into them from each of the origin states.

Listing 5-16. Using collection_list to Collect High-Traffic Destination Cities per Origin State

```
val highCountDestCities = flight_summary.where('count > 5500)
                                    .groupBy("origin_state")
                                    .agg(collect_list("dest_city").
                                    as("dest_cities"))

highCountDestCities.withColumn("dest_city_count", size('dest_cities)).
show(5, false)
+-------------+------------------------------------------+----------------+
| origin_state|               dest_cities                | dest_city_count|
+-------------+------------------------------------------+----------------+
|           AZ| [Seattle, Denver, Los Angeles]           |               3|
|           LA| [Atlanta]                                |               1|
|           MN| [Denver, Chicago]                        |               2|
|           VA| [Chicago, Boston, Atlanta]               |               3|
|           NV| [Denver, Los Angeles, San Francisco] |               3|
+-------------+------------------------------------------+----------------+
```

Aggregation with Pivoting

Pivoting is a way to summarize the data by specifying one of the categorical columns and then performing aggregations on another columns such that the categorical values are transposed from rows into individual columns. Another way of thinking about pivoting is that it is a way to translate rows into columns while applying one or more aggregations. This technique is commonly used in data analysis or reporting. The pivoting process starts with the grouping of one or more columns, then pivots on a column, and finally ends with applying one or more aggregations on one or more columns. Listing 5-17 shows a pivoting example on a small dataset of students where each row contains the student name, gender, weight, and graduation year. You would like to know the average weight of each gender for each graduation year.

Listing 5-17. Pivoting on a Small Dataset

```
import org.apache.spark.sql.Row

case class Student(name:String, gender:String, weight:Int, graduation_year:Int)

val studentsDF = Seq(Student("John", "M", 180, 2015),
                           Student("Mary", "F", 110, 2015),
                           Student("Derek", "M", 200, 2015),
                           Student("Julie", "F", 109, 2015),
                           Student("Allison", "F", 105, 2015),
                           Student("kirby", "F", 115, 2016),
                           Student("Jeff", "M", 195, 2016)).toDF

// calculating the average weight for each gender per graduation year
studentsDF.groupBy("graduation_year").pivot("gender").avg("weight").show()
+----------------+------+------+
| graduation_year|     F|     M|
+----------------+------+------+
|            2015| 108.0| 190.0|
|            2016| 115.0| 195.0|
+----------------+------+------+
```

The previous example has one aggregation, and the gender categorical column has only two possible unique values; therefore, the result table has only two columns. If the gender column has three possible unique values, then there will be three columns in the result table. You can leverage the agg function to perform multiple aggregations, which will create more columns in the result table. See Listing 5-18 for an example of performing multiple aggregations on the same DataFrame as in Listing 5-17.

Listing 5-18. Multiple Aggregations After Pivoting

```
studentsDF.groupBy("graduation_year").pivot("gender")
                 .agg(
                        min("weight").as("min"),
                        max("weight").as("max"),
                        avg("weight").as("avg")
                 ).show()
```

```
+---------------+------+------+------+------+------+------+
|graduation_year| F_min| F_max| F_avg| M_min| M_max| M_avg|
+---------------+------+------+------+------+------+------+
|           2015|   105|   110| 108.0|   180|   200| 190.0|
|           2016|   115|   115| 115.0|   195|   195| 195.0|
+---------------+------+------+------+------+------+------+
```

The number of columns added after the group columns in the result table is the product of the number of unique values of the pivot column and the number of aggregations.

If the pivoting column has a lot of distinct values, you can selectively choose which values to generate the aggregations for. Listing 5-19 shows how to specify values to the pivoting function.

Listing 5-19. Selecting Which Values of Pivoting Columns to Generate the Aggregations For

```
studentsDF.groupBy("graduation_year").pivot("gender", Seq("M"))
                .agg(
                        min("weight").as("min"),
                        max("weight").as("max"),
                        avg("weight").as("avg")
                ).show()
+----------------+------+------+------+
| graduation_year| M_min| M_max| M_avg|
+----------------+------+------+------+
|            2015|   180|   200| 190.0|
|            2016|   195|   195| 195.0|
+----------------+------+------+------+
```

Specifying a list of distinct values for the pivot column actually will speed up the pivoting process. Otherwise, Spark will spend some effort in figuring out a list of distinct values on its own.

Joins

To perform any kind of complex and interesting data analysis or manipulations, you often need to bring together the data from multiple datasets through the process of *joining*. This is a well-known technique in SQL parlance. Performing a join will combine the columns of two datasets (could be different or same), and the combined DataFrame will contain columns from both sides. This will enable you to further analyze the combined dataset in ways that you couldn't with just each individual dataset. Let's take an example of the two datasets from an online e-commerce company. One represents the transactional data that contains information about which products were purchased by which customers (aka a fact table). The other one represents the details about each individual customer (aka a dimension table). By joining these two datasets, you can extract insights about which products are more popular with certain segments of customers in terms of age or location.

This section covers how to perform joining in Spark SQL using the `join` transformation and the various types of join it supports. The last portion of this section describes a few details about how Spark SQL internally performs the joining.

Note   In the world of performing data analysis using SQL, a join is a technique that is used quite often. If you are new to SQL, it is highly recommended that you learn the fundamental concepts and the different kinds of join at `https://en.wikipedia.org/wiki/Join_(SQL)`. A few tutorials about joins are provided at `https://www.w3schools.com/sql/sql_join.asp`.

Join Expressions and Join Types

Performing a join of two datasets requires you to specify two pieces of information. The first one is a join expression that specifies which columns from each dataset should be used to determine which rows from both datasets will be included in the joined dataset. The second one is the join type, which determines what should be included in the joined dataset. Table 5-2 describes the supported join types in Spark SQL.

Table 5-2. Join Types

Type	Description
Inner join (aka equi-join)	Returns rows from both datasets when the join expression evaluates to true.
Left outer join	Returns rows from the left dataset even when the join expression evaluates to false.
Right outer join	Returns rows from the right dataset even when the join expression evaluates to false.
Outer join	Returns rows from both datasets even when the join expression evaluates to false.
Left anti join	Returns rows only from the left dataset when the join expression evaluates to false.
Left semi join	Returns rows only from the left dataset when the join expression evaluates to true.
Cross (aka Cartesian)	Returns rows by combining each row from the left dataset with each row in the right dataset. The number of rows will be a product of the size of each dataset.

To help visualize some of the join types, Figure 5-1 shows a set of Venn diagrams for the common join types (source: `https://en.wikipedia.org/wiki/Join_(SQL)#Outer_join`).

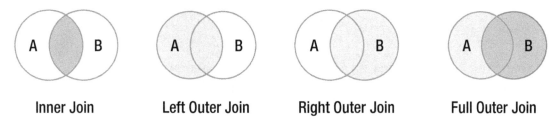

Inner Join   Left Outer Join   Right Outer Join   Full Outer Join

Figure 5-1. *Venn diagrams for common join types*

Working with Joins

To demonstrate how to perform joining in Spark SQL, I'll use two small DataFrames. The first one represents a list of employees, and each row contains the employee name and the department they belong to. The second one contains a list of departments, and each row contains a department ID and department name. Listing 5-20 contains a snippet of code to create these two DataFrames.

Listing 5-20. Creating Two Small DataFrames to Use in the Following Join Type Examples

```
case class Employee(first_name:String, dept_no:Long)
val employeeDF = Seq( Employee("John", 31),
                      Employee("Jeff", 33),
                      Employee("Mary", 33),
                      Employee("Mandy", 34),
                      Employee("Julie", 34),
                      Employee("Kurt", null.
                      asInstanceOf[Int])
          ).toDF
```

```
case class Dept(id:Long, name:String)
val deptDF = Seq( Dept(31, "Sales"),
                               Dept(33, "Engineering"),
                               Dept(34, "Finance"),
                               Dept(35, "Marketing")
                      ).toDF

// register them as views so we can use SQL for perform joins
employeeDF.createOrReplaceTempView("employees")
deptDF.createOrReplaceTempView("departments")
```

Inner Joins

This is the most commonly used join type with the join expression containing the equality comparison of the columns from both datasets. The joined dataset will contain the rows only when the join expression evaluates to true, in other words, when the join column values are the same in both datasets. Rows that don't have matching column values will be excluded from the joined dataset. If the join expression is using the equality comparison, then the number of rows in the joined table will only be as large as the size of the smaller dataset. In Spark SQL, the inner join is the default join type, so it is optional to specify it in the join transformation. Listing 5-21 provides examples of performing an inner join.

Listing 5-21. Performing an Inner Join by the Department ID

```
// define the join expression of equality comparison
val deptJoinExpression = employeeDF.col("dept_no") === deptDF.col("id")

// perform the join
employeeDF.join(deptDF, joinExpression, "inner").show

// no need to specify the join type since "inner" is the default
employeeDF.join(deptDF, joinExpression).show
```

```
+----------+--------+---+------------+
|first_name| dept_no| id|        name|
+----------+--------+---+------------+
|      John|      31| 31|       Sales|
|      Jeff|      33| 33| Engineering|
|      Mary|      33| 33| Engineering|
|     Mandy|      34| 34|     Finance|
|     Julie|      34| 34|     Finance|
+----------+--------+---+------------+
```

```
// using SQL
spark.sql("select * from employees JOIN departments on dept_no == id").show
```

As expected, the joined dataset contains only the rows with matching department IDs from both the employee and department datasets and the columns from both datasets. The output tells you exactly which department each employee belongs to.

The join expression can be specified inside the join transformation or using the where transformation. It is possible to refer to the columns in the join expression using a short-handed version if the column names are unique. If not, then it is required to specify which DataFrame a particular column comes from by using the col function. Listing 5-22 shows different ways of expressing a join expression.

Listing 5-22. Different Ways of Expressing a Join Expression

```
// a shorter version of the join expression
employeeDF.join(deptDF, 'dept_no === 'id).show
```

```
// specify the join expression inside the join transformation
employeeDF.join(deptDF, employeeDF.col("dept_no") === deptDF.col("id")).show
```

```
// specify the join expression using the where transformation
employeeDF.join(deptDF).where('dept_no === 'id).show
```

A join expression is simply a Boolean predicate, and therefore it can be as simple as comparing two columns or as complex as chaining multiple logical comparisons of pairs of columns.

Left Outer Joins

The joined dataset of this join type includes all the rows from an inner join plus all the rows from the left dataset that the join expression evaluates to false. For those nonmatching rows, it will fill in a NULL value for the columns of the right dataset. See Listing 5-23 for an example of doing a left outer join.

Listing 5-23. Performing a Left Outer Join

```
// the join type can be either "left_outer" or "leftouter"
employeeDF.join(deptDF, 'dept_no === 'id, "left_outer").show

// using SQL
spark.sql("select * from employees LEFT OUTER JOIN departments on dept_no
== id").show
```

```
+-----------+--------+-----+------------+
| first_name| dept_no|   id|        name|
+-----------+--------+-----+------------+
|       John|      31|   31|       Sales|
|       Jeff|      33|   33| Engineering|
|       Mary|      33|   33| Engineering|
|      Mandy|      34|   34|     Finance|
|      Julie|      34|   34|     Finance|
|       Kurt|       0| null|        null|
+-----------+--------+-----+------------+
```

As expected, the number of rows in the joined dataset is the same as the number of rows in the employee DataFrame. Since there is no matching department with an ID value of 0, it fills in a NULL value for that row. The result of this particular left outer join enables you to tell which department an employee is assigned to as well as which employees are not assigned to a department.

Right Outer Joins

The behavior of this join type resembles the behavior of the left outer join type, except the same treatment is applied to the right dataset. In other words, the joined dataset includes all the rows from an inner join plus all the rows from the right dataset that the join expression evaluates to false. For those nonmatching rows, it will fill in a NULL value for the columns of the left dataset. See Listing 5-24 for an example of doing a right outer join.

Listing 5-24. Performing a Right Outer Join

```
employeeDF.join(deptDF, 'dept_no === 'id, "right_outer").show

// using SQL
spark.sql("select * from employees RIGHT OUTER JOIN departments on dept_no
== id").show
+-----------+--------+----+------------+
| first_name| dept_no|  id|        name|
+-----------+--------+----+------------+
|       John|      31|  31|       Sales|
|       Mary|      33|  33| Engineering|
|       Jeff|      33|  33| Engineering|
|      Julie|      34|  34|     Finance|
|      Mandy|      34|  34|     Finance|
|       null|    null|  35|   Marketing|
+-----------+--------+----+------------+
```

As expected, the marketing department doesn't have any matching rows from the employee dataset. The joined dataset tells you the department an employee is assigned to as well as which departments have no employees.

Outer Joins (aka Full Outer Joins)

The behavior of this join type is effectively the same as combining the result of both the left outer join and the right outer join. See Listing 5-25 for an example of doing an outer join.

Listing 5-25. Performing an Outer Join

```
employeeDF.join(deptDF, 'dept_no === 'id, "outer").show

// using SQL
spark.sql("select * from employees FULL OUTER JOIN departments on dept_no
== id").show
```

```
+-----------+--------+-----+------------+
| first_name| dept_no|   id|        name|
+-----------+--------+-----+------------+
|       Kurt|       0| null|        null|
|      Mandy|      34|   34|     Finance|
|      Julie|      34|   34|     Finance|
|       John|      31|   31|       Sales|
|       Jeff|      33|   33| Engineering|
|       Mary|      33|   33| Engineering|
|       null|    null|   35|   Marketing|
+-----------+--------+-----+------------+
```

The result from the outer join allows you to see not only which department an employee is assigned to and which departments have employees but also which employees are not assigned to a department and which departments don't have any employees.

Left Anti-Joins

This join type enables you to find out which rows from the left dataset don't have any matching rows on the right dataset, and the joined dataset will contain only the columns from the left dataset. See Listing 5-26 for an example of doing a left anti-join and what the joined dataset looks like.

Listing 5-26. Performing a Left Anti-Join

```
employeeDF.join(deptDF, 'dept_no === 'id, "left_anti").show

// using SQL
spark.sql("select * from employees LEFT ANTI JOIN departments on dept_no ==
id").show
```

```
+----------+--------+
|first_name| dept_no|
+----------+--------+
|      Kurt|       0|
+----------+--------+
```

The result from the left anti-join can easily tell you which employees are not assigned to a department. Notice the right anti-join type doesn't exist; however, you can easily switch the datasets around to achieve the same goal.

Left Semi-Joins

The behavior of this join type is similar to the inner join type, except the joined dataset doesn't include the columns from the right dataset. Another way of thinking about this join type is its behavior is the opposite of the left anti-join, where the joined dataset contains only the matching rows. See Listing 5-27 for an example of doing a left semi-join and what the joined dataset looks like.

Listing 5-27. Performing a Left Semi-Join

```
employeeDF.join(deptDF, 'dept_no === 'id, "left_semi").show

// using SQL
spark.sql("select * from employees LEFT SEMI JOIN departments on dept_no ==
id").show
+-----------+--------+
| first_name| dept_no|
+-----------+--------+
|       John|      31|
|       Jeff|      33|
|       Mary|      33|
|      Mandy|      34|
|      Julie|      34|
+-----------+--------+
```

Cross (aka Cartesian)

In terms of usage, this join type is the simplest to use because the join expression is not needed. Its behavior can be a bit dangerous because it joins every single row in the left dataset with every row in the right dataset. The size of the joined dataset is the product of the size of the two datasets. For example, if the size of each dataset is 1,024, then the size of the joined dataset is more than 1 million rows. For this reason, the way to use this join type is by explicitly using a dedicated transformation in DataFrame, rather than specifying this join type as a string. See Listing 5-28 for an example of doing a cross join and what the joined dataset looks like.

Listing 5-28. Performing a Cross Join

```
// using crossJoin transformation and display the count
employeeDF.crossJoin(deptDF).count
Long = 24

// using SQL and to display up to 30 rows to see all rows in the joined
dataset
spark.sql("select * from employees CROSS JOIN departments").show(30)
```

first_name	dept_no	id	name
John	31	31	Sales
John	31	33	Engineering
John	31	34	Finance
John	31	35	Marketing
Jeff	33	31	Sales
Jeff	33	33	Engineering
Jeff	33	34	Finance
Jeff	33	35	Marketing
Mary	33	31	Sales
Mary	33	33	Engineering
Mary	33	34	Finance
Mary	33	35	Marketing
Mandy	34	31	Sales

```
|    Mandy|      34|  33| Engineering|
|    Mandy|      34|  34|     Finance|
|    Mandy|      34|  35|   Marketing|
|    Julie|      34|  31|       Sales|
|    Julie|      34|  33| Engineering|
|    Julie|      34|  34|     Finance|
|    Julie|      34|  35|   Marketing|
|     Kurt|       0|  31|       Sales|
|     Kurt|       0|  33| Engineering|
|     Kurt|       0|  34|     Finance|
|     Kurt|       0|  35|   Marketing|
+---------+--------+----+------------+
```

Dealing with Duplicate Column Names

Sometimes there is an unexpected issue that comes up after joining two DataFrames with one or more columns that have the same name. When this happens, the joined DataFrame would have multiple columns with the same name. In this situation, it is not easy to refer to one of those columns while performing some kind of transformation on the joined DataFrame. Listing 5-29 simulates this.

Listing 5-29. Simulating a Joined DataFrame with Multiple Column Names That Are the Same

```
// add a new column to deptDF with name dept_no
val deptDF2 = deptDF.withColumn("dept_no", 'id)

deptDF2.printSchema
 |-- id: long (nullable = false)
 |-- name: string (nullable = true)
 |-- dept_no: long (nullable = false)

// now employeeDF with deptDF2 using dept_no column
val dupNameDF = employeeDF.join(deptDF2, employeeDF.col("dept_no") ===
deptDF2.col("dept_no"))
```

```
dupNameDF.printSchema
 |-- first_name: string (nullable = true)
 |-- dept_no: long (nullable = false)
 |-- id: long (nullable = false)
 |-- name: string (nullable = true)
 |-- dept_no: long (nullable = false)
```

Notice the dupNameDF DataFrame now has two columns with the same name, dept_no. Spark will throw an error when you try to project the dupNameDF DataFrame using dept_no in Listing 5-30.

Listing 5-30. Projecting the Column dept_no in the dupNameDF DataFrame

```
dupNameDF.select("dept_no")
```

```
org.apache.spark.sql.AnalysisException: Reference 'dept_no' is ambiguous,
could be: dept_no#30L, dept_no#1050L.;
```

As it turns out, there are several ways to deal with this issue.

Use the Original DataFrame

The joined DataFrame remembers which columns come from which original DataFrame during the joining process. To disambiguate which DataFrame a particular column comes from, you can just tell Spark to prefix it with its original DataFrame name. See Listing 5-31 for how to do this.

Listing 5-31. Using the Original DataFrame deptDF2 to Refer to the dept_no Column in the Joined DataFrame

```
dupNameDF.select(deptDF2.col("dept_no"))
```

Renaming Column Before Joining

To avoid the previous column name ambiguity issue, another approach is to rename a column in one of the DataFrames using the withColumnRenamed transform. Since this is simple, I will leave it as an exercise for you.

Using a Joined Column Name

In the case when the joined column name is the same in both DataFrames, you can leverage a version of the join transformation that automatically removes the duplicate column name from the joined DataFrame. However, if this were a self-join, meaning joining a DataFrame to itself, then there is no way to refer to other duplicate column names. In that case, you would need to use the first technique to rename the columns of one of the DataFrames. Listing 5-32 shows an example of performing a join using a joined column name.

Listing 5-32. Performing a Join Using a Joined Column Name

```
val noDupNameDF = employeeDF.join(deptDF2, "dept_no")

noDupNameDF.printSchema
 |-- dept_no: long (nullable = false)
 |-- first_name: string (nullable = true)
 |-- id: long (nullable = false)
 |-- name: string (nullable = true)
```

Notice there is only one dept_no column in the noDupNameDF DataFrame.

Overview of a Join Implementation

Joining is one of the most expensive operations in Spark. At a high level, there are two different strategies Spark uses to join two datasets. They are shuffle hash join and broadcast join. The main criteria for selecting a particular strategy is based on the size of the two datasets. When the size of both datasets is large, then the shuffle hash join strategy is used. When the size of one of the datasets is small enough to fit into the memory of the executors, then the broadcast join strategy is used. The following sections give the details of how each joining strategy works.

Shuffle Hash Join

Conceptually, joining is about combining the columns of the rows of two datasets that meet the condition specified in the join expression. To do that, those rows with the same column values need to be co-located on the same partition. The shuffle hash join implementation consists of two steps. The first step is to compute the hash value of the columns in the join expression of each row in each dataset and then shuffle those rows with the same hash value to the same partition. To determine which partition a particular row will be moved to, Spark performs a simple arithmetic operation, which computes the modulo of the hash value by the number of partitions. Once the first step is completed, the second step combines the columns of those rows that have the same column hash value. At a high level, these two steps are similar to the steps in the MapReduce programming model.

Figure 5-2 shows the shuffling going on in the shuffle hash join. As mentioned, this is an expensive operation because it requires moving a lot of data from across many machines over a network. When moving data across a network, the data will usually will go through a data serialization and deserialization process. Imagine performing a join on two large datasets where the size of each one is 100GB. In this scenario, it will need to move approximately 200GB of data around. It is not possible to completely avoid a shuffle hash join when joining two large datasets, but it is important to be mindful about reducing the frequency of joining them whenever possible.

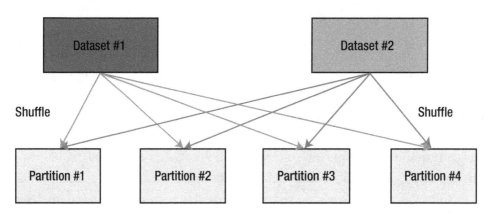

Figure 5-2. *Shuffle hash join*

Broadcast Hash Join

This join strategy is applicable only when one of the datasets is small enough to fit into memory. Knowing that the shuffle hash join is an expensive operation, the broadcast hash join avoids shuffling both datasets and instead shuffles only the smaller one. Similar to the shuffle hash join strategy, this one also consists of two steps. The first one is to broadcast a copy of the entire smaller dataset to each of the partitions of the larger dataset. The second step is to iterate through each row in the larger dataset and look up the corresponding rows in the smaller dataset with matching column values. Figure 5-3 shows the broadcasting of the smaller dataset.

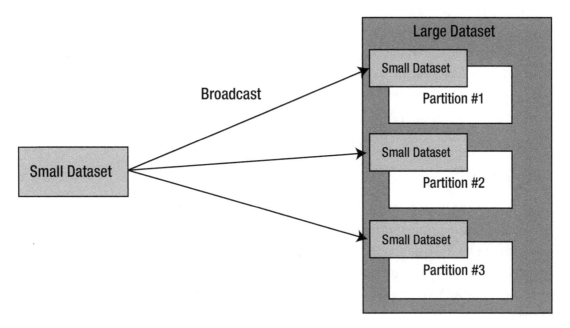

Figure 5-3. *Broadcast hash join*

It is fairly easy to understand that a broadcast hash join is preferred when possible. Spark SQL for the most part can automatically figure out whether to use a broadcast hash join or shuffle hash join based on some statistics it has about datasets while reading them. However, it is feasible to provide a hint to Spark SQL to use a broadcast hash join when using the join transformation. Listing 5-33 provides an example of doing that.

Listing 5-33. Providing a Hint to Use a Broadcast Hash Join to the broadcast deptDF

```
import org.apache.spark.sql.functions.broadcast
```

```
// print out the execution plan to verify broadcast hash join strategy is used
employeeDF.join(broadcast(deptDF), employeeDF.col("dept_no") === deptDF.
col("id")).explain()
```

```
// using SQL
spark.sql("select /*+ MAPJOIN(departments) */ * from employees JOIN
departments on dept_no == id").explain()

== Physical Plan ==
*BroadcastHashJoin [dept_no#30L], [id#41L], Inner, BuildRight
:- LocalTableScan [first_name#29, dept_no#30L]
+- BroadcastExchange HashedRelationBroadcastMode(List(input[0, bigint,
false]))
   +- LocalTableScan [id#41L, name#42]
```

Functions

The DataFrame APIs are designed to operate or transform individual rows in a data set, such as filtering or grouping. If we would like to transform the value of a column of each row in a data set, such as converting a string from upper case to camel case, then we would use a function to do that. Functions are basically methods that are applied to columns. Spark SQL provides a largest set of commonly needed functions as well as an easy way for us to create new ones.

Working with Built-in Functions

To be effective at using Spark SQL to perform distributed data manipulations, you must be proficient working with Spark SQL built-in functions. These built-in functions are designed to generate optimized code for execution at runtime, so it is best to take advantage of them before trying to come up with your own functions. One commonality among these functions is they are designed to take one or more columns of the same row as the input, and they return only a single column as the output. Spark SQL provides more than 200 built-in functions, and they are grouped into different categories. These functions can be used inside DataFrame operations, such as select, filter, groupBy, and so on. For a complete list of built-in functions, please refer to the Spark API Scala documentation at https://spark.apache.org/docs/latest/api/scala/index. html#org.apache.spark.sql.functions$. Table 5-3 classifies them into different categories.

Table 5-3. *A Subset of Built-in Functions for Each Category*

Category	Description
Date time	unix_timestamp, from_unixtime, to_date, current_date, current_timesatmp, date_add, date_sub, add_months, datediff, months_between, dayofmonth, dayofyear, weekofyear, second, minute, hour, month
String	concat, length, levenshtein, locate, lower, upper, ltrim, rtrim, trim, lpad, rpad, repeat, reverse, split, substring, base64
Math	cos, acos, sin, asin, tan, atan, ceil, floor, exp, factorial, log, pow, radian, degree, sqrt, hex, unhex
Cryptography	cr32, hash, md5, sha1, sha2
Aggregation	approx._count_distinct, countDistinct, sumDistinct, avg, corr, count, first, last, max, min, skewness, sum
Collection	array_contain, explode, from_json, size, sort_array, to_json, size
Window	dense_rank, lag, lead, ntile, rank, row_number
Miscellaneous	coalesce, isNan, isnull, isNotNull, monotonically_increasing_id, lit, when

Most of these functions are easy to understand and straightforward to use. The following sections will provide working examples of some of the interesting functions.

Working with Date-Time Functions

The more you use Spark to perform data analysis, the higher chance you have encountering datasets that contain one more date- or time-related columns. The Spark built-in date-time functions broadly fall into the following three categories: converting the date or timestamp from one format to another, performing date-time calculations, and extracting specific values from a date or timestamp.

The date and time conversion functions help with converting a string into either a date, a timestamp, or a Unix time stamp, and vice versa. Internally it uses the Java date format pattern syntax, which is documented at http://docs.oracle.com/javase/tutorial/i18n/format/simpleDateFormat.html. The default date format these

179

functions use is yyyy-MM-dd HH:mm:ss. Therefore, if the date format of a date or timestamp column is different, then you need to provide that pattern to these conversion functions. Listing 5-34 shows an example of converting a date and timestamp in string type to the Spark date and timestamp type.

Listing 5-34. Converting a date and timestamp in string type to Spark Date and Timestamp type.

```
// the last two columns don't follow the default date format
val testDateTSDF = Seq((1, "2018-01-01", "2018-01-01 15:04:58:865", "01-01-
2018", "12-05-2017 45:50"))
                                .toDF("id", "date", "timestamp",
                                "date_str", "ts_str")

// convert these strings into date, timestamp and unix timestamp
// and specify a custom date and timestamp format
val testDateResultDF = testDateTSDF.select(to_date('date).as("date1"),
                                to_timestamp('timestamp).
                                as("ts1"),
                                to_date('date_str,
                                "MM-dd-yyyy").as("date2"),
                                to_timestamp('ts_str,
                                "MM-dd-yyyy mm:ss").as("ts2"),
                                unix_timestamp('timestamp).
                                as("unix_ts")).show(false)

// date1 and ts1 are of type date and timestamp respectively
testDateResultDF.printSchema
 |-- date1: date (nullable = true)
 |-- ts1: timestamp (nullable = true)
 |-- date2: date (nullable = true)
 |-- ts2: timestamp (nullable = true)
 |-- unix_ts: long (nullable = true)

testDateResultDF.show
```

```
+---------+-------------------+---------+-------------------+----------+
|   date1|                ts1|   date2|                ts2|   unix_ts|
+---------+-------------------+---------+-------------------+----------+
|2018-01-01| 2018-01-01 15:04:58| 2018-01-01| 2017-12-05 00:45:50| 1514847898|
+---------+-------------------+---------+-------------------+----------+
```

It is just as easy to convert a date or timestamp to a time string by using the date_format function with a custom date format or using the from_unixtime function to convert a Unix timestamp (in seconds) to a string. See Listing 5-35 for examples of the conversions.

Listing 5-35. Converting a Date, Timestamp, and Unix Timestamp to a String

```
testDateResultDF.select(date_format('date1, "dd-MM-YYYY").as("date_str"),
                        date_format('ts1, "dd-MM-YYYY
                        HH:mm:ss").as("ts_str"),
                        from_unixtime('unix_ts,"dd-MM-YYYY
                        HH:mm:ss").as("unix_ts_str")).show
```

```
+----------+-------------------+-------------------+
|  date_str|             ts_str|        unix_ts_str|
+----------+-------------------+-------------------+
| 01-01-2018| 01-01-2018 15:04:58| 01-01-2018 15:04:58|
+----------+-------------------+-------------------+
```

The date-time calculation functions are useful for figuring out the difference between two dates or timestamps as well as for performing date or time arithmetic. Listing 5-36 has working examples of a date-time calculation.

Listing 5-36. Date-Time Calculation Examples

```
val employeeData = Seq( ("John", "2016-01-01", "2017-10-15"),
                        ("May", "2017-02-06", "2017-12-25"))
                      .toDF("name", "join_date", "leave_date")
```

```
employeeData.show
+-----+----------+----------+
| name|  join_date| leave_date|
+-----+----------+----------+
| John| 2016-01-01| 2017-10-15|
|  May| 2017-02-06| 2017-12-25|
+-----+----------+----------+
```

```
// perform date and month calcuations
employeeData.select('name, datediff('leave_date, 'join_date).as("days"),
                    months_between('leave_date, 'join_date).as("months"),
                    last_day('leave_date).as("last_day_of_mon"))
                    .show
```

```
+-----+-----+----------+---------------+
| name| days|    months| last_day_of_mon|
+-----+-----+----------+---------------+
| John|  653| 21.4516129|     2017-10-31|
|  May|  322|10.61290323|     2017-12-31|
+-----+-----+----------+---------------+
```

```
// perform date addition and substration
val oneDate = Seq(("2018-01-01")).toDF("new_year")
oneDate.select(date_add('new_year, 14).as("mid_month"),
               date_sub('new_year, 1).as("new_year_eve"),
               next_day('new_year, "Mon").as("next_mon")).show
```

```
+----------+------------+----------+
|  mid_month| new_year_eve|   next_mon|
+----------+------------+----------+
| 2018-01-15|   2017-12-31| 2018-01-08|
+----------+------------+----------+
```

The ability to extract specific fields of a date or timestamp value such as year, month, hour, minutes, and second is convenient when working with time-series data. For example, when there is a need to group all the stock transactions by quarter or month or week, then you can just extract that information from the transaction date and group by those values. Listing 5-37 shows how easy it is to extract fields from a date or timestamp.

Listing 5-37. Extracting Specific Fields from a Date Value

```
val valentimeDateDF = Seq(("2018-02-14 05:35:55")).toDF("date")
valentimeDateDF.select(year('date).as("year"),
                                quarter('date).as("quarter"),
                                month('date).as("month"),
                                weekofyear('date).as("woy"),
                                dayofmonth('date).as("dom"),
                                dayofyear('date).as("doy"),
                                hour('date).as("hour"),
                                minute('date).as("minute"),
                                second('date).as("second"))
                        .show
```

```
+-----+--------+------+----+----+----+-----+-------+-------+
| year| quarter| month| woy| dom| doy| hour| minute| second|
+-----+--------+------+----+----+----+-----+-------+-------+
| 2018|       1|     2|   7|  14|  45|    5|     35|     55|
+-----+--------+------+----+----+----+-----+-------+-------+
```

Working with String Functions

Undoubtedly most columns in the majority of datasets are of string type. The Spark SQL built-in string functions provide versatile and powerful ways of manipulating this type of column. Broadly speaking, these functions fall into two buckets. The first one is about transforming a string, and the second one is about applying regular expressions either to replace some part of a string or to extract certain parts of a string based on a pattern.

There are many ways to transform a string. The most common ones are trimming, padding, uppercasing, lowercasing, and concatenating. Listing 5-38 demonstrates the various ways of transforming a string using the various built-in string functions.

Listing 5-38. Different Ways of Transforming a String with Built-in String Functions

```
val sparkDF = Seq(("  Spark  ")).toDF("name")

// trimming
sparkDF.select(trim('name).as("trim"),
                    ltrim('name).as("ltrim"),
```

183

```
                         rtrim('name).as("rtrim"))
              .show
+-----+------+------+
| trim| ltrim| rtrim|
+-----+------+------+
|Spark| Spark| Spark|
+-----+------+------+
```

```
// padding a string to a specified length with given pad string
// first trim spaces around string "Spark" and then pad it so the final
length is 8 characters long
sparkDF.select(trim('name).as("trim"))
              .select(lpad('trim, 8, "-").as("lpad"),
                      rpad('trim, 8, "=").as("rpad"))
              .show
+--------+--------+
|    lpad|    rpad|
+--------+--------+
|---Spark|Spark===|
+--------+--------+
```

```
// transform a string with concatenation, uppercase, lowercase and reverse
val sparkAwesomeDF = Seq(("Spark", "is", "awesome")).toDF("subject",
"verb", "adj")
```

```
sparkAwesomeDF.select(concat_ws(" ",'subject, 'verb, 'adj).as("sentence"))
                     .select(lower('sentence).as("lower"),
                             upper('sentence).as("upper"),
                             initcap('sentence).as("initcap"),
                             reverse('sentence).as("reverse"))
                .show
+----------------+----------------+----------------+----------------+
|           lower|           upper|         initcap|         reverse|
+----------------+----------------+----------------+----------------+
| spark is awesome| SPARK IS AWESOME| Spark Is Awesome| emosewa si krapS|
+----------------+----------------+----------------+----------------+
```

```
// translate from one character to another
sparkAwesomeDF.select('subject, translate('subject, "ar", "oc").
as("translate")).show
+--------+----------+
| subject| translate|
+--------+----------+
|   Spark|     Spock|
+--------+----------+
```

Regular expressions are a powerful and flexible way to replace some portion of a string or extract substrings from a string. The regexp_extract and regexp_replace functions are designed specifically for those purposes. Spark leverages the Java regular expressions library for the underlying implementation of these two string functions.

The input parameters to the regexp_extract function are a string column, a pattern to match, and a group index. There could be multiple matches of the pattern in a string; therefore, the group index (starts with 0) is needed to identify which one. If there are no matches for the specified pattern, this function returns an empty string. See Listing 5-39 for an example of working with the regexp_extract function.

Listing 5-39. Using the regexp_extract String Function to Extract "fox" Using a Pattern

```
val rhymeDF = Seq(("A fox saw a crow sitting on a tree singing \"Caw! Caw!
Caw!\"")).toDF("rhyme")

// using a pattern
rhymeDF.select(regexp_extract('rhyme, "[a-z]*o[xw]",0).as("substring")).show

+------------+
|   substring|
+------------+
|         fox|
+------------+
```

The input parameters to the `regexp_replace` string function are the string column, a pattern to match, and a value to replace with. See Listing 5-40 for an example of the `regexp_replace` function.

Listing 5-40. Using the regexp_replace String Function to Replace "fox" and "crow" with "animal"

```
val rhymeDF = Seq(("A fox saw a crow sitting on a tree singing \"Caw! Caw!
Caw!\"")).toDF("rhyme")

// both lines below produce the same output
rhymeDF.select(regexp_replace('rhyme, "fox|crow", "animal")
.as("new_rhyme")).show(false)
rhymeDF.select(regexp_replace('rhyme, "[a-z]*o[xw]", "animal")
.as("new_rhyme")).show(false)

+---------------------------------------------------------------------+
|                              new_rhyme                              |
+---------------------------------------------------------------------+
|A animal saw a animal sitting on a tree singing "Caw! Caw! Caw!"    |
+---------------------------------------------------------------------+
```

Working with Math Functions

The second most common column type is the numerical type. This is especially true in customer transaction or IoT sensor–related datasets. Most of the math functions are fairly self-explanatory and easy to use. This section covers one very useful and commonly used function called `round`, which performs the half-up rounding of a numeric value based on a given scale. The scale determines the number of decimal points to round up to. There are two variations of this function. The first one takes a column with a floating-point value and a scale, and the second one takes only a column with a floating-point value. The second variation essentially calls the first one with a value of 0 for the scale. Listing 5-41 demonstrates the behavior of the `round` function.

Listing 5-41. Demonstrates the Behavior of round with Various Scales

```
numberDF.select(round('pie).as("pie0"),
                          round('pie, 1).as("pie1"),
                          round('pie, 2).as("pie2"),
                          round('gpa).as("gpa"),
                          round('year).as("year"))
               .show
// because it is a half-up rounding, the gpa value is rounded up to 4.0
+-----+------+-----+----+-----+
| pie0|  pie1| pie2| gpa| year|
+-----+------+-----+----+-----+
|  3.0|   3.1| 3.14| 4.0| 2018|
+-----+------+-----+----+-----+
```

Working with Collection Functions

The collection functions are designed to work with complex data types such as arrays, maps, and structs. This section covers the two specific types of collection functions. The first is about working with the array datatype, and the second one is about working with the JSON data format.

Instead of a single scalar value, sometimes a particular column in a dataset contains a list of values. One way to model that is by using an array data type. For example, let say there is a dataset about tasks that need to be done per day. In this dataset, each row represents a list of tasks per day, so it has a date column, and the other column contains a list of tasks. You can use the array related collection functions to easily get the array size, check for the existence of a value, or sort the array. Listing 5-42 contains examples of working with the various array related functions.

Listing 5-42. Using Array Collection Functions to Manipulate a List of Tasks

```
// create an tasks DataFrame
val tasksDF = Seq(("Monday", Array("Pick Up John", "Buy Milk", "Pay
Bill"))).toDF("day", "tasks")

// schema of tasksDF
tasksDF.printSchema
```

```
|-- day: string (nullable = true)
|-- tasks: array (nullable = true)
|    |-- element: string (containsNull = true)
```

```
// get the size of the array, sort it, and check to see if a particular
value exists in the array
tasksDF.select('day, size('tasks).as("size"),
                          sort_array('tasks).as("sorted_tasks"),
                          array_contains('tasks, "Pay Bill").
                          as("shouldPayBill"))
          .show(false)
```

```
+-------+-----+----------------------------------+-------------+
| day  | size|              sorted_tasks         | shouldPayBill|
+-------+-----+----------------------------------+-------------+
|Monday|    3| [Buy Milk, Pay Bill, Pick Up John] |    true     |
+-------+-----+----------------------------------+-------------+
```

```
// the explode function will create a new row for each element in the array
tasksDF.select('day, explode('tasks)).show
```

```
+-------+-------------+
|   day|          col|
+-------+-------------+
| Monday| Pick Up John|
| Monday|     Buy Milk|
| Monday|     Pay Bill|
+-------+-------------+
```

A lot of unstructured datasets are in the form of JSON, which is a self-describing data format that is used quite often in the industry. One popular example is to encode a Kafka message payload in JSON format. Since this format is widely supported in most popular programming languages, a Kafka consumer written in one of these programming languages can easily decode those Kafka messages. The JSON-related collection functions are useful for converting a JSON string to and from a struct data type. The main functions are from_json, get_json_object, and to_json. Once a JSON string is converted to a Spark struct data type, then you can easily extract those values. See Listing 5-43 for examples of working with the from_json and to_json functions.

Listing 5-43. Examples of Using the from_json and to_json Functions

```
import org.apache.spark.sql.types._
// create a string that contains JSON string
val todos = """{"day": "Monday","tasks": ["Pick Up John","Buy Milk","Pay
Bill"]}"""
val todoStrDF = Seq((todos)).toDF("todos_str")

// at this point, todoStrDF is DataFrame with one column of string type
todoStrDF.printSchema
 |-- todos_str: string (nullable = true)

// in order to convert a JSON string into a Spark struct data type, we need
to describe its structure to Spark
val todoSchema = new StructType().add("day", StringType).
add("tasks",  ArrayType(StringType))

// use from_json to convert JSON string
val todosDF = todoStrDF.select(from_json('todos_str, todoSchema).
as("todos"))

// todos is a struct data type that contains two fields: day and tasks
todosDF.printSchema
|-- todos: struct (nullable = true)
|    |-- day: string (nullable = true)
|    |-- tasks: array (nullable = true)
|    |     |-- element: string (containsNull = true)

// retrieving value out of struct data type using the getItem function of
Column class
todosDF.select('todos.getItem("day"),
                    'todos.getItem("tasks"),
                    'todos.getItem("tasks").getItem(0).as("first_task")
                   ).show(false)
```

```
+---------+------------------------------------------------+-------------+
|todos.day| todos.tasks                                    | first_task  |
+---------+------------------------------------------------+-------------+
|   Monday| [Pick Up John, Buy Milk, Pay Bill]| Pick Up John|
+---------+------------------------------------------------+-------------+
```

```
// to convert a Spark struct data type to JSON string, we can use to_json
function
todosDF.select(to_json('todos)).show(false)
```

```
+----------------------------------------------------------------------+
|                            structstojson(todos)                      |
+----------------------------------------------------------------------+
| {"day":"Monday","tasks":["Pick Up John","Buy Milk","Pay Bill"]}      |
+----------------------------------------------------------------------+
```

Working with Miscellaneous Functions

A few functions in the miscellaneous category are interesting and useful in certain situations. This section covers the following functions: monotonically_increasing_id, when, coalesce, and lit.

Sometimes there is a need to generate monotonically increasing unique, but not necessarily consecutive, IDs for each row in the dataset. It is quite an interesting problem if you spend some time thinking about it. For example, if a dataset has 200 million rows and they are spread across many partitions (machines), how do you ensure the values are unique and increasing at the same time? This is the job of the monotonically_increasing_id function, which generates IDs as 64-bit integers. The key part in its algorithm is that it places the partition ID in the upper 31 bits. Listing 5-44 shows an example of using the monotonically_increasing_id function.

Listing 5-44. monotonically_increasing_id in Action

```
// first generate a DataFrame with values from 1 to 10 and spread them
across 5 partitions
val numDF = spark.range(1,11,1,5)
```

```
// verify that there are 5 partitions
numDF.rdd.getNumPartitions
Int = 5
```

```
// now generate the monotonically increasing numbers and see which ones are
in which partition
numDF.select('id, monotonically_increasing_id().as("m_ii"),
                     spark_partition_id().as("partition")).show
```

```
+---+------------+----------+
| id|        m_ii| partition|
+---+------------+----------+
|  1|           0|         0|
|  2|           1|         0|
|  3|  8589934592|         1|
|  4|  8589934593|         1|
|  5| 17179869184|         2|
|  6| 17179869185|         2|
|  7| 25769803776|         3|
|  8| 25769803777|         3|
|  9| 34359738368|         4|
| 10| 34359738369|         4|
+---+------------+----------+
```

```
// the above table shows the values in m_ii columns have a different range
in each partition.
```

If there is a need to evaluate a value against a list of conditions and return a value, then a typical solution is to use a switch statement, which is available in most high-level programming languages. When there is a need to do this with the value of a column in a DataFrame, then you can use the when function for this use case. See Listing 5-45 for an example of using the when function.

Listing 5-45. Using the when Function to Convert a Numeric Value to a String

```
// create a DataFrame with values from 1 to 7 to represent each day of the week
val dayOfWeekDF = spark.range(1,8,1)

// convert each numerical value to a string

dayOfWeekDF.select('id, when('id === 1, "Mon")
                                  .when('id === 2, "Tue")
                                  .when('id === 3, "Wed")
                                  .when('id === 4, "Thu")
                                  .when('id === 5, "Fri")
                                  .when('id === 6, "Sat")
                                  .when('id === 7, "Sun").as("dow")
                        ).show
+---+----+
| id| dow|
+---+----+
|  1| Mon|
|  2| Tue|
|  3| Wed|
|  4| Thu|
|  5| Fri|
|  6| Sat|
|  7| Sun|
+---+----+
// to handle the default case when we can use the otherwise function of the
column class
dayOfWeekDF.select('id, when('id === 6, "Weekend")
                                  .when('id === 7, "Weekend")
                                  .otherwise("Weekday").as("day_type")
                        ).show
```

```
+--+--------+
|id|day_type|
+--+--------+
| 1| Weekday|
| 2| Weekday|
| 3| Weekday|
| 4| Weekday|
| 5| Weekday|
| 6| Weekend|
| 7| Weekend|
+--+--------+
```

When working with data, it is important to handle null values properly. One of the ways to do that is to convert them to some other values that represent null in your data processing logic. Borrowing from the SQL world, Spark provides a function called coalesce that takes one or more column values and returns the first one that is not null. Each argument in the coalesce function must be of type Column, so if you want to fill in a literal value, then you can leverage the lit function. The way this function works is it takes a literal value as an input and returns an instance of the Column class that wraps the input. See Listing 5-46 for an example of using both the coalesce and lit functions together.

Listing 5-46. Using coalesce to Handle a Null Value in a Column

```
// create a movie with null title
case class Movie(actor_name:String, movie_title:String, produced_year:Long)
val badMoviesDF = Seq( Movie(null, null, 2018L),
                          Movie("John Doe", "Awesome Movie", 2018L)).toDF
// use coalese to handle null value in title column
badMoviesDF.select(coalesce('actor_name, lit("no_name")).as("new_title")).
show
+----------+
| new_title|
+----------+
|   no_name|
|  John Doe|
+----------+
```

Working with User-Defined Functions

Even though Spark SQL provides a large set of built-in functions for most common use cases, there will always be cases where none of those functions can provide the functionality your use cases need. However, don't despair. Spark SQL provides a fairly simple facility to write user-defined functions (UDFs) and use them in your Spark data processing logic or applications in a similar manner as using built-in functions. UDFs are effectively one of the ways you can extend Spark's functionality to meet your specific needs. Another thing that I really like about Spark is that UDFs can be written in either Python, Java, or Scala, and they can leverage and integrate with any necessary libraries. Since you are able to use a programming language that you are most comfortable with to write UDFs, it is extremely easy and fast to develop and test UDFs.

Conceptually, UDFs are just regular functions that take some inputs and provide an output. Although UDFs can be written in either Scala, Java, or Python, you must be aware of the performance differences when UDFs are written in Python. UDFs must be registered with Spark before they are used so Spark knows to ship them to executors to be used and executed. Given that executors are JVM processes that are written in Scala, they can execute Scala or Java UDFs natively inside the same process. If a UDF is written in Python, then an executor can't execute it natively, and therefore it has to spawn a separate Python process to execute the Python UDF. In addition to the cost of spawning a Python process, there is a large cost in terms of serializing data back and forth for every single row in the dataset.

There are three steps involved in working with UDFs. The first one is to write a function and test it. The second step is to register that function with Spark by passing in the function name and its signature to Spark's udf function. The last step is to use UDF in either the DataFrame code or when issuing SQL queries. The registration process is slightly different when using a UDF within SQL queries. Listing 5-47 demonstrates the three steps mentioned earlier with a simple UDF.

Listing 5-47. A Simple UDF in Scala to Convert Numeric Grades to Letter Grades

```scala
// create student grades DataFrame
case class Student(name:String, score:Int)
val studentDF = Seq(Student("Joe", 85),
                                Student("Jane", 90),
                                Student("Mary", 55)).toDF()
// register as a view
studentDF.createOrReplaceTempView("students")

// create a function to convert grade to letter grade
def letterGrade(score:Int) : String = {
  score match {
    case score if score > 100 => "Cheating"
    case score if score >= 90 => "A"
    case score if score >= 80 => "B"
    case score if score >= 70 => "C"
    case _ => "F"
  }
}

// register as a UDF
val letterGradeUDF = udf(letterGrade(_:Int):String)

// use the UDF to convert scores to letter grades
studentDF.select($"name",$"score",
                letterGradeUDF($"score").as("grade")).show
+-----+------+------+
| name| score| grade|
+-----+------+------+
|  Joe|    85|     B|
| Jane|    90|     A|
| Mary|    55|     F|
+-----+------+------+
```

```
// register as UDF to use in SQL
spark.sqlContext.udf.register("letterGrade", letterGrade(_: Int): String)

spark.sql("select name, score, letterGrade(score) as grade from students").show
```

```
+-----+------+------+
| name| score| grade|
+-----+------+------+
|  Joe|    85|     B|
| Jane|    90|     A|
| Mary|    55|     F|
+-----+------+------+
```

Advanced Analytics Functions

The previous sections covered the built-in functions Spark SQL provides for basic analytic needs such as aggregation, joining, pivoting, and grouping. All those functions take one or more values from a single row and produce an output value, or they take a group of rows and return an output.

This section will cover the advanced analytics capabilities Spark SQL offers. The first one is about multidimensional aggregations, which is useful for use cases that involve hierarchical data analysis, where calculating subtotals and totals across a set of grouping columns is commonly needed. The second capability is about performing aggregations based on time windows, which is useful when working with time-series data such as transactions or sensor values from IoT devices. The third one is the ability to perform aggregations within a logical grouping of rows, which is referred to as a *window*. This capability enables you to easily perform calculations such as a moving average, a cumulative sum, or the rank of each row.

Aggregation with Rollups and Cubes

Rollups and cube are basically more advanced versions of grouping on multiple columns, and they are generally used to generate subtotals and grand totals across the combinations and permutations of those columns. The order of the provided set of columns is treated as a hierarchy for grouping.

Rollups

When working with hierarchical data such as the revenue data that spans different departments and divisions, rollups can easily calculate the subtotals and a grand total across them. Rollups respect the given hierarchy of the given set of rollup columns and always start the rolling up process with the first column in the hierarchy. The grand total is listed in the output where all the column values are null. Listing 5-48 demonstrates how a rollup works.

Listing 5-48. Performing Rollups with Flight Summary Data

```
// read in the flight summary data
val flight_summary = spark.read.format("csv")
                                    .option("header", "true")
                                    .option("inferSchema","true")
                                    .load(<path>/chapter5/data/
                                    flights/flight-summary.csv)

// filter data down to smaller size to make it easier to see the rollups result
val twoStatesSummary = flight_summary.select('origin_state, 'origin_city, 'count)
                                    .where('origin_state === "CA"
                                    || 'origin_state === "NY")
                                    .where('count > 1 && 'count < 20)
                                    .where('origin_city =!= "White
                                    Plains")
                                     .where('origin_city =!=
                                    "Newburgh")
                                     .where('origin_city =!=
                                    "Mammoth Lakes")
                                     .where('origin_city =!=
                                    "Ontario")
```

```
// let's see what the data looks like
twoStatesSummary.show
+-------------+--------------+------+
| origin_state|   origin_city| count|
+-------------+--------------+------+
|           CA|     San Diego|    18|
|           CA| San Francisco|     5|
|           CA| San Francisco|    14|
|           CA|     San Diego|     4|
|           CA| San Francisco|     2|
|           NY|      New York|     4|
|           NY|      New York|     2|
|           NY|        Elmira|    15|
|           NY|        Albany|     5|
|           NY|        Albany|     3|
|           NY|      New York|     4|
|           NY|        Albany|     9|
|           NY|      New York|    10|
+-------------+--------------+------+
```

```
// perform the rollup by state, city, then calculate the sum of the count,
and finally order by null last
twoStateSummary.rollup('origin_state, 'origin_city)
                        .agg(sum("count") as "total")
                        .orderBy('origin_state.asc_nulls_last,
                        'origin_city.asc_nulls_last).show
```

```
+-------------+--------------+------+
| origin_state|   origin_city| total|
+-------------+--------------+------+
|           CA|     San Diego|    22|
|           CA| San Francisco|    21|
|           CA|          null|    43|
|           NY|        Albany|    17|
|           NY|        Elmira|    15|
|           NY|      New York|    20|
|           NY|          null|    52|
|         null|          null|    95|
+-------------+--------------+------+
```

This output shows the subtotals per state on the third and seventh lines, and the grand total is shown on the last line with a null value in both the `original_state` and `origin_city` columns. The trick is to sort with the `asc_nulls_last` option, so Spark SQL will order null values last.

Cube

A cube is basically a more advanced version of a rollup. It performs the aggregations across all the combinations of the grouping columns. Therefore, the result includes what a rollup provides as well as other combinations. In our example of cubing by the `origin_state` and `origin_city`, the result will include the aggregation for each of the original cities. The way to use the `cube` function is similar to how you use the `rollup` function. See Listing 5-49 for an example.

Listing 5-49. Performing a Cube Across the origin_state and origin_city Columns

```
// perform the cube across origin_state and origin_city
twoStateSummary.cube('origin_state, 'origin_city)
                          .agg(sum("count") as "total")
                          .orderBy('origin_state.asc_nulls_last,
                          'origin_city.asc_nulls_last).show

// see result below

+-------------+--------------+------+
| origin_state|   origin_city| total|
+-------------+--------------+------+
|           CA|     San Diego|    22|
|           CA| San Francisco|    21|
|           CA|          null|    43|
|           NY|        Albany|    17|
|           NY|        Elmira|    15|
|           NY|      New York|    20|
|           NY|          null|    52|
|         null|        Albany|    17|
|         null|        Elmira|    15|
```

```
|       null|      New York|    20|
|       null|     San Diego|    22|
|       null| San Francisco|    21|
|       null|          null|    95|
+-----------+--------------+------+
```

In the result table, the lines that have a null value in the `origin_state` column represent the aggregation of all the cities in a state. Therefore, the result of a cube will always have more rows than the result of a rollup.

Aggregation with Time Windows

Aggregation with time windows was introduced in Spark 2.0 to make it easy to work with time-series data, which consists of a series of data points in time order. This kind of dataset is common in industries such as finance or telecommunications. For example, the stock market transaction dataset has the transaction date, opening price, close price, volume, and other pieces of information for each stock symbol. Time window aggregations can help with answering questions such as what is the weekly average closing price of Apple stock or the monthly moving average closing price of Apple stock across each week.

Window functions come in a few versions, but they all require a timestamp type column and a window length, which can be specified in seconds, minutes, hours, days, or weeks. The window length represents a time window that has a start time and end time, and it is used to determine which bucket a particular piece of time-series data should belong to. Another version takes additional input for the sliding window size, which tells how much a time window should slide by when calculating the next bucket. These versions of the window function are the implementations of the tumbling window and sliding window concepts in world event processing, and they will be described in more detail in Chapter 6.

The following examples will use the Apple stock transactions, which can be found on the Yahoo Finance web site at `https://in.finance.yahoo.com/q/hp?s=AAPL`. Listing 5-50 calculates the weekly average price of Apple stock based on one year of data.

Listing 5-50. Using the Time Window Function to Calculate the Average Closing Price of Apple Stock

```
val appleOneYearDF = spark.read.format("csv")
                                     .option("header", "true")
                                     .option("inferSchema","true")
                                     .load("<path>/chapter5/data/
                                     stocks/aapl-2017.csv")

// display the schema, the first column is the transaction date
appleOneYearDF.printSchema
 |-- Date: timestamp (nullable = true)
 |-- Open: double (nullable = true)
 |-- High: double (nullable = true)
 |-- Low: double (nullable = true)
 |-- Close: double (nullable = true)
 |-- Adj Close: double (nullable = true)
 |-- Volume: integer (nullable = true)

// calculate the weekly average price using window function inside the
groupBy transformation
// this is an example of the tumbling window, aka fixed window
val appleWeeklyAvgDF = appleOneYearDF.groupBy(window('Date, "1 week"))
                                      .agg(avg("Close").
                                      as("weekly_avg"))

// the result schema has the window start and end time
appleWeeklyAvgDF.printSchema
 |-- window: struct (nullable = true)
 |    |-- start: timestamp (nullable = true)
 |    |-- end: timestamp (nullable = true)
 |-- weekly_avg: double (nullable = true)
```

```
// display the result with ordering by start time and round up to 2 decimal
points
appleWeeklyAvgDF.orderBy("window.start")
                            .selectExpr("window.start", "window.end",
                                        "round(weekly_avg, 2) as
                                        weekly_avg")
                    .show(5)
// notice the start time is inclusive and end time is exclusive
+--------------------+--------------------+---------------+
|               start|                 end|    weekly_avg|
+--------------------+--------------------+---------------+
| 2016-12-28 16:00:00| 2017-01-04 16:00:00|         116.08|
| 2017-01-04 16:00:00| 2017-01-11 16:00:00|         118.47|
| 2017-01-11 16:00:00| 2017-01-18 16:00:00|         119.57|
| 2017-01-18 16:00:00| 2017-01-25 16:00:00|         120.34|
| 2017-01-25 16:00:00| 2017-02-01 16:00:00|         123.12|
+--------------------+--------------------+---------------+
```

The previous example uses a one-week tumbling window, where there is no overlap. Therefore, each transaction is used only once to calculate the moving average. The example in Listing 5-51 uses the sliding window. This means some transactions will be used more than once in calculating the average monthly moving average. The window size is four weeks, and it slides by one week at a time in each window.

Listing 5-51. Use the Time Window Function to Calculate the Monthly Average Closing Price of Apple Stock

```
// 4 weeks window length and slide by one week each time
val appleMonthlyAvgDF = appleOneYearDF.groupBy(window('Date, "4 week", "1
week"))
                                                .agg(avg("Close").
                                                as("monthly_avg"))
// display the results with order by start time
appleMonthlyAvgDF.orderBy("window.start")
                        .selectExpr("window.start", "window.end",
                        "round(monthly_avg, 2) as monthly_avg")
                        .show(5)
```

```
+-------------------+-------------------+-----------+
|              start|                end| monthly_avg|
+-------------------+-------------------+-----------+
| 2016-12-07 16:00:00| 2017-01-04 16:00:00|     116.08|
| 2016-12-14 16:00:00| 2017-01-11 16:00:00|     117.79|
| 2016-12-21 16:00:00| 2017-01-18 16:00:00|     118.44|
| 2016-12-28 16:00:00| 2017-01-25 16:00:00|     119.03|
| 2017-01-04 16:00:00| 2017-02-01 16:00:00|     120.42|
+-------------------+-------------------+-----------+
```

Since the sliding window interval is one week, the previous result table shows that the start time difference between two consecutive rows is one week apart. Between two consecutive rows, there are about three weeks of overlapping transactions, which means a transaction is used more than one time to calculate the moving average.

Window Functions

Up to this point, you know how to use functions such as concat or round to compute an output from one or more column values of a single row and leverage aggregation functions such as max or sum to compute an output for each group of rows. Sometimes there is a need to operate on a group of rows and return a value for every input row. Window functions provide this unique capability to make it easy to perform calculations such as a moving average, a cumulative sum, or the rank of each row.

There are two main steps for working with window functions. The first one is to define a window specification that defines a logical grouping of rows called a *frame*, which is the context in which each row is evaluated. The second step is to apply a window function that is appropriate for the problem that you are trying to solve. You can find more details about the available window functions in the following sections.

The window specification defines three important components the window functions will use. The first component is called *partition by*, and this is where you specify one or more columns to group the rows by. The second component is called *order by*, and it defines how the rows should be ordered based on one or more columns and whether the ordering should be in ascending or descending order. Out of the three components, the last one is more complicated and will require a detailed explanation. The last component is called *frame*, and it defines the boundary of the window with respect to the current row. In other words, the "frame" restricts which rows to be included when calculating a value for the current row. A range of rows to include in a *window frame* can be specified using the row index or the actual value of the order by expression. The last component is applicable for some of the window functions, and therefore it may not be necessary for some scenarios. A window specification is built using the functions defined in the `org.apache.spark.sql.expressions.Window` class. The `rowsBetween` and `rangeBetweeen` functions are used to define the range by row index and actual value, respectively.

Window functions can be categorized into three different types: ranking functions, analytic functions, and aggregate functions. The ranking functions and analytic functions are described in Table 5-4 and Table 5-5, respectively. For aggregate functions, you can use any of the previously mentioned aggregation functions as a window function. You can find a complete list of the window functions at `https://spark. apache.org/docs/latest/api/java/org/apache/spark/sql/functions.html`.

Table 5-4. *Ranking Functions*

Name	Description
rank	Returns the rank or order of rows within a frame based on some sorting order.
dense_rank	Similar to rank, but leaves no gaps in the ranks when there are ties.
percent_rank	Returns the relative rank of rows within a frame.
ntile(n)	Returns the ntile group ID in an ordered window partition. For example, if n is 4, the first quarter of the rows will get a value of 1, the second quarter of rows will get a value of 2, and so on.
row_number	Returns a sequential number starting with 1 with a frame.

Table 5-5. *Analytic Functions*

Name	Description
cume_dist	Returns the cumulative distribution of values with a frame. In other words, the fraction of rows that are below the current row.
lag(col, offset)	Returns the value of the column that is offset rows before the current row.
lead(col, offset)	Returns the value of the column that is offset rows after the current row.

Let's put the aforementioned steps together by working through a small sample dataset to demonstrate window function capabilities. Table 5-6 contains the shopping transaction data of two fictitious users, John and Mary.

Table 5-6. *User Shopping Transactions*

Name	Date	Amount
John	2017-07-02	13.35
John	2016-07-06	27.33
John	2016-07-04	21.72
Mary	2017-07-07	69.74
Mary	2017-07-01	59.44
Mary	2017-07-05	80.14

With this shopping transaction data, let's try using window functions to answer the following questions:

- For each user, what are the two highest transaction amounts?

- What is the difference between the transaction amount of each user and their highest transaction amount?

- What is the moving average transaction amount of each user?

- What is the cumulative sum of the transaction amount of each user?

To answer the first question, you apply the rank window function over a window specification that partitions the data by user and sorts it by the amount in descending order. The ranking window function assigns a rank to each row based on the sorting order of each row in each frame. See Listing 5-52 for the actual code to solve the first question.

Listing 5-52. Apply the Rank Window Function to Find out the Top Two Transactions per User

```
// small shopping transaction data set for two users
val txDataDF= Seq(("John", "2017-07-02", 13.35),
                            ("John", "2017-07-06", 27.33),
                            ("John", "2017-07-04", 21.72),
                            ("Mary",  "2017-07-07", 69.74),
                            ("Mary",  "2017-07-01", 59.44),
                            ("Mary",  "2017-07-05", 80.14))
                         .toDF("name", "tx_date", "amount")

// import the Window class
import org.apache.spark.sql.expressions.Window

// define window specification to partition by name and order by amount in
descending amount
val forRankingWindow = Window.partitionBy("name").orderBy(desc("amount"))

// add a new column to contain the rank of each row, apply the rank
function to rank each row
val txDataWithRankDF = txDataDF.withColumn("rank", rank().
over(forRankingWindow))

// filter the rows down based on the rank to find the top 2 and display the
result
txDataWithRankDF.where('rank < 3).show(10)
+------+-----------+-------+-----+
| name|    tx_date| amount| rank|
+------+-----------+-------+-----+
|  Mary| 2017-07-05|  80.14|    1|
|  Mary| 2017-07-07|  69.74|    2|
|  John| 2017-07-06|  27.33|    1|
|  John| 2017-07-04|  21.72|    2|
+------+-----------+-------+-----+
```

The approach for solving the second question involves applying the max function over the amount column across all the rows of each partition. In addition to partitioning by the username, it also needs to define a frame boundary that includes all the rows in each partition. To do that, you use the `Window.rangeBetween` function with `Window.unboundedPreceding` as the start value and `Window.unboundedFollowing` as the end value. Listing 5-53 defines a window specification according to the logic defined earlier and applies the `max` function over it.

Listing 5-53. Applying the max Window Function to Find the Difference of Each Row and the Highest Amount

```
// use rangeBetween to define the frame boundary that includes all the rows
in each frame
val forEntireRangeWindow = Window.partitionBy("name")
                                 .orderBy(desc("amount"))
                                 .rangeBetween(Window.unboundedPreceding,
                                 Window.unboundedFollowing)

// apply the max function over the amount column and then compute the
difference
val amountDifference = max(txDataDF("amount")).over(forEntireRangeWindow) -
txDataDF("amount")

// add the amount_diff column using the logic defined above
val txDiffWithHighestDF = txDataDF.withColumn("amount_diff",
round(amountDifference, 3))

// display the result
txDiffWithHighestDF.show
+------+-----------+-------+-------------+
|  name|    tx_date| amount|  amount_diff|
+------+-----------+-------+-------------+
|  Mary| 2017-07-05|  80.14|          0.0|
|  Mary| 2017-07-07|  69.74|         10.4|
|  Mary| 2017-07-01|  59.44|         20.7|
|  John| 2017-07-06|  27.33|          0.0|
|  John| 2017-07-04|  21.72|         5.61|
|  John| 2017-07-02|  13.35|        13.98|
+------+-----------+-------+-------------+
```

To compute the transaction amount moving average of each user in the order of transaction date, you will leverage the avg function to calculate the average amount for each row based on a set of rows in a frame. For this particular example, you want each frame to include three rows: the current row plus one row before it and one row after it. Depending a particular use case, the frame might include more rows before and after the current row. Similar to the previous examples, the window specification will partition the data by user, but the rows in each frame will be sorted by transaction date. Listing 5-54 shows how to apply the avg function over the window specification described earlier.

Listing 5-54. Applying the Average Window Function to Compute the Moving Average Transaction Amount

```
// define the window specification
// a good practice is to specify the offset relative to Window.currentRow
val forMovingAvgWindow = Window.partitionBy("name").orderBy("tx_date")
                    .rowsBetween(Window.currentRow-1,Window.currentRow+1)

// apply the average function over the amount column over the window
specification
// also round the moving average amount to 2 decimals
val txMovingAvgDF = txDataDF.withColumn("moving_avg",
                                    round(avg("amount").
                                    over(forMovingAvgWindow), 2))

// display the result
txMovingAvgDF.show
+------+----------+-------+-----------+
|  name|   tx_date| amount| moving_avg|
+------+----------+-------+-----------+
|  Mary| 2017-07-01|  59.44|      69.79|
|  Mary| 2017-07-05|  80.14|      69.77|
|  Mary| 2017-07-07|  69.74|      74.94|
|  John| 2017-07-02|  13.35|      17.54|
|  John| 2017-07-04|  21.72|       20.8|
|  John| 2017-07-06|  27.33|      24.53|
+-------+----------+-------+-----------+
```

To compute the cumulative sum of the transaction amount for each user, you will apply the sum function over a frame that consists of all the rows up to the current row. The partition by and order by clauses are the same as the moving average example. Listing 5-55 shows how to apply the sum function over the window specification described earlier.

Listing 5-55. Applying the sum Window function to compute the cumulative sum of transaction amount

```
// define the window specification with each frame includes all the
previous rows and the current row
val forCumulativeSumWindow = Window.partitionBy("name").orderBy("tx_date")
                                    .rowsBetween(Window.unbounded
                                    Preceding,Window.currentRow)

// apply the sum function over the window specification
val txCumulativeSumDF = txDataDF.withColumn("culm_sum",
                                    round(sum("amount").over
                                    (forCumulativeSumWindow),2))

// display the result
txCumulativeSumDF.show
+------+----------+-------+---------+
|  name|   tx_date| amount| culm_sum|
+------+----------+-------+---------+
|  Mary| 2017-07-01|  59.44|    59.44|
|  Mary| 2017-07-05|  80.14|   139.58|
|  Mary| 2017-07-07|  69.74|   209.32|
|  John| 2017-07-02|  13.35|    13.35|
|  John| 2017-07-04|  21.72|    35.07|
|  John| 2017-07-06|  27.33|     62.4|
+------+----------+-------+---------+
```

The default frame of a window specification includes all the preceding rows and up to the current row. For the previous example, it is not necessary to specify the frame, so you should get the same result.

The previous window function examples were written using the DataFrame APIs. It is possible to achieve the same goals using SQL with the PARTITION BY, ORDER BY, ROWS BETWEEN, and RANGE BETWEEN key words. The frame boundary can be specified using the following key words: UNBOUNDED PRECEDING, UNBOUNDED FOLLOWING, CURRENT ROW, <value> PRECEDING, and <value> FOLLOWING. Listing 5-56 shows examples of using the window functions with SQL.

Listing 5-56. Example of a Window Function in SQL

```
// register the txDataDF as a temporary view called tx_data
txDataDF.createOrReplaceTempView("tx_data")

// use RANK window function to find top two highest transaction amount
spark.sql("select name, tx_date, amount, rank from
            (
              select name, tx_date, amount,
                      RANK() OVER (PARTITION BY name ORDER BY amount
                      DESC) as rank from tx_data
            ) where rank < 3").show

// difference between  maximum transaction amount
spark.sql("select name, tx_date, amount, round((max_amount - amount),2) as
amount_diff from
             (
               select name, tx_date, amount, MAX(amount) OVER
                   (PARTITION BY name ORDER BY amount DESC
                    RANGE BETWEEN UNBOUNDED PRECEDING AND UNBOUNDED
                    FOLLOWING
                   ) as max_amount from tx_data)"
          ).show
```

```
// moving average
spark.sql("select name, tx_date, amount, round(moving_avg,2) as moving_avg from
            (
                select name, tx_date, amount, AVG(amount) OVER
                    (PARTITION BY name ORDER BY tx_date
                        ROWS BETWEEN 1 PRECEDING AND 1 FOLLOWING
                    ) as moving_avg from tx_data)"
        ).show

// cumulative sum
spark.sql("select name, tx_date, amount, round(culm_sum,2) as moving_avg from
            (
                select name, tx_date, amount, SUM(amount) OVER
                    (PARTITION BY name ORDER BY tx_date
                        ROWS BETWEEN UNBOUNDED PRECEDING AND CURRENT ROW
                    ) as culm_sum from tx_data)"
        ).show
```

When using the window functions in SQL, the partition by, order by, and frame window must be specified in a single statement.

Catalyst Optimizer

The easiest way to write efficient data processing applications is to not worry about it and get your data processing applications automatically optimized. That is the promise of the Spark Catalyst, which is a query optimizer and is the second major component in the Spark SQL module. It plays a major role in ensuring the data processing logic written in either DataFrame APIs or SQL runs efficiently and quickly. It was designed to minimize end-to-end query response times as well as to be extensible such that Spark users can inject user code into the optimizer to perform custom optimization. At a high level, the Spark Catalyst translates the user-written data processing logic into a logical plan, then optimizes it using heuristics, and finally converts the logical plan to a physical plan. The final step is to generate code based on the physical plan. Figure 5-4 provides a visual representation of the steps.

The idea of taking user expressions of what needs to be done and then figuring out the most efficient means of executing those steps is an idea that has been around a long time in the RDBMS world. However, the novelties introduced in the Spark Catalyst are the extensibility and the way it was developed using the functional programming constructs in Scala. These two novelties enable the Spark Catalyst to mature quickly through the Spark user community contributions.

The following sections will provide some brief details of each step in the Catalyst optimization process as well as show a few examples of the generated query plan.

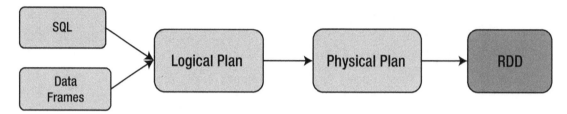

Figure 5-4. *Catalyst optimizer*

Logical Plan

The first step in the Catalyst optimization process is to create a logical plan from either a DataFrame object or the abstract syntax tree of the parsed SQL query. The logical plan is an internal representation of the user data processing logic in the form of a tree of operators and expression. Next, the Catalyst analyzes the logical plan to resolve references to ensure they are valid. Then it applies a set of rule-based and cost-based optimizations to the logical plan. Both of these types of optimization follow the principle of pruning unnecessary data as early as possible and minimizing per-operator cost.

The rule-based optimizations include constant folding, project pruning, predicate pushdown, and others. For example, during this optimization phase, the Catalyst may decide to move the filter condition before performing a join. For curious minds, the list of rule-based optimizations is defined in the `org.apache.spark.sql.catalyst.optimizer.Optimizer` class.

The cost-based optimizations were introduced in Spark 2.2 to enable Catalyst to be more intelligent in selecting the right kind of join based on the statistics of the data being processed. The cost-based optimization relies on the detailed statistics of the columns participating in the filter or join conditions, and that's why the statistics collection framework was introduced. Examples of the statistics include the cardinality, the number of distinct values, max/min, average/max length, and so on.

Physical Plan

Once the logical plan is optimized, the Catalyst will generate one or more physical plans using the physical operators that match the Spark execution engine. In addition to the optimizations performed in the logical plan phase, the physical plan phase performs its own ruled-based optimizations, including combining projections and filtering into a single operation as well as pushing the projections or filtering predicates all the way down to the data sources that support this feature, i.e., Parquet. Again, these optimizations follow the data pruning principle described earlier. The final step the Catalyst performs is to generate the Java bytecode of the cheapest physical plan.

Catalyst in Action

This section shows how to use the explain function of the DataFrame class to display the logical and physical plans.

To see both the logical plan and the physical plan, you can call the explain function with the extended argument as a Boolean true value. Otherwise, this function displays only the physical plan.

The small and somewhat silly example first reads the movie data in Parquet format, then performs filtering based on produced_year, then adds a column called produced_decade and projects the movie_title and produced_decade columns, and finally filters rows based on produced_decade. The goal here is to prove that the Catalyst performs the predicate pushdown and filtering condition optimizations. See Listing 5-57 for how to generate the logical and physical plans.

Listing 5-57. Using the explain Function to Generate the Logical and Physical Plans

```
// read movies data in Parquet format
val moviesDF = spark.read.load("<path>/book/chapter4/data/movies/movies.
parquet")

// perform two filtering conditions
val newMoviesDF = moviesDF.filter('produced_year > 1970)
                                    .withColumn("produced_decade",
                                    'produced_year + 'produced_
                                    year % 10)
```

```
                                      .select('movie_title,
                                      'produced_decade).where
                                      ('produced_decade > 2010)

// display the logical and physical plans
newMoviesDF.explain(true)

== Parsed Logical Plan ==
'Filter ('produced_decade > 2010)
+- Project [movie_title#408, produced_decade#415L]
   +- Project [actor_name#407, movie_title#408, produced_year#409L,
      (produced_year#409L + (produced_year#409L % cast(10 as bigint)))
      AS produced_decade#415L]
      +- Filter (produced_year#409L > cast(1970 as bigint))
         +- Relation[actor_name#407,movie_title#408,produced_year#409L]
            parquet

== Analyzed Logical Plan ==
movie_title: string, produced_decade: bigint
Filter (produced_decade#415L > cast(2010 as bigint))
+- Project [movie_title#408, produced_decade#415L]
   +- Project [actor_name#407, movie_title#408, produced_year#409L,
      (produced_year#409L + (produced_year#409L % cast(10 as bigint)))
      AS produced_decade#415L]
      +- Filter (produced_year#409L > cast(1970 as bigint))
         +- Relation[actor_name#407,movie_title#408,produced_year#409L]
            parquet

== Optimized Logical Plan ==
Project [movie_title#408, (produced_year#409L + (produced_year#409L % 10))
AS produced_decade#415L]
+- Filter ((isnotnull(produced_year#409L) && (produced_year#409L > 1970))
   && ((produced_year#409L + (produced_year#409L % 10)) > 2010))
   +- Relation[actor_name#407,movie_title#408,produced_year#409L] parquet

== Physical Plan ==
*Project [movie_title#408, (produced_year#409L + (produced_year#409L % 10))
AS produced_decade#415L]
```

```
+- *Filter ((isnotnull(produced_year#409L) && (produced_year#409L > 1970))
   && ((produced_year#409L + (produced_year#409L % 10)) > 2010))
   +- *FileScan parquet [movie_title#408,produced_year#409L] Batched:
      true, Format: Parquet, Location: InMemoryFileIndex[file:<path>/
      book/chapter4/data/movies/movies.pa..., PartitionFilters: [],
      PushedFilters: [IsNotNull(produced_year), GreaterThan(produced_year,
      1970)], ReadSchema: struct<movie_title:string,produced_year:bigint>
```

If you carefully analyze the optimized logical plan, you will see that it combines both filtering conditions into a single filter. The physical plan shows that Catalyst both pushes down the filtering of produced_year and performs the projection pruning to the FileScan step.

Project Tungsten

Starting in 2015, the Spark designers observed that the Spark workloads were increasingly bottlenecked by CPU and memory rather than I/O and network communication. It is a bit counterintuitive but not too surprising, given the advancements on the hardware side like 10Gbps network links and high-speed SSD. Project Tungsten was created to improve the efficiency of using memory and CPU in Spark applications and to push the performance closer to the limits of modern hardware. There are three initiatives in the Tungsten project.

- Manage memory explicitly by using off-heap management techniques to eliminate the overhead of the JVM object model and minimize garbage collection.

- Use intelligent cache-aware algorithms and data structures to exploit memory hierarchy.

- Use whole-stage code generation to minimize virtual function calls by combining multiple operators into a single Java function.

The hard and interesting work that went into the Tungsten project has dramatically improved the Spark execution engine since Spark 2.0. Much of the work in the Tungsten project happens behind the scenes in the execution engine. The following example demonstrates a small glimpse into the whole-stage code generation initiative by examining the physical plan. In the following output, whenever an asterisk (*) appears before an operator, it means the whole-stage code generation is enabled. Listing 5-58 displays the physical plan of filtering and summing integers in a DataFrame.

Listing 5-58. Demonstrating the Whole-Stage Code Generation by Looking at the Physical Plan

```
spark.range(1000).filter("id > 100").selectExpr("sum(id)").explain()

== Physical Plan ==
*HashAggregate(keys=[], functions=[sum(id#13L)], output=[sum(id)#23L])
+- Exchange SinglePartition
   +- *HashAggregate(keys=[], functions=[partial_sum(id#13L)],
      output=[sum#25L])
      +- *Filter (id#13L > 100)
         +- *Range (0, 1000, step=1, splits=8)
```

The whole-stage code generation combines the logic of filtering and summing integers into a single Java function.

Summary

This chapter covered a lot of useful and powerful features available in the Spark SQL module.

- Aggregation is one of the mostly commonly used features in the world of big data analytics. Spark SQL provides many of the commonly needed aggregation functions such as sum, count, avg, and so on. Aggregation with pivoting provides a nice way of summarizing the data as well as transposing columns into rows.

- Doing any useful and meaningful data processing often requires joining two or more datasets. Spark SQL supports many of the standard join types that exist in the SQL world.

- Spark SQL comes with a rich set of built-in functions, which should cover most of the common needs for working with strings, math, dates and times, and so on. If none of them meets a particular needs of a use case, then it is fairly easy to write a user-defined function that can be used with both the DataFrame APIs and SQL queries.

- Window functions are powerful and advanced analytics functions because they can compute a value for each row in the input group. They are particular useful for computing moving average, a cumulative sum, or the rank of each row.

- The Catalyst optimizer enables you to write efficient data processing applications without having to reason about them too much. The cost-based optimizer was introduced in Spark 2.2 to enable Catalyst to be more intelligent about selecting the right kind of join implementation based on the collected statistics of the data being processed.

- Project Tungsten is the workhorse behind the scenes that speeds up the execution of data process applications by employing a few advanced techniques to improve the efficiency of using memory and CPU.

CHAPTER 6

Spark Streaming

In addition to batch data processing, streaming data processing has become a must-have capability for any business that wants to harness the value of real-time data to either increase their competitive advantage or to improve their user experience. With the advent of the Internet of Things, the volume and velocity of real-time data have increased even more than before. For Internet companies such as Facebook, LinkedIn, and Twitter, millions of social activities happening every second on their platforms are represented as streaming data.

At a high level, streaming processing is about the continuous processing of unbounded streams of data. Doing this at scale, in a fault-tolerant and consistent manner, is quite a challenging task. Luckily, the stream processing engines such as Spark, Flink, Samza, Heron, and Kafka have been steadily and dramatically maturing over the last few years to enable businesses to build and operate complex stream processing applications.

More and more interesting use cases of real-time data processing have emerged as the community understands how best to apply the increasingly mature streaming engines to their business needs. For example, Uber leverages streaming processing capabilities to understand the number of riders and drivers on its platform at near real-time, and these near real-time insights influence business decisions such as moving excess drivers from low-demand areas to higher-demand areas in a city. Most Internet companies leverage some kind of A/B experimentation system to perform A/B testing when releasing new features or trying a new design. Streaming processing enables a faster reaction to the experiments by reducing the time it takes to understand an experiment's effectiveness from days to hours. Fraud detection is an area that has embraced stream processing because of the benefits it gains from instant insights of fraud activities so that they can be either stopped or monitored. For large companies that have hundreds of online services, a common need is to monitor their health by

© Hien Luu 2018
H. Luu, *Beginning Apache Spark 2*, https://doi.org/10.1007/978-1-4842-3579-9_6

processing the large volume of generated logs at near real-time via streaming data processing. There are many more interesting real-time data processing use cases, and some of them will be shared in this chapter.

This chapter starts with describing a few useful stream processing concepts and then provides a short introduction to the stream processing engine landscape. Then the remaining sections of this chapter will describe the Spark streaming processing engine in detail and the APIs it provides.

Stream Processing

In the world of big data, batch data processing became widely known with the introduction of Hadoop. The popular MapReduce framework is one of the components in the Hadoop ecosystem, and it became the king of batch data processing because of its capabilities and robustness. After a period of innovation in the batch data processing area, most challenges in this space are now well understood. Since then, the big data open source community has shifted its focus and innovations to the streaming data processing space.

Batch data processing is about running the computational logic through a fixed input dataset and producing a result at the end. This means the processing will stop when it gets to the end of the dataset. By contrast, stream processing is about running the computational logic through an unbounded dataset, and therefore the processing is continuous and long running. Although the difference between batch data and streaming data is mainly about the finiteness, streaming data processing is much more complex and challenging than batch data processing because of the unbounded data nature, the incoming order of the real-time data, the different rates that the data will arrive, and the expectation of correctness and low latency in the face of machine failure.

In the world of batch data processing, it is not uncommon to hear that it takes hours to finish a complex batching data processing job because of the size of the input datasets. In the world of streaming data processing, there is an expectation that streaming processing engines will provide low latency and high throughput by delivering incoming streams of data as quickly and efficiently as possible so they can react or extract insight quickly. Performing any interesting and meaningful streaming data processing usually involves maintaining some kind of state in a fault-tolerant manner. For example, a stock trading streaming application would like to maintain and display the top 10 or 20 most actively traded stocks through the day. To accomplish this goal, the running count of each stock must be maintained either by the streaming processing engine on behalf of the application or by the application itself. Usually the state is maintained in memory and backed by some resilient storage such as disk, so the state is resilient to machine failures.

Streaming data processing doesn't work in a silo. Sometimes there is a need to work together with batch data processing to enrich the incoming streaming data. A good example of this is when a page view streaming application needs to compute the page view statistics of its users based on user location; then it needs to join user clicks and streaming data with member data. A good streaming processing engine should provide an easy way to join batch data with streaming data without much effort.

One of the common use cases of streaming data processing is to perform some aggregations of incoming data and then write that summarized data out to an external data sink to be consumed by either a web application or a data analytics engine. The desire here is to have an end-to-end, exactly once guarantee of the data in the face of failure, whether that is because of machine failures or some bugs in the data processing application. The key here is how the streaming processing engine deals with failure such that the incoming data is not lost as well as not double counted.

As streaming processing engines mature, they provide not only the desired distributed system properties such as fast, scalable, and fault tolerant, but they also provide easy and developer-friendly ways of performing data streaming computation by up-leveling the abstraction from low-level APIs to high-level declarative languages such as SQL. With this advancement, it is much easier to build a self-service streaming platform to enable product teams to quickly make meaningful business decisions by tapping into the data or events that are generated by various products in the company. Remember, one of the goals in data streaming processing is to extract business insights in a timely manner so businesses can either react quickly or make business actions.

In summary, streaming data processing has its own set of unique challenges, which are a result of processing data that is continuous and unbounded. It is important to be mindful about these challenges as you set out to build long-running streaming data processing applications or when evaluating a particular streaming processing engine. The challenges are as follows:

- Maintaining a potentially large state in a reliable manner for data streaming applications

- Efficiently and quickly delivering messages for applications to process

- Dealing with streaming data that arrives out of order

- Joining with batch data to enrich the incoming streaming data

- End-to-end, exactly once guarantee delivery of data even where there is failure

- Dealing with an uneven data arrival rate

Concepts

To be effective at performing streaming data processing, it is imperative to understand the following core and universal concepts. These important concepts are very much applicable to developing streaming applications on any streaming processing engine. Knowing these concepts will be useful when evaluating streaming processing engines; they also enable you to ask the right questions to find out how much support a particular streaming processing engine provides in each of these areas:

- Data delivery semantics

- Notion of time

- Windowing

Data Delivery Semantics

When a piece of data enters a streaming processing engine, it has the responsibility of delivering it to the streaming application for processing. There are three types of guarantees that a streaming processing engine can provide even under failure scenarios.

- *At most once*: This implies that a streaming processing engine guarantees that a piece of data will be delivered to an application no more than one time, but it could be zero times. In other words, there is a chance that a piece of data will be lost, and therefore an application will not see it at all. For some use cases, this is acceptable, but it is not for some other use cases. One of those use cases is a financial transaction processing application. Losing data can result in not charging customers and therefore a reduction in revenue.

- *At least once*: This implies that a streaming processing engine guarantees that a piece of data will be delivered to an application one or more times. There is no data lost in this case; however, there is a potential for double or triple counting. In the example of financial transaction processing applications, it means that a transaction is applied multiple times, which results in complaints from customers. This guarantee is stronger than at most once because no data will be lost.

- *Exactly once*: This implies that a streaming processing engine guarantees that a piece of data will be delivered to an application exactly one time only, no more and no less. In this case, there is no data loss and no double counting. Most modern and popular streaming processing engines provide this kind of guarantee. Of the three guarantees, this one is the most desirable for building critical business streaming applications.

One way of looking at these delivery semantics is they fall into a spectrum, where at most once is the weakest guarantee and exactly once is the strongest guarantee, which is depicted in Figure 6-1.

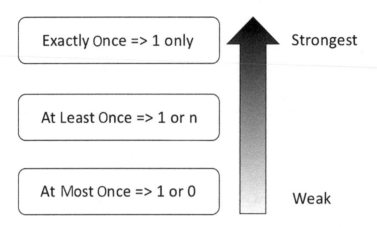

Figure 6-1. *Delivery semantics spectrum*

When evaluating a streaming processing engine, it is important to not only understand the level of guarantee it provides but also understand the implementation behind this guarantee. Most modern streaming processing engines employ a combination of check-pointing and write-ahead log techniques to provide an exactly once guarantee.

Notion of Time

In the world of streaming data processing, the notion of time is important because it enables you to understand what's going on in terms of time. For example, in the case of a real-time anomaly detection application, the notion of time gives you insights into the number of suspicious transactions occurring in the last five minutes or at a certain part of the day.

There are two important types of time: event time and processing time. As depicted in Figure 6-2, event time represents the time when the piece of data was created, and typically this information is encoded in the data. For example, in the case of IoT devices that take an ocean temperature in a certain part of the world, the event time is when the temperature was taken. The encoding of the temperature data may consist of the temperature itself and a timestamp. The processing time represents the time when the stream processing engine processes a piece of data. In the example of the ocean temperature IoT devices, the processing time is the clock time of the streaming processing engine at the time it starts to perform transformations or aggregations on the temperature data.

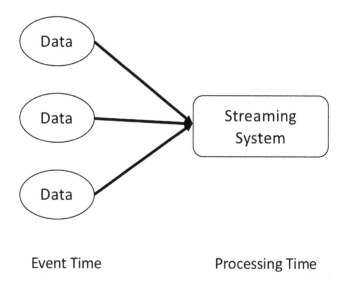

Event Time   Processing Time

Figure 6-2. *Event time and processing*

To truly understand what's going behind the incoming stream of data, it is imperative to be able to process the incoming data in terms of event time because the event time represents the point in time that the data was created. In an ideal state, the data will arrive and be processed shortly after it was created, and therefore the gap between the event time and processing time is small. In reality, that is often not the case, and therefore the lag varies over time according to the conditions that prevent the data from arriving immediately after it was created. The greater the lag, the greater the need to be able to process data using the event time and not using the processing time. Figure 6-3 illustrates the relationship between event time and processing time; it also shows an example of what the lag looks like in reality. The notion of time is very much related to the windowing concept, which is described next. To deal with an unbounded incoming stream of data, one common practice in the streaming data processing world is to divide the incoming data into chunks by using the start and end times as the boundary. It is fairly obvious that it makes more sense to use the event time as the temporal boundaries.

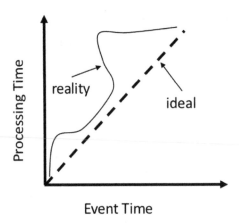

Figure 6-3. *The lag between event time and processing time*

Windowing

Given the unbounded nature of streaming data, it is not feasible to have a global view of the incoming streaming data. Hence, to extract any meaningful value from the incoming data, you need to process it in chunks. For example, given a traffic count sensor that emits a count of the number of cars every 20 seconds, it is not feasible to compute a final sum. Instead, it is more logical to ask how many cars pass that sensor every minute or every five minutes. In this case, you need to partition the traffic-counting data into chunks of one minute or five minutes, respectively. Each chunk is called a *window*.

Windowing is a common streaming data processing pattern where the unbounded incoming stream of data is divided into chunks based on temporal boundaries, which can either be event time or processing time, although the former is used more commonly to reflect the actual reality of the data. However, given that the data may not arrive in the order it was created or it may be delayed because of network congestion, it is not possible to always have all the data that was created in that time window.

There are three commonly used windowing patterns, and most modern streaming processing engines support them. Figure 6-4 shows the three patterns.

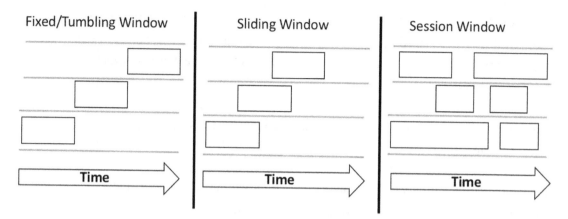

Figure 6-4. *Three commonly used windowing patterns*

A fixed/tumbling window basically divides the incoming stream of data into fixed-size segments, where each one has a window length, a start time, and an end time. Each incoming piece of data will be slotted into one and only one fixed/tumbling window. With this small batch of data in each window, it is easy to reason about when performing aggregations such as sum, max, or average.

A sliding window is another way of dividing the incoming stream of data into fixed-size segments, where each one has a window length and a sliding interval. If the sliding interval is the same size as the window length, then it is the same as the fixed/tumbling window. The example in Figure 6-4 shows that the sliding interval is smaller than the window length. This implies that one or more pieces of data will be included in more than one sliding window. Because of the overlapping of the windows, the aggregation will produce a smoother result than in the fixed/tumbling window.

The session window type is commonly used to analyze user behavior on a web site. Unlike the fixed/tumbling and sliding window, it has no predetermined window length. Rather, it is determined usually by a gap of inactivity that is greater than some threshold. For example, the length of a session window on Facebook is determined by the duration of activities that a user does, such as browsing the user feeds, sending messages, and so on.

Stream Processing Engine Landscape

There is no shortage of innovations from the open source community in coming up with solutions for streaming data processing. In fact, at the moment, there are multiple streaming processing engines. Some of the earlier streaming processing engines were born out of necessity, some of the later ones were born out of research projects, and some evolved from batching processing engines. This section presents a few of the popular streaming processing engines: Apache Storm, Apache Samza, Apache Flink, Apache Kafka Streams, Apache Apex, and Apache Beam.

Apache Storm is one of the pioneers in the area of streaming data processing, and its popularity is mainly associated with the large-scale streaming processing that Twitter does. Apache Storm's initial release was in 2011, and it became an Apache top-level project in 2014. In 2015, Twitter abandoned Apache Storm and switched over to Heron, which is the next generation of Apache Storm. Heron is more resource efficient and provides much better throughput than Apache Storm.

Apache Samza was created at LinkedIn to help solve its streaming processing needs, and it was open sourced in 2013. It was designed to work closely with Kafka and to run on top of Hadoop YARN for process isolation, security, and fault tolerance. Apache Samza was designed to process streams, which are composed of ordered, partitioned, replayable, and fault-tolerant sets of immutable messages.

Apache Flink started out as a fork of the research project called Stratosphere: Information Management on the Cloud. It became an Apache top-level project in 2015, and ever since then it has been steadily gaining popularity as a high-throughput and low-latency streaming engine. One key difference between Apache Flink and Apache Storm and Apache Samza is that Apache Flink supports both batch and streaming processing in the same engine.

Apache Kafka has evolved from a distributed publish-subscribe messaging system to a distributed streaming platform. It was created at LinkedIn and became a top-level Apache project in 2012. Unlike other streaming processing engines, Kafka's stream processing capabilities are packaged as a light-weight library, which makes it easy to write real-time streaming applications.

Apache Apex is a relatively newcomer to this space. It was developed at a company called DataTorrent, which decided to open source it in 2016. Apache Apex is considered a Hadoop YARN native platform that unifies stream and batch processing.

Apache Beam is quite an interesting project that came out of Google in 2016. The main idea behind this project was to provide a powerful and easy-to-use model for both streaming and batch processing that is portable across a variety of runtime platforms, such as Apache Flink, Apache Spark, and Google Cloud DataFlow. In other words, think of Apache Beam as an uber-API for big data.

There are two standard stream processing models, and each of the previous streaming processing engines (except Apache Beam) is subscribed to one of them. The two models are called *record-at-a-time* and *micro-batching*, as shown in Figure 6-5.

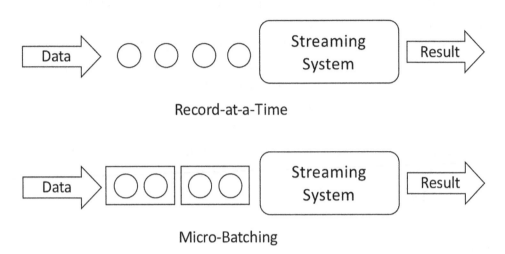

Figure 6-5. *Two different models of streaming processing*

Both models have inherent advantages and disadvantages. The record-at-a-time model does what it sounds like; it immediately processes each piece of input data as it arrives. As a result, this model provides the lowest possible latency. The micro-batching model waits and accumulates a small batch of input data based on a configurable batching interval and then processes each batch in parallel. It is fairly obvious that the micro-batching model can't provide the same level of latency as the other model. In terms of throughput, though, the micro-batch has a much higher rate because a batch of data is processed in an optimized manner, and therefore the cost per each piece of data is low compared to the other model. One interesting side note is that it is fairly easy to build a micro-batching model on top of a record-of-a-time model.

Of all the streaming processing engines listed, only Apache Spark employs the micro-batching model; however, there is already some work underway to support the record-at-a-time model.

Spark Streaming Overview

One of the contributing factors to the popularity of Apache Spark's unified data processing platform is the ability to perform streaming data processing as well as batch data processing.

With the high-level description of the intricacies and challenges of stream processing as well as a few core concepts out of the way, the remainder of this chapter will focus on the Spark streaming topic. First, it will provide a short and high-level understanding of some of the capabilities of Spark's first-generation streaming processing engine called DStream. Then the bulk of the chapter will provide details about Spark's second streaming processing engine called Structured Streaming. New Spark streaming applications should be developed on top of Structured Streaming to take advantage of some of the unique and advanced features it provides.

Spark DStream

The first generation of the Spark streaming processing engine was introduced in 2012, and the main programming abstraction in this engine is called a *discretized stream*, or DStream. The way it works is by employing the micro-batching model to divide the incoming stream of data into batches, which are then processed by the Spark batch processing engine. This makes a lot of sense when an RDD is the main programming abstraction model. Each batch is internally represented by an RDD. The number of pieces of data in a batch is a function of the incoming data rate and the batch interval. Figure 6-6 shows the way DStream works at a high level.

Figure 6-6. *Spark DStream*

A DStream can be created from an input data stream from sources such as Kafka, AWS Kinesis, a file, or a socket. One of the key pieces of information that is needed when creating a DStream is the batch interval, which can be in seconds or in milliseconds. With a DStream, you can apply a high-level data processing function such as `map`, `filter`, reduce, or reduceByKey on the incoming stream of data. Additionally, you can perform windowing operations such as reducing and counting over either a fixed/tumbling or a sliding window by providing a window length and a slide interval. One important note is that the window length and slide interval must be multiples of a batch interval. For example, if the batch interval is three seconds and the fixed/tumbling interval is used, then the window length and slide interval can be six seconds. Maintaining arbitrary state while performing computations across batches of data is supported in DStream, but it is a manual process and a bit cumbersome. One of the cool things you can do with a DStream is to join it with either another DStream or an RDD that represents static data. After all the processing logic is complete, you can use a DStream to write the data out to external systems such as a database, a file system, or HDFS.

Any new Spark streaming applications should be developed on the second generation Spark streaming processing engine called Structured Streaming, which will be covered in the next section. For the remainder of this section, you will look at a small word count Spark DStream application; the goal is to give you a sense of what a typical Spark DStream application looks like. Listing 6-1 contains the code for the word count application, which is an example from Apache Spark (see https://bit.ly/2G8N3OG).

Listing 6-1. Apache Spark DStream Word Count Application

```
object NetworkWordCount {
  def main(args: Array[String]) {

    // Create the context with a 1 second batch size
    val sparkConf = new SparkConf().setAppName("NetworkWordCount")
    val ssc = new StreamingContext(sparkConf, Seconds(1))

    val host = "localhost"
    val port = 9999

    val lines = ssc.socketTextStream(host, port, StorageLevel.MEMORY_AND_
DISK_SER)
    val words = lines.flatMap(_.split(" "))
    val wordCounts = words.map(x => (x, 1)).reduceByKey(_ + _)

    wordCounts.print()
```

```
    ssc.start()
    ssc.awaitTermination()
  }
}
```

There are a few important steps when putting together a DStream application. The entry point to a DStream application is `StreamingContext`, and one of the required inputs is a batch interval, which defines a time duration that Spark uses to batch incoming data into an RDD for processing. It also represents a trigger point for when Spark should execute the streaming application computation logic. For example, if the batch interval is three seconds, then Spark batches all the data that arrives within that three-second interval; after that interval elapses, it will turn that batch of data into an RDD and process it according to the processing logic you provide. Once a `StreamingContext` is created, the next step is to create an instance DStream by defining an input source. The previous example defines the input source as a socket that reads lines of text. After this point, then you provide the processing logic for the newly created DStream. The processing logic in the previous example is not complex. Once an RDD for a collection of lines is available after one second, then Spark executes the logic of splitting each line into words, converting each word into a tuple of the word and a count of 1, and finally summing up the count of the same word. Finally, the counts are printed out on the console. Remember that a streaming application is a long-running application; therefore, it requires a signal to start the task of receiving and processing the incoming stream of data. That signal is given by calling the `start()` function of `StreamingContext`, and this is usually done at the end of the file. The `awaitTermination()` function is used to wait for the execution of the streaming application to stop as well as a mechanism to prevent the driver from exiting while your streaming application is running. In a typically program, once the last line of code is executed, it will exit. However, a long-running streaming application needs to keep going once it is started and will end only when you explicitly stop it.

Spark Structured Streaming

Structured Streaming is Spark's second-generation streaming engine. It was designed to be much faster, more scalable, and more fault tolerant and to address the shortcomings in the first-generation streaming engine. It was designed for developers to build end-to-end streaming applications that can react to data in real-time using a simple programming model that it is built on top of the optimized and solid foundation of the Spark SQL engine. One distinguishing aspect of Structured Streaming is that it provides a unique and easy way for engineers to build streaming applications.

Building production-grade streaming applications requires overcoming many challenges, and with that in mind, the Structured Streaming engine was designed to help deal with these challenges:

- Handling end-to-end reliability and guaranteeing correctness

- Performing complex transformations on a variety of incoming data

- Processing data based on the event time and dealing with out-of-order data easily

- Integrating with a variety of data sources and data sinks

The following sections will cover various aspects of the Structured Streaming engine and the support it provides to deal with these challenges.

Overview

There are two key ideas in Structured Streaming. The first one is treating streaming computation just like the way batch computation is treated, meaning treating the incoming data stream as an input table, and as a new set of data arrives, treating that as a new set of rows being appended to the input table, just like in Figure 6-7.

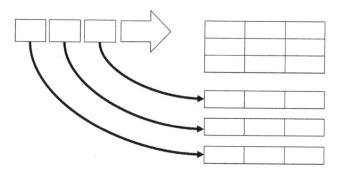

Figure 6-7. *Treating streaming data as a table being continuously updated*

Another way to think of a stream of incoming data is as nothing more than a table being continuously appended. This simple yet radical idea has many implications. One of them is the ability to leverage the existing Structured APIs for DataFrame and Dataset in Scala, Java, or Python to perform streaming computations and have the Structured Streaming engine take care of running them incrementally and continuously as the new streaming data arrives. Figure 6-8 provides a visual comparison between performing batch and stream processing in Spark. The other implication is that the same Catalyst engine discussed in the previous chapter is used to optimize the streaming computation expressed via the Structured APIs. The knowledge you gain from working with the Structured APIs is directly transferrable to building streaming applications running on the Spark Structured Streaming engine. The only remaining parts to be learned are the ones that are specific to the streaming processing domain, such as event-time processing and maintaining state.

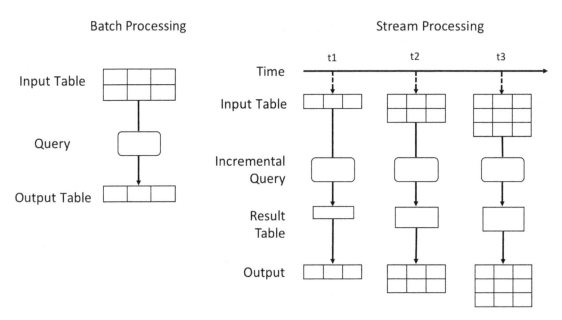

Figure 6-8. *Comparing batch processing and streaming processing in Spark*

The second key idea is the transactional integration with the storage systems to provide an end-to-end, exactly once guarantee. The goal here is to ensure that the serving applications that read data from the storage systems see a consistent snapshot of the data that has been processed by the streaming applications. Traditionally, it is a developer's responsibility to ensure there is no duplicate data or data loss when sending data from a streaming application to an external storage system. This is one of the pain points that was raised by streaming application developers. Internally, the Structure Streaming engine already provides an exactly once guarantee, and now that same guarantee is extended to external storage systems, provided those systems support transactions.

Starting with Apache Spark 2.3, the Structured Streaming engine's processing model has been expanded to support a new model called *continuous processing*. The previous processing model was the micro-batching model, which is the default one. Given the nature of the micro-batching processing model, it is suitable for use cases that can tolerate end-to-end latency in the range of 100 milliseconds. For other use cases that need end-to-end latency as low as 1 millisecond, they should use the continuous processing model; however, it has an experimental status as of Apache Spark 2.3, and it has a few restrictions in terms of what streaming computations are allowed.

Core Concepts

This section covers a set of core concepts you need to understand before building a streaming application. The main parts of a streaming application consist of specifying one or more streaming data sources, providing the logic for manipulating the incoming data streams in the form of DataFrame transformations, defining the output mode and the trigger, and finally specifying a data sink to write the result to. Since both the output mode and the trigger have default values, they are optional if their default values meet your use case. Figure 6-9 outlines the steps mentioned earlier. The optional ones are marked with an asterisk.

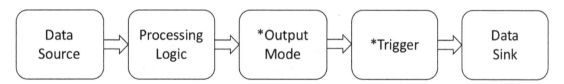

Figure 6-9. *The core pieces of a Structured Streaming application*

Each of these concepts will be described in detail in the following sections.

Data Sources

Let's start with data sources. With batching processing, the data source is a static dataset that resides on some storage system like a local file system, HDFS, or S3. The data sources in Structured Streaming are quite different. The data they produce is continuous and may never end, and the producing rate can vary over time. Structured Streaming provides the following out-of-the-box sources:

- *Kafka source*: require Apache Kafka with version 0.10 or higher. This is the most popular data source in a production environment. Working with this data source will require a fundamental of understanding of how Kafka works. Connecting to and reading data from a Kafka topic requires a specific set of settings that must be provided. Please refer to the Kafka Integration Guide on the Spark website for more details.

- *File source*: Files are located on either the local file system, HDFS, or S3. As new files are dropped into a directory, this data source will pick them up for processing. Commonly used file formats are supported, such as text, CSV, JSON, ORC, and Parquet. See the `DataStreamReader` interface for an up-to-date list of supported file formats. A good practice when working with this data source is to completely write the input files and then move them into the path of this data source.

- *Socket source*: This is for testing purposes only. It reads UTF-8 data from a socket listening on a certain host and port.

- *Rate source*: This is for testing and benchmark purposes only. This source can be configured to generate a number of events per second, where each event consists of a timestamp and a monotonically increased value. This is the easiest source to work with while learning Structured Streaming.

One important property a data source needs to provide for Structured Streaming to deliver an end-to-end, exactly once guarantee is a way to track a read position in the stream. For example, a Kafka data source provides a Kafka offset to track the read position of a partition of a topic. This property determines whether a particular data source is fault tolerant. Table 6-1 describes some of the options for each out-of-the box data source.

Table 6-1. *Out-of-the-Box Data Sources*

Name	Fault Tolerant	Configurations
File	Yes	`path`: Path to the input directory `maxFilesPerTrigger`: Maximum number of new files to read per trigger `latestFirst`: Whether to process the latest files (in terms of modification time)
Socket	No	The following are required: `host`: Host to connect to `port`: Port to connect to
Rate	Yes	`rowsPerSecond`: Number of rows to generate per second `rampUpTime`: Ramp-up time in seconds before reaching `rowsPerSecond` `numPartitions`: Number of partitions
Kafka	Yes	`kafka.bootstrap.servers`: A comma-separated list of `host:port` of Kafka brokers `subscribe`: A comma-separated list of topics Please refer to the Kafka Integration Guide on the Spark website for more details (`https://spark.apache.org/docs/latest/structured-streaming-kafka-integration.html`).

Apache Spark 2.3 introduced the DataSource V2 APIs, which is an official supported set of interfaces for Spark developers to develop custom data sources that can easily integrate with Structured Streaming. With this well-defined set of APIs, the number of custom Structured Streaming sources will dramatically increase in the near future.

Output Modes

Output modes are a way to tell Structure Streaming how the output data should be written to a sink. This concept is unique to streaming processing in Spark. There are three options.

- *Append mode*: This is the default mode if output mode is not specified. In this mode, only new rows that were appended to the result table will be sent to the specified output sink.

- *Complete mode*: The entire result table will be written to the output sink.

- *Update mode*: Only the rows that were updated in the result table will be written to the output sink. For the rows that were not changed, they will not be written out.

Output mode is an concept that will take some time getting used to because there are a few dimensions to it. Given the three options, it is only natural to wonder under what circumstances one would use one output mode versus the other ones. It will make more sense when you will go through a few examples.

Trigger Types

Trigger is another important concept to understand. The Structured Streaming engine uses the trigger information to determine when to run the provided streaming computation logic in your streaming application. Table 6-2 describes the different trigger types.

Table 6-2. Trigger Types

Type	Description
Not specified (default)	For this default type, Spark will use the micro-batch mode and process the next batch of data as soon as the previous batch of data has completed processing.
Fixed interval	For this type, Spark will use the micro-batch mode and process the batch of data based on the user-provided interval. If for whatever reason the processing of the previous batch of data takes longer than the interval, then the next batch of data is processed immediately after the previous one is completed. In other words, Spark will not wait until the next interval boundary.
One-time	This trigger type is meant to be used for one-time processing of the available batch of data, and Spark will immediately stop the streaming application once the processing is completed. This trigger type is useful when the data volume is extremely low, and therefore it is more cost effective to spin up a cluster and process the data only a few times a day.
Continuous	This trigger type invokes the new continuous processing mode that is designed for a certain streaming applications that require very low latency. This is new and experimental processing mode in Spark 2.3.

Data Sinks

Data sinks are at the opposite end of the data sources. They are meant for storing the output of streaming applications. It is important to recognize which sinks can support which output mode and whether they are fault tolerant. A short description of each sink is provided here, and the various options for each sink are outlined in Table 6-3.

- *Kafka sink*: require Apache Kafka with version 0.10 or higher. There is a specific set of settings to connect to a Kafka cluster. Please refer to the Kafka Integration Guide on the Spark website for more details.

- *File sink*: This is a destination on a file system, HDFS, or S3. Commonly used file formats are supported, such as text, CSV, JSON, ORC, and Parquet. See the `DataStreamReader` interface for an up-to-date list of supported file formats.

- *Foreach sink*: This is meant for running arbitrary computations on the rows in the output.

- *Console sink*: This is for testing and debugging purposes only and when working with low-volume data. The output is printed to the console on every trigger.

- *Memory sink*: This is for testing and debugging purposes only when working with low-volume data. It uses the memory of the driver to store the output.

Table 6-3. *Out-of-the-Box Data Sinks*

Name	Supported Output Modes	Fault Tolerant	Configurations
File	Append	Yes	`path`: This is the path to the input directory. All the popular file formats are supported. See `DataFrameWriter` for more details.
Foreach	Append, Update, Complete	Depends	This is a very flexible sink, and it is implementation specific. See the following details.
Console	Append, Update, Complete	No	`numRows`: This is the number of rows to print every trigger. The default is 20 rows. `truncate`: This specifies whether to truncate if each row is too long. The default is true.
Memory	Append, Complete	No	N/A
Kafka	Append, Update, Complete	Yes	`kafka.bootstrap.servers`: This is a comma-separated list of `host:port` of Kafka brokers. `topic`: This is a Kafka topic to write data to. Please refer to the Kafka Integration Guide on the Spark website for more details (`https://spark.apache.org/docs/latest/structured-streaming-kafka-integration.html`).

One important property a data sink must support for Structured Streaming to deliver an end-to-end, exactly once guarantee is to be idempotent for handling reprocessing. In other words, it must be able to handle multiple writes (that occur at different times) with the same data such that the outcome is the same as if there was only a single write. The multiple writes is a result of reprocessing data during a failure scenario.

To help solidify an understanding of the core concepts mentioned earlier, the next section will provide examples of how the various pieces fit together when putting together a Structured Streaming application in Spark.

Watermarking

Watermarking is a commonly used technique in streaming processing engines to deal with data that arrives at a much later time than other data that was created at about the same time. Late data presents challenges to streaming processing engines when the streaming computation logic requires it to maintain some kind of state. Examples of this scenario are when there are aggregations or joining going on. Streaming application developers can specify a threshold to let the Structured Streaming engine know how late the data is expected to be in terms of the event time. With this information, the Structured Streaming engine can decide whether a piece of late data will be processed or discarded. More important, Structured Streaming uses the specified threshold to determine when old state can be discarded. Without this information, Structured Streaming will need to maintain all the state indefinitely, and this will cause out-of-memory issues for streaming applications. Any production Structured Streaming applications that perform some kind of aggregations or joining will need to specify a watermark. This is an important concept, and more details about this topic will be discussed and illustrated in later sections.

Note   Apache Kafka has become one of the most popular open source technologies in the big data landscape. It plays a critical role in the architecture of a big data platform by acting as the glue between the various data producers and consumers. At a high level, Kafka is a distributed and fault-tolerant pub-sub messaging system for ingesting real-time data streams. The unit of data with Kafka is called a *message*. Messages are organized into topics, which are split into partitions to enable the ability to consume the messages in parallel. The messages of each partition are stored in a file with the structure that is similar to a commit log. Each partition data file contains an ordered, immutable sequence of messages. A sequential ID is assigned to each message and is commonly referred to as the *offset*. As new messages arrive to a partition, they are simply appended to the end of the partition file. This key design point is what enables Kafka to handle a high ingestion rate. Each partition can be replicated to multiple replicas. The append-only style of writing messages to a partition and the partition replication are the key contributors to how Kafka provides redundancy and scalability. Each topic has a configuration for a retention period based on either size or age, after which messages are marked for deletion. For more details about Kafka, please visit `https://kafka.apache.org/documentation/`.

Structured Streaming Application

This section will go through a Spark Structured Streaming example application to see how the aforementioned concepts are mapped to code. The following example is about processing a small set of mobile action events from a file data source. Each event consists of three fields:

- *id*: Represents the unique ID of a phone. In the provided sample data set, the phone ID will be something like phone1, phone2, phone3, and so on.

- *action*: Represents an action taken by a user. Possible values of the action are open and close.

- *ts*: Represents the timestamp when the action was taken by user. This is the event time.

The mobile event data is split into three JSON files, and they are available in the chapter6/data/mobile directory. To simulate the data streaming behavior, the JSON files will be copied into the input folder in a certain order, and then the output is examined to validate your understanding.

Let's explore the mobile event data by using DataFrames to read the data. See Listing 6-2.

Listing 6-2. Reading in Mobile Data and Printing Out Its Schema

```
val mobileDataDF = spark.read.json("<path>/chapter6/data/mobile")

mobileDataDF.printSchema
 |-- action: string (nullable = true)
 |-- id: string (nullable = true)
 |-- ts: string (nullable = true)

file1.json
{"id":"phone1","action":"open","ts":"2018-03-02T10:02:33"}
{"id":"phone2","action":"open","ts":"2018-03-02T10:03:35"}
{"id":"phone3","action":"open","ts":"2018-03-02T10:03:50"}
{"id":"phone1","action":"close","ts":"2018-03-02T10:04:35"}
```

```
file2.json
{"id":"phone3","action":"close","ts":"2018-03-02T10:07:35"}
{"id":"phone4","action":"open","ts":"2018-03-02T10:07:50"}
```

```
file3.json
{"id":"phone2","action":"close","ts":"2018-03-02T10:04:50"}
{"id":"phone5","action":"open","ts":"2018-03-02T10:10:50"}
```

By default, Structured Streaming requires a schema when reading data from a file-based data source. This makes sense because initially the directory might be empty, so therefore Structured Streaming wouldn't be able to infer the schema. However, if you really want it to infer the schema, you can set the configuration spark.sql.streaming. schemaInference to true. In this example, you will explicitly create a schema. Listing 6-3 contains a snippet of code for creating the schema for the mobile event data.

Listing 6-3. Creating a Schema for Mobile Event Data

```
import org.apache.spark.sql.types._
import org.apache.spark.sql.functions._

val mobileDataSchema = new StructType().add("id", StringType, false)
                                       .add("action", StringType, false)
                                       .add("ts", TimestampType, false)
```

Let's start with a simple use case for processing the mobile event data. The goal is to generate a count per action type using a fixed window with a ten-second window length. The three lines of code in Listing 6-4 will help achieve this goal. The first line of code demonstrates the usage of a file-based data source by using the DataStreamReader to read data from a directory. The expected data format is in JSON, and the schema is defined in Listing 6-3. The returned object is a DataFrame, which you are familiar with from Chapter 4. However, this DataFrame is a streaming DataFrame, so when the isStreaming function is invoked, the returned value should be true. The streaming computation logic in this simple application is expressed in the second line of code, which performs the group by transformation using the action column and a fixed window based on the ts column. A keen reader probably already recognizes this, but just to emphasize the point about event time, the fixed window in the group by transformation is based on the timestamp embedded inside the mobile event data. The third line of code is an important one because it defines the output mode and data sink, and most importantly it tells the Structured Streaming engine to start incrementally running our streaming computation logic expressed in the second line. To go into more detail, the third line of code uses the DataFrameWriter instance of the actionCountDF DataFrame to specify the console as the data sink, meaning the output will be printed to a console for you to examine. It then defines the output mode as "complete" so you can see all the records in the result table. Finally, it invokes the start() function of the DataStreamWriter to start the execution, which means the file-based data source will start processing files that are dropped into the /<path>/chapter6/data/input directory. Another important thing to note is that the start function will return an instance of a StreamingQuery class, which represents a handle to a query that is executing continuously in the background as new data arrives. You can use the mobileConsoleSQ streaming query to examine the status and progress of the computation in the streaming application.

Before you type in the three lines of code in Listing 6-4, make sure the input folder is empty.

Listing 6-4. Generating a Count per Action Type in a Ten-Second Sliding Window

```
val mobileSSDF = spark.readStream.schema(mobileDataSchema).json("/<path>/
chapter6/data/input")

mobileSSDF.isStreaming

val actionCountDF = mobileSSDF.groupBy(window($"ts", "10 minutes"),
$"action").count

val mobileConsoleSQ = actionCountDF.writeStream
                                .format("console").option("truncate",
                                "false")
                                .outputMode("complete")
                                .start()
```

To start seeing the output in the console like in Listing 6-5, copy file1.json from the chapter6/data/mobile directory to the chapter6/data/input directory. The following output should show up in the console. The output tells you there is only one window from 10:00 to 10:10, and within this window there is one close action and three open actions, which should match the four lines of events in files1.json. Now repeat the same process with file file2.json, and the output should match Listing 6-6. The data file file2.json contains one event with an open action and another with a close action, and both fall into the same window as earlier. Therefore, the counts are updated to two close actions and four open actions, respectively, for the action type.

Listing 6-5. Output from Processing file1.json

```
----------------------------------------------------------
Batch: 0
----------------------------------------------------------
+--------------------------------------------+-------+------+
|                                      window| action| count|
+--------------------------------------------+-------+------+
| [2018-03-02 10:00:00, 2018-03-02 10:10:00]|  close|     1|
| [2018-03-02 10:00:00, 2018-03-02 10:10:00]|   open|     3|
+--------------------------------------------+-------+------+
```

Listing 6-6. Output from Processing file2.json

```
----------------------------------------------------------
Batch: 1
----------------------------------------------------------
+--------------------------------------------+-------+------+
|                                      window| action| count|
+--------------------------------------------+-------+------+
|[2018-03-02 10:00:00, 2018-03-02 10:10:00]|  close|     2|
|[2018-03-02 10:00:00, 2018-03-02 10:10:00]|   open|     4|
+--------------------------------------------+-------+------+
```

At this point, let's invoke a few functions of the query stream mobileConsoleSQ (an instance of the StreamingQuery class) to examine the status and progress. The status() function will tell you what's going at the current status of the query stream, which can be either in wait mode or in the middle of processing the current batch of events. The lastProgress() function provides some metrics about the processing of the last batch of events including processing rates, latencies, and so on. Listing 6-7 contains the sample output from both of these functions.

Listing 6-7. Output from Calling the status() and lastProgress() Functions

```scala
scala> mobileConsoleSQ.status
res14: org.apache.spark.sql.streaming.StreamingQueryStatus =
{
  "message" : "Waiting for data to arrive",
  "isDataAvailable" : false,
  "isTriggerActive" : false
}

scala> mobileConsoleSQ.lastProgress
res17: org.apache.spark.sql.streaming.StreamingQueryProgress =
{
  "id" : "2200bc3f-077c-4f6f-af54-8043f50f719c",
  "runId" : "0ed4894c-1c76-4072-8252-264fe98cb856",
  "name" : null,
  "timestamp" : "2018-03-18T18:18:12.877Z",
  "batchId" : 2,
  "numInputRows" : 0,
  "inputRowsPerSecond" : 0.0,
  "processedRowsPerSecond" : 0.0,
  "durationMs" : {
    "getOffset" : 1,
    "triggerExecution" : 1
  },
  "stateOperators" : [ {
    "numRowsTotal" : 2,
    "numRowsUpdated" : 0,
    "memoryUsedBytes" : 17927
  } ],
  "sources" : [ {
    "description" : "FileStreamSource[file:<path>/chapter6/data/input]",
    "startOffset" : {
      "logOffset" : 1
    },
```

```
"endOffset" : {
  "logOffset" : 1
},
"numInputRows" : 0,
"inputRowsPerSecond" : 0.0,...
```

Let's finish processing the last file of the mobile event data. It's the same as file2.json. Copy file3.json to the input directory, and the output should look something like Listing 6-8. File file3.json contains one close action that belongs to the first window and an open action that falls into a new window from 10:10 to 10:20. In total, there are eight actions. Seven of them fall into the first window, and one action falls into the second window.

Listing 6-8. Output from Processing file3.json

```
-------------------------------------------------------------
Batch: 2
-------------------------------------------------------------
+---------------------------------------------+-------+------+
|                                       window| action| count|
+---------------------------------------------+-------+------+
|[2018-03-02 10:00:00, 2018-03-02 10:10:00]|  close|     3|
|[2018-03-02 10:00:00, 2018-03-02 10:10:00]|   open|     4|
|[2018-03-02 10:10:00, 2018-03-02 10:20:00]|   open|     1|
+---------------------------------------------+-------+------+
```

For a production and long-running streaming application, it is necessary to call the StreamingQuery.awaitTermination() function, which is a blocking call to prevent the driver process from exiting, and to let the streaming query continuously run and process new data as it arrives into the data source.

While learning and playing around with Structured Streaming, sometimes you want to stop a streaming query to change either the output mode, the trigger, or other configurations. You can use the StreamingQuery.stop() function to stop the data source from receiving new data and stop the continuous execution of logic in the streaming query. See Listing 6-9 for examples of managing streaming queries.

Listing 6-9. Managing a Streaming Query

```
// this is blocking call
mobileSQ.awaitTermination()

// stop a streaming query
mobileSQ.stop

// another way of stopping all streaming queries in a Spark application
for(qs <- spark.streams.active) {
    println(s"Stop streaming query: ${qs.name} - active: ${qs.isActive}")
    if (qs.isActive) {
      qs.stop
    }
}
```

Streaming DataFrame Operations

The previous example shows that once a data source is configured and defined, the `DataStreamReader` will return an instance of a DataFrame, which is the same DataFrame class you are familiar with from Chapter 4 and Chapter 5. This means you can use most of the familiar operations and Spark SQL functions to express your application streaming computation logic. However, it is important to note that not all operations in the DataFrame are supported for a streaming DataFrame. This is because some of them are not applicable in the context of streaming data processing. Examples of such operations include limit, distinct, and sort.

Selection, Project, and Aggregation Operations

One of the selling points of Structured Streaming is a set of unified APIs for batch processing and stream processing in Spark. With a streaming DataFrame, it is feasible to apply any of the select and filter transformations to it, as well as any of the Spark SQL functions that operate on individual columns. In addition, basic aggregations and the advanced analytics functions covered in Chapter 5 are available to a streaming DataFrame as well. To complete the similarity comparison of the two DataFrame types (static and streaming), a streaming DataFrame can be registered as a temporary view and then apply SQL queries on it. Listing 6-10 provides an example of using filtering and applying Spark SQL functions on top of the `mobileSSDF` DataFrame in Listing 6-4.

Listing 6-10. Applying Filtering and Spark SQL Functions on a Streaming DataFrame

```
import org.apache.spark.sql.functions._
val cleanMobileSSDF = mobileSSDF.filter($"action" === "open" || $"action"
=== "close")
                              .select($"id", upper($"action"), $"ts")

// create a view to apply SQL queries on
cleanMobileSSDF.createOrReplaceTempView("clean_mobile")
spark.sql("select count(*) from clean_mobile")
```

It is important to note the following DataFrame transformations are not supported yet in a streaming DataFrame either because they are too complex to maintain state or because of the unbounded nature of streaming data.

- Multiple aggregations or a chain of aggregations on a streaming DataFrame.

- Limit and take N rows.

- Distinct transformation. However, there is a way to deduplicate data using a unique identifier.

- Sorting on a streaming DataFrame without any aggregation. However, sorting is supported after some form of aggregation.

Any attempt to use one of the unsupported operations will result in an `AnalysisException` exception and a message like "operation XYZ is not supported with streaming DataFrames/Datasets."

Join Operations

One of the coolest things you can do with a streaming DataFrame is to join it with either a static DataFrame or another streaming DataFrame. However, joining is a complex operation, and the tricky part is not all of the data for a streaming DataFrame is available at the time of joining. Therefore, the result of a join is generated incrementally at each trigger point, similar to how the result of an aggregation is generated.

Starting with Spark 2.3, Structured Streaming supports joining two streaming DataFrames. Given the unbounded nature of a streaming DataFrame, Structured Streaming must maintain the past data of both streaming DataFrames to match with any future, yet-to-be-received data. To avoid the explosion of the streaming state that Structured Streaming must maintain, a watermark can be optionally provided for both streaming DataFrames, and a constraint on event time must be defined in the join condition. Let's go through an IoT use case of joining two data sensor–related data streams of a data center. The first one contains the temperature reading of the various locations in a data center, and the second one contains the load information of each computer in the same data center. The join condition of these two streams is based on the location. Listing 6-11 contains code about providing watermarks and a constraint on the event time in the join condition.

Listing 6-11. Joining Two Streaming DataFrames

```
import org.apache.spark.sql.functions.expr

// the specific streaming data source information is not important in this
example
val tempDataDF = spark.readStream. ...
val loadDataDF = spark.readStream. ...

val tempDataWatermarkDF = tempDataDF.withWaterMark("temp_taken_time",
"1 hour")
val loadDataWatermarkDF = loadDataDF.withWaterMark("load_taken_time",
"2 hours")

// join on the location id as well as the event time constraint
tempWithLoadDataDF = tempDataWatermarkDF.join(loadDataWatermarkDF,
   expr(""" temp_location_id = load_location_id AND
           load_taken_time >= temp_taken_time AND
           load_taken_time <= temp_taken_time + interval 1 hour
       """)
)
```

There are more restrictions on the outer joins when joining a static DataFrame and a streaming DataFrame and when joining two streaming DataFrames. Table 6-4 provides some details about this.

Table 6-4. *Some Details About Joining Streaming DataFrames*

Left Side+Right Side	Join Type	Note
Static+Streaming	Inner	Supported.
Static+Streaming	Left outer	Not supported.
Static+Streaming	Right outer	Supported.
Static+Streaming	Full outer	Not supported.
Streaming+Streaming	Inner	Supported.
Streaming+Streaming	Left outer	Conditionally supported. You must specify the watermark on the right side and the time constraint.
Streaming+Streaming	Right outer	Conditionally supported. You must specify the watermark on the left and the time constraint.
Streaming+Streaming	Full outer	Not supported.

Working with Data Sources

The previous section described each of the built-in sources that Structured Streaming provides. This section will go into more detail and will provide sample code for working with them.

Both the Socket and Rate data sources are designed for testing and learning purposes only, and they shouldn't be used in production.

Working with the Socket Data Source

The Socket data source is fairly easy to work with, and It only requires information about about the host and port to connect. Before starting a streaming query for the Socket data source, it is important to start a socket server first using a network command-line utility like nc on Mac or netcat on Windows. In this example, the nc network utility is used. You need two terminals. The first one is for starting up a socket server with port number 9999; the command is nc -lk 9999. The second terminal runs the Spark shell with the code in Listing 6-12.

Listing 6-12. Reading Streaming Data from the Socket Data Source

```
val socketDF = spark.readStream.format("socket")
                            .option("host", "localhost")
                            .option("port", "9999").load()

val words = socketDF.as[String].flatMap(_.split(" "))
val wordCounts = words.groupBy("value").count()

val query = wordCounts.writeStream.format("console")
                              .outputMode("complete")
                              .start()
```

Now go back to the first window, type Spark is great, and hit the Enter key. Then type Spark is awesome and hit the Enter key. Hitting the Enter key tells the Netscat server to send whatever was typed to the socket listener. If everything went well, there should two output batches in the Spark shell console, as in Listing 6-13, and each one contains the count of each word. Since Structured Streaming maintains state across batches, it was able to update the count of the Spark and is words to 2.

Listing 6-13. Output of the Socket Data Source in the Spark Shell Console

```
-------------------------------------------
Batch: 0
-------------------------------------------

+------+------+
| value| count|
+------+------+
| great|     1|
|    is|     1|
| Spark|     1|
+------+------+
```

```
----------------------------------------------
Batch: 1
----------------------------------------------
+-------+------+
|  value| count|
+-------+------+
|  great|     1|
|     is|     2|
|awesome|     1|
|  Spark|     2|
+-------+------+
```

When you are done with testing the Socket data source, you can stop the streaming query by calling on the stop function, as shown in Listing 6-14. As expected, after the streaming query is stopped, typing anything in the first terminal will not result in anything being displayed in the Spark shell.

Listing 6-14. Stopping a Streaming Query of the Socket Data Source

```
query.stop
```

Working with the Rate Data Source

Similar to the Socket data source, the Rate data source was designed for testing and learning purposes only. It supports a few options, and one of them is the number of rows to generate per second. If that number is high, then another optional configuration can be provided for the ramp-up time to get to the number of rows per second. Each piece of data the Rate source produces contains only two columns: the timestamp and the auto-increment value. Listing 6-15 contains the code for printing out the data from the Rate data source and what the first batch looks like in the console.

Listing 6-15. Working with the Rate Data Source

```
// configure it to generate 10 rows per second
val rateSourceDF = spark.readStream.format("rate")
                           .option("rowsPerSecond","10")
                           .load()
```

```
val rateQuery = rateSourceDF.writeStream
                            .outputMode("update")
                            .format("console")
                            .option("truncate", "false")
                            .start()
-------------------------------------------
Batch: 1
-------------------------------------------
+----------------------+------+
|             timestamp| value|
+----------------------+------+
|2018-03-19 10:30:21.952|    0|
|2018-03-19 10:30:22.052|    1|
|2018-03-19 10:30:22.152|    2|
|2018-03-19 10:30:22.252|    3|
|2018-03-19 10:30:22.352|    4|
|2018-03-19 10:30:22.452|    5|
|2018-03-19 10:30:22.552|    6|
|2018-03-19 10:30:22.652|    7|
|2018-03-19 10:30:22.752|    8|
|2018-03-19 10:30:22.852|    9|
+----------------------+------+
```

One interesting thing to note is the number in the value column is guaranteed to be consecutive across all the partitions. Listing 6-16 illustrates what the output looks like with three partitions.

Listing 6-16. The Output of the Rate Data Source with the Partition ID

```
import org.apache.spark.sql.functions._

// with 3 partitions
val rateSourceDF2 = spark.readStream.format("rate")
                                    .option("rowsPerSecond","10")
                                    .option("numPartitions",3).load()
```

```
// add partition id column to examine
val rateWithPartitionDF = rateSourceDF2.withColumn("partition_id",
spark_partition_id())

val rateWithPartitionQuery = rateWithPartitionDF.writeStream
                                               .outputMode("update")
                                               .format("console")
                                               .option("truncate", "false")
                                               .start()

// output of batch one
-------------------------------------------------
Batch: 1
-------------------------------------------------

+-----------------------+------+------------+
|              timestamp| value| partition_id|
+-----------------------+------+------------+
|2018-03-24 08:46:43.412|    0|           0|
|2018-03-24 08:46:43.512|    1|           0|
|2018-03-24 08:46:43.612|    2|           0|
|2018-03-24 08:46:43.712|    3|           1|
|2018-03-24 08:46:43.812|    4|           1|
|2018-03-24 08:46:43.912|    5|           1|
|2018-03-24 08:46:44.012|    6|           2|
|2018-03-24 08:46:44.112|    7|           2|
|2018-03-24 08:46:44.212|    8|           2|
|2018-03-24 08:46:44.312|    9|           2|
+-----------------------+------+------------+
```

The previous output shows that the ten rows are spread across three partitions, and the values are consecutive as if they were generated for a single partition. If you are curious about the implementation of this data source, then check out https://github.com/apache/spark/blob/master/sql/core/src/main/scala/org/apache/spark/sql/execution/streaming/RateSourceProvider.scala.

Working with the File Data Source

The File data source is the simplest to understand and work with. Let's say there is a need to process new files that are periodically copied into a directory. This is the perfect data source for this use case. Out of the box, it supports all the commonly used file formats including text, CSV, JSON, ORC, and Parquet. For a complete list of supported file formats, please consult the DataStreamReader interface. Among the four options that the File data source supports, only the input directory to read files from is required.

As new files are copied into a specified directory, the File data source will pick up all of them for processing. It is possible to configure the File data source to selectively pick up only a fixed number of new files for processing. The option to use to specify the number of files is the maxFilesPerTrigger option. Listing 6-17 provides an example of reading JSON mobile data events from a directory and using the same schema defined in Listing 6-3. Another interesting optional option that the File data source supports is whether to process the latest files before the older files. The last timestamp of a file is used to determine which file is newer than another file. The default behavior is to process files from oldest to latest. This particular option is useful when there is a large backlog of files to process and you want to process the new files first.

Listing 6-17. Working with the File Data Source

```
val mobileSSDF = spark.readStream.schema(mobileDataSchema).json("<directory
name>")

// if we want to specify maxFilesPerTrigger
val mobileSSDF =  spark.readStream.schema(mobileDataSchema).
                               option("maxFilesPerTrigger",
                               5).json("<directory name>")

// if we want to process new files first
val mobileSSDF =  spark.readStream.schema(mobileDataSchema).
                               option("latestFirst", "true").
                               json("<directory name>")
```

Working with the Kafka Data Source

A Kafka data source is probably the most commonly used one in production streaming applications. To be effective at working with this data source, you need a certain amount of basic knowledge of working with Kafka. At a high level, this data source acts as a Kafka consumer; therefore, the information it needs is similar to the kind a Kafka consumer needs. There are two required pieces of information and a handful of optional ones.

The two required pieces of information are a list of Kafka servers to connect to and information about one or more topics to read the data from. To support the various ways of choosing which topics and partitions of topics to read data from, it supports three different ways of specifying this information. You just need to pick the one that best suits your use case. Table 6-5 contains details about the two required options.

Table 6-5. *Required Options for the Kafka Data Source*

Option	Value	Description
kafka.bootstrap. servers	host1:port1, host2:port2	This is a comma-separated list of Kafka broker servers. Consult your Kafka administrators for the host name and port number to use.
subscribe	topic1, topic2	This is a comma-separated list of topic names for this data source to read data from.
subscribePattern	topic.*	This is a regex pattern to express which topics to read data from. This is a little bit more flexible than the subscribe option.
assign	{ topic1: [1,2], topic2: [3,4] }	With this option, you can specify the specific list of partitions of the topics to read data from. This information must be provided in JSON format.

After these required options are specified, then you can optionally specify the options in Table 6-6, which contains only a few of the commonly used ones. For a complete list of optional options, please consult Structured Streaming and the Kafka Integration Guide at `https://spark.apache.org/docs/latest/structured-streaming-kafka-integration.html`. The reason these options are optional is because they have default values.

The `startingOffsets` and `endingOffsets` options are a way for you to have fine-grained control of processing data in Kafka from a specific point in a particular partition of a particular topic. This kind of flexibility is extremely useful in scenarios when reprocessing is needed because of either failure or some bugs were introduced in a new version of the software or when retraining a machine learning model. The ability to reprocess data in Kafka is one of the reasons that Kafka is popular in the world of big data processing. It may be obvious, but `startingOffsets` is used by the Kafka data source to figure out where to start reading the data from in Kafka, and therefore, once the processing is going, this option is no longer used. The `endingOffsets` option is used by the Kafka data source to figure out when to stop reading the data from Kafka. For example, if you want your streaming application to read the latest data from Kafka and continue with processing new incoming data, then the value of both `startingOffsets` and `endingOffsets` would be the latest.

Table 6-6. *Optional Options for the Kafka Data Source*

Option	Default Value	Value	Description
starting Offsets	latest	earliest, latest JSON string of starting offset for each topic, i.e., { "topic1": { "0":45, "1": -1}, "topic2": { "0":-2} }	earliest means the beginning of a topic. latest means whatever the latest data is in a topic. When using the JSON string format, -2 represents the earliest offset in a specific partition, and -1 represents the latest offset in a specific partition.
ending Offsets	latest	latest JSON string, i.e., { "topic1": { "0":45, "1": -1}, "topic2": { "0":-2} }	latest means the latest data in a topic. When using the JSON string format, -1 represents the latest offset in a specific partition. Naturally -2 is not applicable for this option.
maxOffsets PerTrigger	none	Long, i.e., 500	This option is a rate limit mechanism to control the number of records to process per trigger interval. If a value is specified, it represents the total number of records across all the partitions, not per partition.

By default, the Kafka data source is not included in the Apache Spark binary available at `https://spark.apache.org/downloads.html`. If you are going to use the Kafka data source from the Spark shell, then it is important to start the Spark shell with an extra option to ask it to download and include the right JAR file. The deployment section of Structured Streaming and the Kafka integration documentation (`https://spark.apache.org/docs/latest/structured-streaming-kafka-integration.html`) provides the information about the extra option. It looks something like Listing 6-18.

Listing 6-18. Start Spark Shell with the Kafka Data Source JAR File

```
./bin/spark-shell --packages org.apache.spark:spark-sql-
kafka-0-10_2.11:2.3.0

// if the above package is not provided, the following problem will be encountered

java.lang.ClassNotFoundException: Failed to find data source: kafka. Please
find packages at http://spark.apache.org/third-party-projects.html
  at org.apache.spark.sql.execution.datasources.DataSource$.lookupDataSource
  (DataSource.scala:635)
  at org.apache.spark.sql.streaming.DataStreamReader.load(DataStreamReader.
  scala:159)
```

Let's start with a simple example of processing the data from the beginning of a Kafka topic called `pageviews` and continue processing new data as it arrives in Kafka. See Listing 6-19 for the code.

Listing 6-19. Kafka Data Source Example

```
import org.apache.spark.sql.functions._

val pvDF = spark.readStream.format("kafka")
                                        .option("kafka.bootstrap.
                                        servers","localhost:9092")
                .option("subscribe", "pageviews")
                .option("startingOffsets", "earliest")
                .load()
```

```
pvDF.printSchema
 |-- key: binary (nullable = true)
 |-- value: binary (nullable = true)
 |-- topic: string (nullable = true)
 |-- partition: integer (nullable = true)
 |-- offset: long (nullable = true)
 |-- timestamp: timestamp (nullable = true)
 |-- timestampType: integer (nullable = true)
```

One thing that is unique about the Kafka data source is that the streaming DataFrame it returns has a fixed schema, which looks something like Listing 6-19. The value column contains the actual content of each message in Kafka, and the column type is binary. Kafka doesn't really care about the content of each message, and therefore it treats it as a binary blob. The rest of columns in the schema contains the metadata of each message. If the content of the messages was serialized in some binary format at the time of sending to Kafka, then you would need a way to deserialize it using either Spark SQL functions or an UDF before those messages can be processed in Spark. In the following example, the content is a string, so you simply need to cast it to a String type. For demonstration purposes, Listing 6-20 performs the casting of the value column as well as selecting a few metadata-related columns to display.

Listing 6-20. Casting Message Content to String Type

```
val pvValueDF = pvDF.selectExpr("partition","offset","CAST(key AS STRING)",
"CAST(value AS STRING)")
                    .as[(String, Long, String, String)]
```

The examples in Listing 6-21 contain a few variations of specifying the Kafka topic, partition, and offset to read messages from Kafka.

Listing 6-21. Various Examples of Specifying Kafka Topic, Partition, and Offset

```
// reading from multiple topics with default startingOffsets and endingOffsets
val kafkaDF = spark.readStream.format("kafka")
                              .option("kafka.bootstrap.server
                              s","server1:9092,server2:9092")
                      .option("subscribe", "topic1,topic2")
                      .load()
```

```
// reading from multiple topics using subscribePattern
val kafkaDF = spark.readStream.format("kafka")
                              .option("kafka.bootstrap.servers","server1:90
                              92,server2:9092")
                              .option("subscribePattern", "topic*").load()
// reading from a particular offset of a partition using JSON format
// the triple quotes format in Scala is used to escape double quote in JSON
   string
Val kafkaDF = spark.readStream.format("kafka")
                              .option("kafka.bootstrap.
                              servers","localhost:9092")
                              .option("subscribe", "topic1,topic2")
                              .option("startingOffsets", """
                              {"topic1": {"0":51} } """)
                              .load()
```

Working with the Custom Data Source

Prior to Spark 2.3, the Data Source APIs have limitations and are not very extensible. Therefore, it is quite challenging for Spark developers to build custom data sources. Starting with Spark 2.3, the Data Source V2 APIs were introduced to address the issues in V1 as well as to provide a set of new APIs that are clean, extensible, and easy to work with. The Data Source V2 APIs are available in Scala only.

This section is meant to provide a quick overview of the interfaces and main APIs that are involved in building a custom data source using the Data Source V2 APIs. A few good references to examine are the implementations of the built-in data sources such as classes RateSourceProvider.scala, RateSourceProviderV2.scala, and KafkaSourceProvider.scala.

All custom data sources must implement a marker interface called DataSourceV2, and then it can select whether to implement interface ContinuousReadSupport or MicroBatchReadSupport or both. For example, KafkaSourceProvider.scala implements both interfaces because it allows users to choose which processing mode to use based on a use case. Each of the two interfaces acts has a factory method for creating an instance of ContinuousReader or MicroBatchReader, respectively. The bulk of the custom data source implementation will be in implementing the APIs defined in these two interfaces.

I've implemented a fun and non-fault-tolerant data source that reads wiki edits from the Wikipedia IRC server. It is fairly easy to use Spark Structured Streaming to analyze the wiki edits of various Wikipedia sites. See README.md in the GitHub repository (https://github.com/beginning-spark/book/tree/master/chapter6/custom-data-source) for more details. To use this custom data source in the Spark shell, the first step is to download the streaming_sources-assembly-0.0.1.jar JAR file from the previous GitHub repository. Listing 6-22 describes the remaining steps.

Listing 6-22. Analyzing Wiki Edits with a Custom Data Source

```
// start up spark-shell with streaming_sources-assembly-0.0.1.jar
bin/spark-shell --jars <path>/streaming_sources-assembly-0.0.1.jar

// once spark-shell is successfully started

// define the data source provider name
val provideClassName = "org.structured_streaming_sources.wikedit.
WikiEditSourceV2"

// use custom data and subscribe to English Wikipedia edit channel
val wikiEditDF = spark.readStream.format(provideClassName).
option("channel", "#en.wikipedia").load()

// examine the schema of wikiEditDF streaming DataFrame

wikiEditDF.printSchema

 |-- timestamp: timestamp (nullable = true)
 |-- channel: string (nullable = true)
 |-- title: string (nullable = true)
 |-- diffUrl: string (nullable = true)
 |-- user: string (nullable = true)
 |-- byteDiff: integer (nullable = true)
 |-- summary: string (nullable = true)
```

```
// select only a few columns for analysis
val wikiEditSmallDF = wikiEditDF.select("timestamp", "user", "channel", "title")

// start streaming query and write out the wiki edits to console
val wikiEditQS = wikiEditSmallDF.writeStream.format("console").option
("truncate", "false").start()

// wait for a few seconds for data to come in and the result might look like below
+----------------------+------------+-------------+------------------------+
|           timestamp|        user|      channel|                   title|
+----------------------+------------+-------------+------------------------+
| 2018-03-24 15:36:39.409| 6.62.103.211| #en.wikipedia|       Thomas J.R. Hughes|
| 2018-03-24 15:36:39.412| .92.206.108| #en.wikipedia|List of international schools|
+----------------------+------------+-------------+------------------------+

// to stop the query stream
wikiEditQS.stop
```

Notice the custom data source name is a fully qualified class name of the data source provider. It is not short like the built-in data sources because those already registered their short names in a file called `org.apache.spark.sql.sources.DataSourceRegister`.

Working with Data Sinks

The last step in a streaming application usually involves writing out the computation result to some external system or storage system. Structure Streaming provides five built-in sinks. Three of them are for production usage, and the remaining two are for testing purposes. The following sections will go into detail on each one and will provide sample code for working with them.

Working with the File Data Sink

The File data sink is a pretty straightforward data sink to understand and to work with. The only required option you need to provide is the output directory. Since the File data sink is fault-tolerant, Structured Streaming will require a checkpoint location to write the progress information and other metadata to help with the recovery when there is a failure.

The example in Listing 6-23 configures the Rate data source to generate ten rows per second, send the generated rows to two partitions and write the data out in JSON format to the specified directory.

Listing 6-23. Writing Data from the Rate Data Source to the File Sink

```
val rateSourceDF = spark.readStream.format("rate")
                               .option("rowsPerSecond","10")
                               .option("numPartitions","2")
                               .load()

val rateSQ = rateSourceDF.writeStream.outputMode("append")
                               .format("json")
                               .option("path", "/tmp/output")
                               .option("checkpointLocation", "/tmp/
                               ss/cp")
                               .start()

// use the line below to stop the writing the data
rateSQ.stop
```

Since the number of partitions was configured as two, two files are written out to the output folder each time Structured Streaming writes out the data at each trigger point. So, if you examine the output folder, you will see files with names that start with either part-00000 or part-00001. The Rate data source was configured with ten rows per second, and there are two partitions; therefore, each output contains five rows, as shown in Listing 6-24.

Listing 6-24. The Content of Each Output File

```
{"timestamp":"2018-03-24T17:42:08.182-07:00","value":205}
{"timestamp":"2018-03-24T17:42:08.282-07:00","value":206}
{"timestamp":"2018-03-24T17:42:08.382-07:00","value":207}
{"timestamp":"2018-03-24T17:42:08.482-07:00","value":208}
{"timestamp":"2018-03-24T17:42:08.582-07:00","value":209}
```

Working with the Kafka Data Sink

In Structured Streaming, writing the data of a streaming DataFrame to a Kafka data sink is a little simpler than reading data from a Kafka data source. The Kafka data sink can be configured with the four options listed in Table 6-7. Three of the options are required. The important options to understand are the key and value, which are related to the structure of a Kafka message. As mentioned earlier, the unit of data in Kafka is a message, which essentially is a key-value pair. The role of the value is fairly obvious, which is to hold the actual content of a message, and it has no meaning to Kafka. As far as Kafka is concerned, the value is just a bunch of bytes. The key, however, is considered by Kafka as a piece of metadata, and it is saved along with the value in the Kafka message. When a message is sent to the Kafka and a key is provided, Kafka utilizes it as a routing mechanism to determine which partition a particular Kafka message should be sent to by hashing the key and performs a modulo on the number of partitions a topic has. This implies that all messages with the same key will be routed to the same partition. If a key is not provided in the message, then Kafka can't guarantee which partition that message is sent to, and Kafka employs a round-robin algorithm to balance the messages between partitions.

Table 6-7. *Options for the Kafka Data Sink*

Option	Value	Description
kafka.bootstrap. servers	host1:port1, host2:port2	This is a comma-separated list of Kafka broker servers. Consult your Kafka administrators for the host name and port number to use.
topic	topic1	This is a single topic name.
key	A string or binary	This key is used to determine which partition a Kafka message should be sent to. All Kafka messages with the same key will go to the same partition. This is an optional option.
value	A string or binary	This is the content of a message. To Kafka, it is simply just an array of bytes, and it has no meaning to Kafka.

There are two ways to provide a topic name. The first way is to provide the topic name in the configuration when setting up a Kafka data sink, and the second way is by defining a column in the streaming DataFrame called topic; the value of that column will be used as the topic name.

If the column called key exists in the streaming DataFrame, then the value of that column will be used as the message key. Since the key is an optional piece of metadata, it is not absolutely required to have this column in the streaming DataFrame. On the other hand, the value must be provided, and the Kafka data sink expects a column named value in the streaming DataFrame.

Listing 6-25 provides an example of setting a Rate data source and then writes the data to a Kafka topic called rates. If you are planning to use the Spark shell to try the following code, make sure to start the Spark shell with an appropriate argument as described earlier to include the org.apache.spark:spark-sql-kafka-0-10_2.11:2.3.0 JAR file and its dependencies.

Note   The simplest way to get started with Kafka is to download the Confluent Platform package and then follow the Getting Started guide. More information is available at https://docs.confluent.io/current/getting-started. html. Once the download is complete, uncompress the compressed TAR file into a directory. To start up the servers (Zookeeper, Kafka Broker, Schema Registry), use the command line ./bin/confluent start. Each of those server listens on a specific port. All the command-line tools are available in the bin directory, and almost all of them require the host and port for either Zookeeper or Kafka Broker. Before running the code in Listing 6-25, make sure to create a topic called rates. Here is the command to do that: bin/kafka-topics --create --zookeeper localhost:2181 --replication-factor 1 --partitions 2 --topic rates. To list out a list of active topics, use this command: ./bin/kafka-topics --zookeeper localhost:2181 --list.

Listing 6-25. Writing Data from the Rate Data Source to a File Sink

```
import org.apache.spark.sql.functions._

// setting up the rate data source with 10 rows per second and use two
partitions
val ratesSinkDF = spark.readStream.format("rate")
                              .option("rowsPerSecond","10")
                              .option("numPartitions","2").load()

// transform the ratesSinkDF to create a column called "key" and "value" column
// the value column contains a JSON string that contains two fields:
   timestamp and value
val ratesSinkForKafkaDF = ratesSinkDF.select($"value".cast("string") as "key",
                                    to_json(struct("timestamp",
                                    "value")) as "value")

// setup a streaming query to write data to Kafka using topic "rates"
val rateSinkSQ = ratesSinkForKafkaDF.writeStream
                              .outputMode("append")
                              .format("kafka")
                              .option("kafka.bootstrap.servers",
                              "localhost:9092")
                              .option("topic","rates")
                              .option("checkpointLocation",
                              "/Users/hluu/tmp/ss/cp")
                              .start()

// it doesn't take long to write a lot of messages to Kafka, so after a few
second, feel free to stop the
// rateSinkSQL
rateSinkSQ.stop
```

To read data back from the rates topic in Kafka, use the sample code listed in Listing 6-21 and substitute an appropriate value for options such as kafka.bootstrap.servers and the topic name. The data that comes back from the rates topic in Kafka will looking something like Listing 6-26.

Listing 6-26. Sample of Data from Kafka

```
+---------+-------+-------+----------------------------------------------------------+
|partition| offset|   key|                                                     value|
+---------+-------+-------+----------------------------------------------------------+
|        1|   9350| 583249| {"timestamp":"2018-03-25T09:53:52.582-07:00","value":583249}|
|        1|   9351| 583250| {"timestamp":"2018-03-25T09:53:52.682-07:00","value":583250}|
|        1|   9352| 583251| {"timestamp":"2018-03-25T09:53:52.782-07:00","value":583251}|
|        1|   9353| 583256| {"timestamp":"2018-03-25T09:53:53.282-07:00","value":583256}|
|        1|   9354| 583261| {"timestamp":"2018-03-25T09:53:53.782-07:00","value":583261}|
|        1|   9355| 583266| {"timestamp":"2018-03-25T09:53:54.282-07:00","value":583266}|
|        1|   9356| 583267| {"timestamp":"2018-03-25T09:53:54.382-07:00","value":583267}|
|        1|   9357| 583274| {"timestamp":"2018-03-25T09:53:55.082-07:00","value":583274}|
|        1|   9358| 583275| {"timestamp":"2018-03-25T09:53:55.182-07:00","value":583275}|
|        1|   9359| 583276| {"timestamp":"2018-03-25T09:53:55.282-07:00","value":583276}|
+---------+-------+-------+----------------------------------------------------------+
```

Working with the Foreach Data Sink

Compared to the other built-in data sinks that Structure Streaming provides, the Foreach data sink is an interesting one because it provides complete flexibility in terms of how data should be written, when to write out the data, and where to write the data to. In fact, it was designed to be an extensible as well as pluggable data sink. This flexibility and extensibility comes with a responsibility because you are responsible for the logic of writing out the data when using this data sink. The contract this data sink places on you is the ForeachWriter abstract class (https://spark.apache.org/docs/latest/api/scala/index.html#org.apache.spark.sql.ForeachWriter). Since this abstract class is in Scala, it means that at the moment this data sink is available only in Scala and Java. In a nutshell, you need to provide an implementation of the ForeachWriter, which consists of three methods: open, process, and close. They will get called whenever there is a list of rows generated as the output after a trigger. Working with this data sink requires some intimate details about how Spark works as well the interactions between the two parties and the responsibilities of each side.

- An instance of the `ForeachWriter` abstract class implementation will be created on the driver side, and it will be sent to the executors in your Spark cluster for execution. This has two implications. First, the implementation of the `ForeachWriter` must be serializable; otherwise, an instance of it can't be shipped across the network to the executors. Second, if there are any initializations during the creation of the implementation, they will happen on the driver side. So if you want to open a database connection or socket connect, that should not happen during the class initialization but rather somewhere else.

- The number of partitions in a streaming DataFrame determines how many instances of the `ForeachWriter` implementation will be created. This is similar to the behavior of the `Dataset.foreachPartition` method.

- The three methods defined in the `ForeachWriter` abstract class will be invoked on the executors.

- The best place to perform initializations such as opening a database connection or socket connect is in the open method. However, the open method is called each time there is data to be written out; therefore, that logic must be intelligent and efficient.

- The open method signature has two input parameters: the partition ID and version. The return type is Boolean. The combination of these two parameters uniquely represent a set of rows that needs to be written out. The value of the version is a monotonically increasing ID that increases with every trigger. Based on the value of the partition ID and version parameters, the open method needs to decide whether it needs to write out the sequence of rows and return the appropriate Boolean value to the Structure Streaming engine.

- If the open method returns true, then the process method is called for each row of the output of a trigger.

- Whenever the open method is called and regardless of the value it returns, the close method will also be called. If there was an error during the call to the process method, that error will be passed into the close method. The intention for calling the close method is to give you a chance to clean up any necessary state that was created during the open or process method invocation. The only time the close method is not called is when the JVM of the executor crashes or the open method throws a Throwable exception.

In short, this data sink provides you with the ultimate flexibility in writing out the data of a streaming DataFrame. The sample code in Listing 6-27 contains a simple implementation of the ForeachWriter abstract class by writing the data from the Rate data source out to the console.

Listing 6-27. Sample Code for Working with the Foreach Data Sink

```scala
// define an implementation of the ForeachWriter abstract class
import org.apache.spark.sql.{ForeachWriter,Row}

class ConsoleWriter(private var pId:Long = 0, private var ver:Long = 0)
extends ForeachWriter[Row] {
    def open(partitionId: Long, version: Long): Boolean = {
       pId = partitionId
       ver = version
       println(s"open => ($partitionId, $version)")
       true
    }

    def process(row: Row) = {
      println(s"writing => $row")
    }

    def close(errorOrNull: Throwable): Unit = {
      println(s"close => ($pId, $ver)")
    }
}
```

```
// setup the Rate data source
val ratesSourceDF = spark.readStream.format("rate")
                                    .option("rowsPerSecond","10")
                                    .option("numPartitions","2")
                                    .load()

// setup the Foreach data sink
val rateSQ = ratesSourceDF.writeStream.foreach(new ConsoleWriter).start()

// sample output from the console
open => (1, 1)
writing => [2018-03-25 13:03:41.867,5]
writing => [2018-03-25 13:03:41.367,0]
writing => [2018-03-25 13:03:41.967,6]
writing => [2018-03-25 13:03:41.467,1]
writing => [2018-03-25 13:03:42.067,7]
writing => [2018-03-25 13:03:41.567,2]
writing => [2018-03-25 13:03:42.167,8]
writing => [2018-03-25 13:03:41.667,3]
writing => [2018-03-25 13:03:42.267,9]
close => (1, 1)

// to close the rateSQ streaming query
rateSQ.stop
```

Working with the Console Data Sink

This data sink is extremely easy to work with, and it does exactly what it sounds like.
It is not a fault-tolerant data sink, and it is designed to be used for debugging purposes
or while learning Structured Streaming. It has only two options: the number of rows to
display and whether to truncate the output if too long. Each one of these options has a
default value, as shown in Table 6-8. The underlying implementation of this data sink
uses the same logic as in the DataFrame.show method to display the data in a streaming
DataFrame.

Table 6-8. *Options for the Console Data Sink*

Option	Default Value	Description
numRows	20	The number of rows to print to console
truncate	true	Whether to truncate with the content of each column is longer than 20 characters

The example in Listing 6-28 shows the Console data sink in action and not using the default value for the previous options.

Listing 6-28. Sample Code for Working with the Console Data Sink

```
// setting up a data source
val ratesDF = spark.readStream.format("rate")
                        .option("rowsPerSecond","10")
                        .option("numPartitions","2")
                        .load()

Val ratesSQ = ratesDF.writeStream.outputMode("append")
                        .format("console")
                        .option("truncate",false)
                        .option("numRows",50)
                        .start()
```

Working with the Memory Data Sink

Similar to the Console data sink, this data sink is easy to understand and work with. In fact, it is so easy because it has no options that you need to configure. It is not a fault-tolerant data sink, and it is designed to be used for debugging purposes or while learning Structured Streaming. The data it collects is sent to the driver and stored in the driver as an in-memory table. In other words, the amount of data you can send to the Memory data sink is bound by the amount of memory the driver JVM has. You may be wondering whether the data is in memory and how you query it and see it. While setting up this data sink, you can specify a query name as an argument to the DataStreamWriter.queryName function, and then you can issue SQL queries against the in-memory table. Unlike the Console data sink, once the data is sent to the in-memory table, you can further analyze or process the data using pretty much all the features available in the Spark SQL component. If the amount of data is large and wouldn't fit into memory, the next best option is to use the File data sink to write the data out in the Parquet format.

The sample code in Listing 6-29 writes the data from the Rate data source into an in-memory table and you issue queries about it.

Listing 6-29. Sample Code for Working with the Memory Data Sink

```
val ratesDF  = spark.readStream.format("rate")
                            .option("rowsPerSecond","10")
                            .option("numPartitions","2")
                            .load()

// write data out to Memory data sink with in-memory table name as "rates"
val ratesSQ = ratesDF.writeStream.outputMode("append")
                            .format("memory")
                            .queryName("rates").start()

// we issue SQL queries against the "rates" in-memory table
spark.sql("select * from rates").show(10,false)
+-----------------------+------+
|              timestamp| value|
+-----------------------+------+
| 2018-03-25 14:02:59.461|     0|
| 2018-03-25 14:02:59.561|     1|
| 2018-03-25 14:02:59.661|     2|
| 2018-03-25 14:02:59.761|     3|
| 2018-03-25 14:02:59.861|     4|
| 2018-03-25 14:02:59.961|     5|
| 2018-03-25 14:03:00.061|     6|
| 2018-03-25 14:03:00.161|     7|
| 2018-03-25 14:03:00.261|     8|
| 2018-03-25 14:03:00.361|     9|
+-----------------------+------+
```

```
// count the number of rows in the "rates" in-memory table
spark.sql("select count(*) from rates").show
+---------+
| count(1)|
+---------+
|      100|
+---------+

// to stop the ratesSQ query stream
ratesSQ.stop
```

One thing to note is that the in-memory `rates` will still be around even after the streaming query `ratesSQ` has stopped. However, once a new streaming query is started with the same name, then the data from in-memory is truncated.

Before you leave this section, it is important to understand which outputs are supported by each type of data sink. Table 6-9 provides a quick summary table for reference. The details about output modes will be covered in the next section.

Table 6-9. *Data Sinks and Their Support Output Modes*

Sink	Supported Output Modes	Notes
File	Append	Supports writing out new rows only and no updates
Kafka	Append, Update, Complete	
Foreach	Append, Update, Complete	Depending on the `ForeachWriter` implementation
Console	Append, Update, Complete	
Memory	Append, Complete	Doesn't support in-place updates

Deep Dive on Output Modes

The earlier "Output Modes" section provided a basic description of each of the output modes. This section will provide more details about them as well as ways to understand which output mode is applicable for which streaming query type.

Broadly speaking, there are two types of streaming query. The first type is called the *stateless type*, and it performs only basic transformations on the incoming streaming data and then writes out the data to a data sink. The second type is called the *stateful type*, which needs to maintain some amount of state, whether that is done implicitly or explicitly. The stateful type usually performs some kind of aggregations or uses the Structured Streaming APIs like `mapGroupsWithState` or `flatMapGroupsWithState` to maintain some arbitrary state needed for a particular use case, for example, maintaining user session data.

Let's start with the simple, stateless streaming query type. A typical use case for this kind of streaming query is the real-time streaming ETL where it continuously reads real-time streaming data such as page view events that are continuously produced by online services to capture which pages are being viewed by which users. In this kind of use case, it usually performs the following:

- Filtering, transforming, and cleaning

    - Real-world data is messy and dirty, and the structure may be not well suited for repeated analysis.

- Converting to a more efficient storage format

    - Text file formats such as CVS and JSON are human readable but inefficient for repeated analysis, especially if the data volume is large such as hundreds of terabytes. More efficient binary formats like ORC, Parquet, or Avro are commonly used to reduce file size and improve analysis speed.

- Partitioning data by certain columns

    - While writing the data out to a data sink, it is possible to partition the data based on the value of commonly used columns to speed up the repeated analysis by various teams in an organization.

As you can see, the previous tasks don't require a streaming query to maintain any kind of state before writing the data out to a data sink. As new data comes in, it is cleaned, transformed, and possibly restructured and immediately written out. Therefore, the only applicable output mode for this stateless streaming type is Append. The Complete output mode is not applicable because that will require Structured Streaming to maintain all the previous data, which may be too large to maintain. The Update output mode is not applicable because only new data is being written out. However, when this output mode is used for a stateless streaming query, Structured Streaming recognizes this and treats it the same as the Append output mode. The cool thing is when an inappropriate output mode is used for a streaming query, the Structured Streaming engine will let you know. Listing 6-30 shows what happens when an inappropriate output mode is used.

Listing 6-30. Using the Complete Output Mode with a Stateless Streaming Query

```
val ratesDF  = spark.readStream.format("rate")
                              .option("rowsPerSecond","10")
                              .option("numPartitions","2")
                              .load()

// simple transformation
val ratesOddEvenDF = ratesDF.withColumn("even_odd", $"value" % 2 === 0)

// write out to Console data sink using complete output mode
val ratesSQ = ratesOddEvenDF.writeStream.outputMode("complete")
                                        .format("console")
                                        .option("truncate",false)
                                        .option("numRows",50)
                                        .start()

// An exception from Structured Streaming during the analysis phase
org.apache.spark.sql.AnalysisException: Complete output mode not supported
when there are no streaming aggregations on streaming DataFrames/Datasets;
```

Now let's move on to the stateful streaming query type. When a stateful steaming query performs an aggregation via a groupBy transformation, the state of that aggregation is maintained implicitly by the Structured Streaming engine. As more data comes in, the result of the aggregation on new data is updated into the result table. At each trigger point, either the updated data or all the data in the result table is written out to a data sink, depending on the output mode. This implies that using the Append output mode is inappropriate because that violates the semantics of that output mode, which specifies that only new rows that were appended to the result table will be sent to the specified output sink. In other words, only the Complete and Update output modes are appropriate for the stateful query type with the aggregation state implicitly maintained by the Structured Streaming engine. The output of a streaming query using the Complete output mode is always equal or more than the output of the same streaming query using the Update output mode. Listing 6-31 contains the code to illustrate the difference in the output.

Listing 6-31. The Output Differences Between the Update and Complete Modes

```
// import statements
import org.apache.spark.sql.types._
import org.apache.spark.sql.functions._

val mobileDataSchema = new StructType().add("id", StringType, false)
                                .add("action", StringType, false)
                                .add("ts", TimestampType, false)

val mobileDF = spark.readStream.schema(mobileDataSchema)
                                .json("<path>/chapter6/data/input")

val actionCountDF = mobileDF.groupBy($"action").count

val completeModeSQ = actionCountDF.writeStream.format("console")
                                        .option("truncate", "false")
                                        .outputMode("complete").
                                        start()

val updateModeSQ = actionCountDF.writeStream.format("console")
                                        .option("truncate", "false")
                                        .outputMode("complete").start()

// at this point copy file1.json, file2.json, file3.json and newaction.jso
from
// mobile directory to the input directory

// the output of the streaming query with complete mode is below
-----------------------------------------------
Batch: 3
-----------------------------------------------
+-------+------+
| action| count|
+-------+------+
|  close|     3|
|  swipe|     1|
|  crash|     1|
|   open|     5|
+-------+------+
```

```
// the output of the streaming query with update mode is below
---------------------------------------------
Batch: 3
---------------------------------------------
+-------+------+
| action| count|
+-------+------+
|  swipe|    1|
|  crash|    1|
+-------+------+
```

The previous output of the streaming query with the Complete output mode contains all the action types in the result table. The previous output of the streaming query with the Update output mode contains only the actions in file newaction.json that the result table hasn't seen before.

Again, if an inappropriate output mode is used for the stateful query type, the Structured Streaming engine will let you know, as shown in Listing 6-32.

Listing 6-32. Using an Inappropriate Append Output Mode with a Stateful Streaming Query

```
// use an inappropriate output for stateful streaming query, see exception below
val actionCountSQ = actionCountDF.writeStream.format("console").
outputMode("append").start()
```

```
org.apache.spark.sql.AnalysisException: Append output mode not supported
when there are streaming aggregations on streaming DataFrames/DataSets
without watermark;
```

There is an exception to the previous logic. If a watermark is provided to the stateful streaming query with aggregation, then all the output modes are applicable. The reason the semantics of the Append output is not violated anymore is because the Structured Streaming engine will drop the old aggregation state data that is older than the specified watermark, which means new rows can be added to the result table once the watermark is crossed.

Undoubtedly, the output mode is one of the most complicated concepts in Structured Streaming to understand because there are multiple dimensions that come together to determine which output modes are appropriate to use. The Structured Streaming programming guide provides a compatibility matrix, which can be found at `https://spark.apache.org/docs/latest/structured-streaming-programming-guide.html#output-modes`.

Deep Dive on Triggers

The trigger setting determines when the Structured Streaming engine will run the streaming computation logic expressed in a streaming query, which includes all the transformations as well as writing out the data to the data sink. Another way of thinking about it is that the trigger setting controls when the data will be written out to a data sink as well as which processing mode to use. Starting in Spark 2.3, a new processing mode called Continuous was introduced.

The "Trigger Types" section described the types that are supported in Structured Streaming. This section will go into more detail and provide sample code for specifying the different trigger types.

Up until now, all the stream query examples have used the default trigger type because a trigger type was not specified. This default trigger type chooses the micro-batch mode as the processing mode, and the logic in the streaming query is executed not based on time but as soon as the previous batch of data has completed processing. This implies there is less predictability in terms of how often the data is written out.

If a little more predictability is desired, then the Fixed interval trigger can be specified to cause the logic in the streaming query to be executed at a certain interval based on the user-provided interval, for example, every 30 seconds. In terms of processing mode, this trigger type uses the micro-batch mode. The interval can be specified in a string format or as a Scala `Duration` or Java `TimeUnit`. Listing 6-33 contains examples for using the Fixed interval trigger.

Listing 6-33. Examples of Using the Fixed Interval Trigger Type

```
import org.apache.spark.sql.streaming.Trigger

// setting up with 3 rows per second
val ratesDF  = spark.readStream.format("rate")
                              .option("rowsPerSecond","3")
                              .option("numPartitions","2")
                              .load()
// trigger the streaming query execution every 3 seconds and write out to
console
val ratesSQ = ratesDF.writeStream.outputMode("append")
                              .format("console")
                              .option("numRows",50)
                              .option("truncate",false)
                              .trigger(Trigger.ProcessingTime("3 seconds"))
                              .start()

// we should expect to see about 9 rows in every 3 seconds
+-----------------------+---------+
|               timestamp|    value|
+-----------------------+---------+
|2018-03-26 07:14:11.176|        0|
|2018-03-26 07:14:11.509|        1|
|2018-03-26 07:14:11.843|        2|
|2018-03-26 07:14:12.176|        3|
|2018-03-26 07:14:12.509|        4|
|2018-03-26 07:14:12.843|        5|
|2018-03-26 07:14:13.176|        6|
|2018-03-26 07:14:13.509|        7|
|2018-03-26 07:14:13.843|        8|
+-----------------------+---------+
```

```
// specifying the interval using Scala Duration type
import scala.concurrent.duration._

val ratesSQ = ratesDF.writeStream.outputMode("append")
                                 .format("console")
                                 .option("numRows",50)
                                 .option("truncate",false)
                                 .trigger(Trigger.ProcessingTime(3.seconds))
                                 .start()
```

The Fixed interval trigger doesn't always guarantee that the execution of a streaming query will happen at exactly each user-specified interval. There are two reasons for this. The first one is fairly obvious; if there is no data arriving for processing, then there is nothing to process, and therefore nothing is written out to the data sink. The second reason is when the processing time of the previous batch exceeds the interval, the next execution of a streaming query will start as soon as the processing completes. In other words, it will not wait for the next interval boundary.

The one-time trigger does what it sounds like. It executes the logic in a streaming query in micro-batch mode and writes out the data to a data sink one time, and then the processing stops. It may sound a bit silly for this trigger type to exist; however, it is useful in both development and production environments. While in the development phase, usually the streaming computation logic is developed in an iterative manner, and in each iteration you would like to test the logic. This trigger type simplifies the develop-test iteration a bit. For a production environment, this trigger type is suitable for use cases where the volume of incoming streaming data is low, and therefore it is only necessary to run the data processing logic a few times a day. Instead of launching a Spark cluster and leaving it running all the time, the frequency of launching Spark and executing the streaming processing logic one time is based on the desired processing frequency of that particular use case. It is quite simple to specify this one-time trigger type, and Listing 6-34 shows how to do that.

Listing 6-34. Example of Using a One-Time Trigger Type

```
import org.apache.spark.sql.streaming.Trigger

val mobileSQ =  mobileDF.writeStream.outputMode("append")
                                .format("console")
                                .trigger(Trigger.Once())
                                .start()
```

The last trigger type is called a Continuous trigger type. This new, exciting, and experimental processing mode was introduced in Spark 2.3 to address the use cases that need end-to-end millisecond latency. In this new processing mode, Structured Streaming launches long-running tasks to continuously read, process, and write data to a data sink. This implies the incoming data will be processed and written out to data sink as soon as it arrives in the data source, and the end-to-end latency is a few milliseconds. In addition, an asynchronous checkpoint mechanism, which is used for recording the progress of the streaming query, was introduced to not interrupt the long-running tasks from providing consistent millisecond-level latencies. A good use case to leverage this Continuous trigger type is credit card fraudulent transaction detection. At a high level, the Structure Streaming engine figures out which processing mode to use based on the trigger type, which is depicted in Figure 6-10.

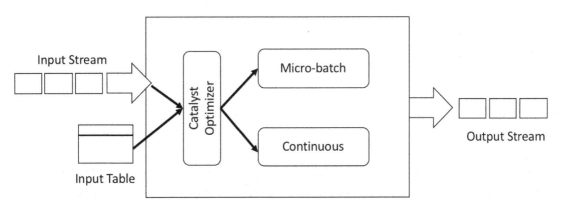

Figure 6-10. *Structured Streaming supports two different processing modes*

As of Spark 2.3, only the projection and selection operations are allowed in the Continuous processing mode, such as select, where, map, flatmap, and filter. In this processing mode, all Spark SQL functions are supported except aggregation functions.

To use the Continuous processing mode for a streaming query, all you need to do is specify a Continuous trigger with a desired checkpoint interval like in Listing 6-35.

Listing 6-35. Examples of Specifying a Continuous Trigger Type

```
import org.apache.spark.sql.streaming.Trigger

// setting a Rate data source with two partitions
val ratesDF  = spark.readStream.format("rate")
                           .option("numPartitions","2").load()
// write out the data to console and using continuous trigger with 2 second
interval for writing out progress
val rateSQ = ratesDF.writeStream.format("console")
                           .trigger(Trigger.Continuous("2 second"))
                           .start()
// sample output from console
+--------------------+------+
|           timestamp| value|
+--------------------+------+
|2018-03-26 21:43:...|     0|
|2018-03-26 21:43:...|     2|
|2018-03-26 21:43:...|     4|
|2018-03-26 21:43:...|     6|
|2018-03-26 21:43:...|     1|
|2018-03-26 21:43:...|     3|
|2018-03-26 21:43:...|     5|
|2018-03-26 21:43:...|     7|
+--------------------+------+
```

The ratesDF streaming DataFrame was set up to have two partitions; therefore, Structured Streaming launched two running tasks in the Continuous processing mode, and that is why the output shows all the even numbers appearing together and all the odd numbers appearing together.

Summary

Structured Streaming is the second-generation streaming processing engine of Apache Spark. It provides an easy way to build and reason about fault-tolerant and scalable streaming applications. This chapter covered a lot of ground, including core concepts in the streaming processing domain and the core parts of Structured Streaming.

- Streaming processing is an exciting domain that can help solve many new and interesting use cases in the era of big data.

- Building production streaming data applications is much more challenging than building batch data processing applications because of the nature of the unbounded data and the unpredictability of the data arrival rate and out-of-order data.

- To be effective at building streaming data applications, you must be comfortable with the three core concepts in the streaming processing domain. They are data delivery semantics, notion of time, and windowing.

- Stream processing engines have drastically and dramatically matured in the last few years, and now there are many options to pick from. The popular ones are Apache Flink, Apache Samza, Apache Kafka, and Apache Spark.

- Spark DStream is the first-generation streaming processing engine of Apache Spark, and it was built on top of the RDD programming model.

- The Structured Streaming processing engine was designed for developers to build end-to-end streaming applications that can react to data in real-time using a simple programming model built on top of the optimized and solid foundation of the Spark SQL engine.

- The unique idea in Structured Streaming is to treat streaming data as an unbounded input table and, as a new set of data arrives, treat that as a new set of new rows being appended to the input table.

- The core components in a streaming query are the data source, streaming operations, output mode, trigger, and data sink.

- Structured Streaming provides a set of built-in data sources as well as data sinks. The built-in data sources are File, Kafka, Socket, and Rate. The built-in data sinks are File, Kafka, Console, and Memory.

- The output mode determines how the data is output to a data sink, and there are three options: Append, Update, and Complete.

- A trigger is a mechanism for the Structure Streaming engine to determine when to run the streaming computation. There are several options to choose from: micro-batch, fixed interval micro-batch, one-time micro-batch, and continuous. The last one is for use cases that demand millisecond latency, and it is in an experimental state as of Spark 2.3.

CHAPTER 7

Spark Streaming (Advanced)

The previous chapter introduced the core concepts of streaming processing, the features that the Spark Structured Streaming processing engine provides, and the basic steps of putting together a streaming application. Real-world streaming applications usually need to extract insights or patterns from the incoming real-time data at scale and feed that information into downstream applications to make business decisions or to save that information in some storage system for further analysis or visualization purposes. Another aspect of real-world streaming applications is that they are continuously running to process real-time data as it comes in. Therefore, they must be resilient against failures. The first half of this chapter covers event-time processing and stateful processing features in Structured Streaming and how they can help with extracting insights or patterns from incoming real-time data. The second half of this chapter explains the support Structured Streaming provides to help streaming applications to be fault tolerant against failures and to monitor the status and progress of streaming applications.

Event Time

The ability to process incoming real-time data based on the data creation time is a must-have feature for any serious streaming processing engine. This is important because to truly understand and accurately extract insights or patterns from streaming data, you need to be able to process them based on when that data or those events happened, not when they were processed. Oftentimes, the event-time processing is in the context of some sort of aggregation, which includes the event time and zero or more pieces of additional information about the event.

© Hien Luu 2018
H. Luu, *Beginning Apache Spark 2*, https://doi.org/10.1007/978-1-4842-3579-9_7

Let's take the example of the mobile action events described in Chapter 6. Instead of applying the aggregations over the action type, you can apply the aggregations over a time window, which could be a fixed window or sliding window type (described in Chapter 6). In addition, you can easily add the action type to the grouping key to further group the mobile action events by time bucket and action type.

The following example will process the mobile data event; Listing 7-1 shows its schema. The ts column represents the time when an event was created, in other words, when a user opens or closes an application. The mobile event data is located in the <path>/chapter6/data/mobile directory, which contains file1.json, file2.json, file3.json, and newaction.json. Listing 7-2 displays the rows in each of the files.

Listing 7-1. Mobile Data Event Schema

```
mobileDataDF.printSchema

 |-- action: string (nullable = true)
 |-- id: string (nullable = true)
 |-- ts: timestamp (nullable = true)
```

Listing 7-2. Mobile Event Data in file1.json, file2.json, file3.json, newaction.json

```
// file1.json
{"id":"phone1","action":"open","ts":"2018-03-02T10:02:33"}
{"id":"phone2","action":"open","ts":"2018-03-02T10:03:35"}
{"id":"phone3","action":"open","ts":"2018-03-02T10:03:50"}
{"id":"phone1","action":"close","ts":"2018-03-02T10:04:35"}

// file2.json
{"id":"phone3","action":"close","ts":"2018-03-02T10:07:35"}
{"id":"phone4","action":"open","ts":"2018-03-02T10:07:50"}

// file3.json
{"id":"phone2","action":"close","ts":"2018-03-02T10:04:50"}
{"id":"phone5","action":"open","ts":"2018-03-02T10:10:50"}

// newaction.json
{"id":"phone2","action":"crash","ts":"2018-03-02T11:09:13"}
{"id":"phone5","action":"swipe","ts":"2018-03-02T11:17:29"}
```

Fixed Window Aggregation Over an Event Time

A fixed window (aka a tumbling window) operation essentially discretizes a stream of incoming data into nonoverlapping buckets based on a fixed window length. For each piece of incoming data, it will be placed into one of the buckets based on its event time. Performing aggregations is just a matter of going through each bucket and applying the aggregation logic, whether that is doing a count or sum. Figure 7-1 illustrates the fixed window aggregation logic.

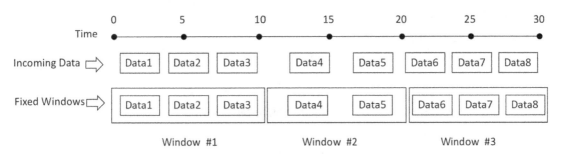

Figure 7-1. *Fixed window operation*

An example of fixed window aggregation is to perform a counting aggregation of the number of mobile events per each fixed window of ten minutes long. The window length is usually determined by the needs of a particular use case as well as the data volume. The result of this aggregation gives you high-level insights into the rate of the mobile event that was generated per window. If you are interested in mobile usage throughout the day and by the hour, then maybe the window length of 60 minutes is more appropriate. Listing 7-3 contains the code for performing the counting aggregation and the aggregation result. As expected, there are only a total ten mobile data events in all four files listed, and the total count in the output matches that number.

Listing 7-3. Processing Mobile Event Data with a Ten-Minute Window

```
import org.apache.spark.sql.types._
import org.apache.spark.sql.functions._

val mobileDataSchema = new StructType() .add("id", StringType, false)
                                        .add("action", StringType, false)
                                        .add("ts", TimestampType, false)
```

```scala
val mobileSSDF = spark.readStream.schema(mobileDataSchema)
                            .json("<path>/chapter6/data/input")

val windowCountDF = mobileSSDF.groupBy(window($"ts", "10 minutes")).count

val mobileConsoleSQ = windowCountDF.writeStream.format("console")
                                        .option("truncate", "false")
                                        .outputMode("complete")
                                        .start()
// stop the streaming query
mobileConsoleSQ.stop

// output
+------------------------------------------------+------+
|                                          window| count|
+------------------------------------------------+------+
| [2018-03-02 10:00:00, 2018-03-02 10:10:00]|     7|
| [2018-03-02 10:10:00, 2018-03-02 10:20:00]|     1|
| [2018-03-02 11:00:00, 2018-03-02 11:10:00]|     1|
| [2018-03-02 11:10:00, 2018-03-02 11:20:00]|     1|
+------------------------------------------------+------+

windowCountDF.printSchema

 |-- window: struct (nullable = false)
 |    |-- start: timestamp (nullable = true)
 |    |-- end: timestamp (nullable = true)
 |-- count: long (nullable = false)
```

When performing an aggregation with a window, the output window is actually a struct type, which contains the start and end times.

In addition to specifying a window in the groupBy transformation, you can specify additional columns from the event itself. The following example will perform the aggregation with a window and the action. This gives you additional insights into the count of each by window and action type. It requires only a small change to the previous example to accomplish this. Listing 7-4 contains only the lines that needed changes.

Listing 7-4. Processing the Mobile Event Data with a Ten-Minute Window and Action Type

```
val windowActionCountDF= mobileSSDF.groupBy(window($"ts", "10 minutes"),
$"action").count

val windowActionCountSQ = windowActionCountDF.writeStream.format("console")
                                         .option("truncate", "false")
                                         .outputMode("complete")
                                         .start()
// result
+-------------------------------------------+-------+------+
|                                     window| action| count|
+-------------------------------------------+-------+------+
| [2018-03-02 10:00:00, 2018-03-02 10:10:00]| close |    3 |
| [2018-03-02 11:00:00, 2018-03-02 11:10:00]| crash |    1 |
| [2018-03-02 11:10:00, 2018-03-02 11:20:00]| swipe |    1 |
| [2018-03-02 10:00:00, 2018-03-02 10:10:00]| open  |    4 |
| [2018-03-02 10:10:00, 2018-03-02 10:20:00]| open  |    1 |
+-------------------------------------------+-------+------+

// stop the query stream
windowActionCountSQ.stop()
```

Each line in the previous result table contains insight about the count of each action in each ten-minute window. If there was a lot of crash actions around a certain window, that insight can help figure out whether there was a release around that time frame.

Sliding Window Aggregation Over an Event Time

In addition to the fixed window type, there is another windowing type called *sliding window*. Defining a sliding window requires two pieces of information, the window length and a sliding interval, which is usually smaller than the window length. Given the aggregation computation is sliding over the incoming stream of data, the result is usually smoother than the result of the fixed window type. Therefore, this windowing type is often used to compute moving averages. An important thing to note about a sliding window is that a piece of data can fall into more than one window because of the overlapping, as illustrated in Figure 7-2.

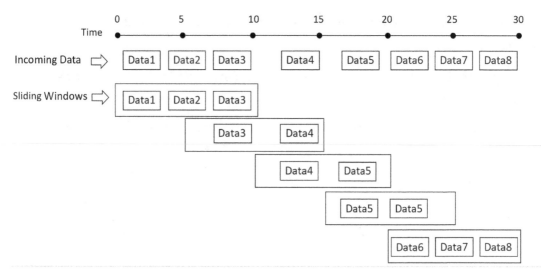

Figure 7-2. *Fixed window operation*

To illustrate the sliding window aggregation over the incoming data, you will use a small synthetic data about the temperature of computer racks in a data center. Imagine each computer rack emits its temperature at a certain interval, and you want to generate a report of the average temperature among all computer racks as well as per rack over a window length of ten minutes and a sliding interval of five minutes. This dataset is located in the <path>/chapter7/data/iot directory, which contains file1.json and file2.json. Listing 7-5 shows the temperature data.

Listing 7-5. Temperature Data of Two Racks

```
// file1.json
{"rack":"rack1","temperature":99.5,"ts":"2017-06-02T08:01:01"}
{"rack":"rack1","temperature":100.5,"ts":"2017-06-02T08:06:02"}
{"rack":"rack1","temperature":101.0,"ts":"2017-06-02T08:11:03"}
{"rack":"rack1","temperature":102.0,"ts":"2017-06-02T08:16:04"}

// file2.json
{"rack":"rack2","temperature":99.5,"ts":"2017-06-02T08:01:02"}
{"rack":"rack2","temperature":105.5,"ts":"2017-06-02T08:06:04"}
{"rack":"rack2","temperature":104.0,"ts":"2017-06-02T08:11:06"}
{"rack":"rack2","temperature":108.0,"ts":"2017-06-02T08:16:08"}
```

The code in Listing 7-6 first reads the temperature data and then performs a groupBy transformation on a sliding window over the ts column. For each sliding window, the avg() function is applied on the temperature column. To make it easy to inspect the output, it will write the data out to a memory data sink with a query name of iot. Then you can issue SQL queries against this temporary table.

Listing 7-6. Average Temperature of All the Computer Racks over a Sliding Window

```
import org.apache.spark.sql.types._
import org.apache.spark.sql.functions._

// define schema
val iotDataSchema = new StructType().add("rack", StringType, false)
                                    .add("temperature", DoubleType, false)
                                    .add("ts", TimestampType, false)

val iotSSDF = spark.readStream.schema(iotDataSchema).json("<path>/chapter7/
data/iot")

// group by a sliding window and perform average on the temperature column
val iotAvgDF = iotSSDF.groupBy(window($"ts", "10 minutes", "5 minutes"))
                                    .agg(avg("temperature") as "avg_temp")

// write the data out to memory sink with query name as iot
val iotMemorySQ = iotAvgDF.writeStream.format("memory")
                                    .queryName("iot")
                                    .outputMode("complete")
                                    .start()

// display the data in the order of start time
spark.sql("select * from iot").orderBy($"window.start").show(false)

// output
+------------------------------------------+---------+
|                                    window| avg_temp|
+------------------------------------------+---------+
| [2017-06-02 07:55:00, 2017-06-02 08:05:00]|  99.5   |
| [2017-06-02 08:00:00, 2017-06-02 08:10:00]| 101.25  |
| [2017-06-02 08:05:00, 2017-06-02 08:15:00]| 102.75  |
| [2017-06-02 08:10:00, 2017-06-02 08:20:00]| 103.75  |
| [2017-06-02 08:15:00, 2017-06-02 08:25:00]| 105.0   |
+------------------------------------------+---------+
```

```
// stop the streaming query
iotMemorySQ.stop
```

The previous output shows there are five windows in the synthetic data set. Notice the start time of each window is five minutes apart, which is because of the length of the sliding interval specified earlier in the groupBy transformation. The temperature column indicates the average temperature is increasing, which is alarming. At this point, it is unclear whether the temperature of all the computer racks are increasing or only certain ones. To help with identifying which computer racks, Listing 7-7 will add the rack column to the groupBy transformation, and it will show only the lines that are different than Listing 7-6.

Listing 7-7. Average Temperature of Each Rack Over a Sliding Window

```
// group by a sliding window and rack column
val iotAvgByRackDF = iotSSDF.groupBy(window($"ts", "10 minutes", "5
minutes"), $"rack")
                            .agg(avg("temperature") as "avg_temp")

// write out to memory data sink with iot_rack query name
val iotByRackConsoleSQ = iotAvgByRackDF.writeStream
                                .format("memory")
                                .queryName("iot_rack")
                                .outputMode("complete")
                                .start()

spark.sql("select * from iot_rack").orderBy($"rack", $"window.start").
show(false)
```

```
+-----------------------------------------------+------+---------+
|                                         window| rack | avg_temp|
+-----------------------------------------------+------+---------+
| [2017-06-02 07:55:00, 2017-06-02 08:05:00]| rack1| 99.5    |
| [2017-06-02 08:00:00, 2017-06-02 08:10:00]| rack1| 100.0   |
| [2017-06-02 08:05:00, 2017-06-02 08:15:00]| rack1| 100.75  |
| [2017-06-02 08:10:00, 2017-06-02 08:20:00]| rack1| 101.5   |
| [2017-06-02 08:15:00, 2017-06-02 08:25:00]| rack1| 102.0   |
```

```
| [2017-06-02 07:55:00, 2017-06-02 08:05:00]| rack2|  99.5   |
| [2017-06-02 08:00:00, 2017-06-02 08:10:00]| rack2| 102.5   |
| [2017-06-02 08:05:00, 2017-06-02 08:15:00]| rack2| 104.75  |
| [2017-06-02 08:10:00, 2017-06-02 08:20:00]| rack2| 106.0   |
| [2017-06-02 08:15:00, 2017-06-02 08:25:00]| rack2| 108.0   |
+-------------------------------------------+------+---------+

// stop query stream
iotByRackConsoleSQ.stop()
```

The output table clearly shows the average temperature of rack 1 is below 103, and it is rack 2 that you should be concerned about.

Aggregation State

The previous examples of performing aggregations of over a fixed window or a sliding window with an event time and additional information show how easy it is to perform commonly used and complex streaming processing operations in Spark Structured Streaming. While it seems easy from the outside, internally both the Structured Streaming engine and the Spark SQL engine work cooperatively together to maintain the intermediate aggregation result in a fault-tolerant manner while executing the streaming aggregation. In fact, anytime an aggregation is performed on a streaming query, the intermediate aggregation state must be maintained. This state is maintained in a key-value pairs structure, similar to a hash map, where the key is the group name and the value is the intermediate aggregation value. In the previous example of aggregation by a sliding window and rack ID, the key would be the combined value of the start and end times of the window, and the rack name and the value would be the average temperature.

The intermediate state is stored in an in-memory, versioned, key-value "state store" on the Spark executors, and it is written out to a write-ahead log, which should be configured to reside in a stable storage system like HDFS. At every trigger point, the state is read and updated in the in-memory state store and then written out to the write-ahead log. In the case of a failure and when a Spark Structured Streaming application is restarted, the state is restored from the write-ahead log and resumes from that point. This fault-tolerant state management obviously incurs some resource and processing overhead in the Structured Streaming engine. The amount of overhead is proportional to the amount of state it needs to maintain Therefore, it is important keep the amount of state in an acceptable size; in other words, the size of the state should not grow indefinitely.

Given the nature of sliding windows, the number of windows will grow indefinitely. This implies that performing sliding window aggregation will require the intermediate state to grow indefinitely unless there is a way to drop the old state that is no longer updated. This is accomplished using a technique called *watermarking*.

Watermarking: Limit State and Handle Late Data

Watermarking is a commonly used technique in streaming processing engines to deal with late data as well as to limit the amount of state needed to maintain it. Streaming data in the real world often arrives out of order as well as arrives late because of network congestion, network disruption, or the data generator like the mobile device is not online. As a developer of real-time streaming applications, it is important to know what you want to do with the data that arrives later than a certain threshold. In other words, what is an acceptable amount of time you expect most of the data will arrive by in relative to the others? Most likely the answer to the previous question is it depends on the use case. Late data will be dropped on the floor and will not be processed.

From the perspective of Structured Streaming, a watermark is a moving threshold in the event time that trails behind the maximum event time seen so far. As new data arrives with a newer event time, the maximum event time is updated, which will cause the watermark to move as well. Figure 7-3 illustrates an example where the watermark is defined as ten minutes. The watermark line is represented by the solid line, and it is trailing behind the maximum event time line, which is represented by the dotted line. Each rectangular box represents a piece of data, and its event time is immediately below the box. The piece of data with event-time 10:07 arrives a bit late, around 10:12; however, that still falls within the threshold between 10:03 and 10:13. Therefore, it will be processed as usual. The piece of data with event-time 10:15 falls in the same category. However, the piece of data with event-time 10:04 arrives really late, around 10:22, which falls below the watermark line, and therefore it will be ignored and not processed.

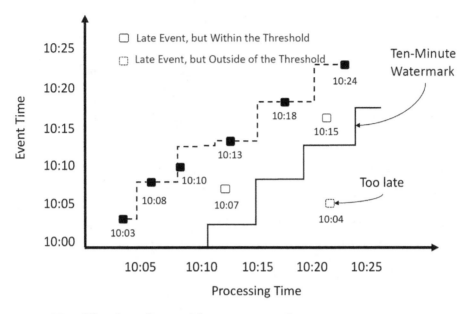

Figure 7-3. *Handling late data with a watermark*

One of the biggest benefits of specifying the watermark is to enable the Structured Streaming engine to safely remove the aggregation state of the windows that are older than the watermark. Production streaming applications that perform any kind of aggregation should specify a watermark to avoid out-of-memory issues. Without a doubt, watermarking is an essential tool to deal with the messy part of real-time streaming data.

Structured Streaming makes it easy to specify a watermark as part of the streaming DataFrame. You just need to provide two pieces of data to the Watermark API, the event time column and the threshold, which can be in seconds, minutes, or hours. To demonstrate the watermark in action, you can work through a simple example of processing two JSON files in the <path>/chapter7/data/mobile directory, and a watermark is specified as ten minutes. Listing 7-8 shows the data in those two files. The data is set up in such a way that each row in the file1.json file falls into its own ten-minute window. The first row in the file2.json file falls into the 10:20:00 to 10:30:00 window, and even though it arrives late, its timestamp still falls within an acceptable threshold, and therefore it will be processed. The last row of file2.json is a simulation of late data where its timestamp is in the 10:10:00 to 10:20:00 window, and since that falls outside the watermark threshold, it will be ignored and not processed.

Listing 7-8. Mobile Event Data in Two JSON Files

```
// file1.json
{"id":"phone1","action":"open","ts":"2018-03-02T10:15:33"}
{"id":"phone2","action":"open","ts":"2018-03-02T10:22:35"}
{"id":"phone3","action":"open","ts":"2018-03-02T10:33:50"}

// file2.json
{"id":"phone4","action":"open","ts":"2018-03-02T10:29:35"}
{"id":"phone5","action":"open","ts":"2018-03-02T10:11:35"}
```

To simulate the processing, first create a directory called `input` under the directory `<path>/chapter7/data`. Then run the code in Listing 7-9. The next step is to copy the `file1.json` file to the input directory and examine the output. The final step is to copy the `file2.json` file to the input directory and examine the output.

Listing 7-9. Code for Processing Mobile Data Events with Late Arrival

```
import org.apache.spark.sql.types._
import org.apache.spark.sql.functions._

val mobileDataSchema = new StructType().add("id", StringType, false)
                                       .add("action", StringType, false)
                                       .add("ts", TimestampType, false)

val mobileSSDF = spark.readStream.schema(mobileDataSchema).json("<path>/
book/chapter7/data/input")


//setup a streaming DataFrame with a watermark and group by ts and action column.
val windowCountDF = mobileSSDF.withWatermark("ts", "10 minutes")
                             .groupBy(window($"ts", "10 minutes"), $"action")
                             .count

val mobileMemorySQ = windowCountDF.writeStream
                                  .format("console")
                                  .option("truncate", "false")
                                  .outputMode("update")
                                  .start()
```

```
// the output from processing file11.json
// as expected each row falls into its own window
+--------------------------------------------+-------+------+
|                                      window| action| count|
+--------------------------------------------+-------+------+
| [2018-03-02 10:20:00, 2018-03-02 10:30:00]| open  |   1  |
| [2018-03-02 10:30:00, 2018-03-02 10:40:00]| open  |   1  |
| [2018-03-02 10:10:00, 2018-03-02 10:20:00]| open  |   1  |
+--------------------------------------------+-------+------+

// the output from processing file2.json
// notice the count for window 10:20 to 10:30 is now updated to 2
// and there was no change to the window 10:10:00 and 10:20:00
+--------------------------------------------+-------+------+
|                                      window| action| count|
+--------------------------------------------+-------+------+
| [2018-03-02 10:20:00, 2018-03-02 10:30:00]| open  |   2  |
+--------------------------------------------+-------+------+
```

As stated earlier, since the timestamp of the last line in the file2.json file falls outside the ten-minute watermark threshold, it was not processed at all. If the call to the Watermark API is removed, then the output would look something like Listing 7-10. The count to the window 10:10 and 10:20 is updated to 2.

Listing 7-10. Output of Removing the Call to the Watermark API

```
+--------------------------------------------+-------+------+
|                                      window| action| count|
+--------------------------------------------+-------+------+
| [2018-03-02 10:20:00, 2018-03-02 10:30:00]| open  |  2   |
| [2018-03-02 10:10:00, 2018-03-02 10:20:00]| open  |  2   |
+--------------------------------------------+-------+------+
```

A watermark is a useful feature, so it is important to understand the conditions under which the aggregation state is properly cleaned up.

- The output mode can't be the complete mode and must be in either update or append mode. The reason is that the semantics of the complete mode dictate all aggregate data must be maintained, and to not violate those semantics, the watermark can't drop any intermediate state.

- The aggregation via the groupBy transformation must be directly on the event-time column or a window on the event-time column.

- The event-time column specified in the Watermark API and the groupBy transformation must be the same one.

- When setting up a streaming DataFrame, the Watermark API must be called before the groupBy transformation is called; otherwise, it will be ignored.

Arbitrary Stateful Processing

As mentioned, the intermediate state of aggregations by key or event window is automatically maintained by Structured Streaming. However, not all event-time processing can be satisfied by simply aggregating on one or more columns and with or without windowing. For example, you want to send out an alert or email or a pager when three consecutive temperature readings with a value greater than 100 degrees are seen in the IoT temperature dataset. Another example is about maintaining user sessions, where the length of each session is not determined by a fixed amount of time but rather by a user's activities and lack thereof. To solve these two examples and similar use cases, you need the ability to apply arbitrary processing logic on each group of data, to control the window length for each group of data, and to maintain arbitrary state across trigger points. This is where Structured Streaming arbitrary state processing comes in.

Arbitrary Stateful Processing with Structured Streaming

Structured Streaming provides a callback mechanism for streaming applications to perform arbitrary stateful processing, and it will take care of ensuring the intermediate state is maintained and stored in a fault-tolerant manner. This style of processing essentially boils down to the ability to perform one of the following tasks, which are illustrated in Figure 7-4:

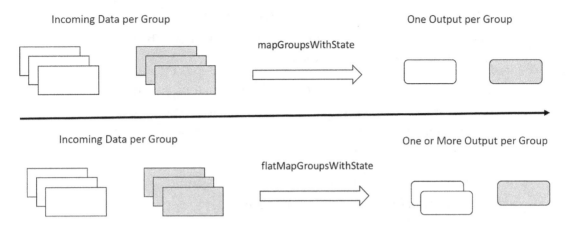

Figure 7-4. *Visual description of the two arbitrary stateful processing tasks*

- Map over groups of data, apply arbitrary processing on each group of data, and then output only a single row per group.

- Map over groups of data, apply arbitrary processing on each group of data, and then output any number of rows per group, including none.

For each of these tasks, Structured Streaming provides a specific API to handle it. For the first one, the API is called mapGroupsWithState, and for the second one, the API is called flatMapGroupsWithState. These APIs are available starting with Spark 2.2 and only in Scala and Java.

When working with any kind of callback mechanism, it is important to have a clear understanding of the contract between the framework and callback function regarding when and how often it gets called as well as the details of the input arguments. In this particular case, the sequence goes something like this:

- To perform arbitrary stateful processing on a streaming DataFrame, you must first specify the grouping by calling the groupByKey transformation and provide a column to group by; it then returns an instance of the KeyValueGroupedDataset class.

- From an instance of the KeyValueGroupedDataset class, you can call either the mapGroupsWithState or flatMapGroupsWithState function. Each one of two APIs requires a different set of input parameters.

- When calling the `mapGroupsWithState` function, you need to provide the timeout type and a user-defined callback function. The timeout part will be explained in a moment.

- When calling the `flatMapGroupsWithState` function, you need to provide an output mode, the timeout type, and a user-defined callback function. Both the output mode and timeout parts will be explained in a moment.

The following is the contract between Structured Streaming and the user-defined callback function mentioned earlier:

- The user-defined callback function will be invoked repeatedly for each group in each trigger. For each invocation, it is meant for each group that has data in the trigger. If a particular group doesn't have any data in a trigger, then there will be no invocation for that group. Therefore, you shouldn't assume this function is invoked in every trigger for every group.

- Each time the user-defined callback function is called, the following information will be passed in:

  - The value of the group key.

  - All the data of a group. There is no guarantee they are in any particular order.

  - A previous state of a group, which was returned by a previous invocation of the same group. A group state is managed by a state holder class called `GroupState`. When there is a need to update the state of a group, you must call the update function of this class with the new state. The information in the state for each group is defined by a user-defined class. When calling the update function, the provided user-defined state can't be null.

As you learned from the previous chapter, whenever there is a need to maintain an intermediate state, then only certain output modes are allowed. As of Spark 2.3, only the update output mode is supported when calling the `mapGroupsWithState` API; however, both append and update modes are supported when calling the `flatMapGroupsWithState` API.

Handling State Timeouts

In the case of event-time aggregations with a watermark, the timeout of the intermediate state is internally managed by Structured Streaming, and there isn't any way to influence it. On the other hand, Structured Streaming arbitrary stateful processing provides the flexibility of controlling the intermediate state timeout. Since you have the ability to maintain an arbitrary state, it makes sense to have control over the intermediate state timeout for this specific use case.

Structured Streaming stateful processing provides three different timeout types. The first one is based on the processing time, and the other one is based on the event time. The timeout type is configured at the global level, meaning it is for all the groups within a particular streaming DataFrame. The timeout amount can be configured for each individual group and can be changed at will. If the intermediate state is configured with a timeout, it is important to check whether it has timed out or not before processing the given list of values in the callback function. In some use cases, a timeout is not needed, and the third timeout type is designed for this scenario. The timeout type is defined inside class GroupStateTimeout, and you specify the type when calling either the mapGroupsWithState or flatMapGroupsWithState function. The timeout duration is specified using either the GroupState.setTimeoutDuration or GroupState.setTimeoutTimeStamp function for processing timeouts and event timeouts, respectively.

Keen readers may be wondering what happens when an intermediate state of a specific group has timed out. The contract Structured Streaming provides regarding this situation is that it will call the user-defined callback function with an empty list of values as well as set the flag GroupState.hasTimedOut to true.

Of the three different timeout types, the event-time timeout is the most complicated one and will be covered first. An event-time timeout implies that it is based on the time in the event, and therefore setting a watermark in the streaming DataFrame via DataFrame.withWatermark is required for this timeout type. To control the timeout per group, you need to provide a timestamp value to the GroupState.setTimeoutTimestamp function during the processing of a particular group. The intermediate state of a group is timed out when the watermark advances beyond the provided timestamp. In the user sessionization use case, as a user interacts with the website, the user session is extended by simply updating the timeout timestamp based on the user's latest interaction time plus some threshold. This is to ensure that as long as a user interacts with the website, the user session remains active, and the intermediate date will not be timed out.

The processing timeout type works in a similar fashion as the event-time timeout type; however, the difference is that it is based on the wall clock of the server, which is constantly advancing forward. To control the timeout per group, you provide a time duration to the `GroupState.setTimeoutDuration` function during the processing of a particular group. The time duration can be something like 1 minute, 1 hour, or 2 days. The intermediate state of a group is timed out when the clock has advanced past the provided duration. Since this timeout type depends on the system clock, it is important to consider the case when the time zone changes or when there is clock skew.

This may be obvious to keen readers, but it is important to recognize that if there is no data in the stream for a while, there won't be any triggers, and therefore the user-defined callback function will not be called. In addition, the watermark will not advance, and the timeout function call will not happen.

At this point, you should have a good understanding of how arbitrary state processing in Structured Streaming works and which APIs are involved. The following section will work through a couple of examples to demonstrate how to implement arbitrary state processing.

Arbitrary State Processing in Action

This section will demonstrate the arbitrary state processing in Structured Streaming by working through two use cases.

- The first one is about extracting patterns from the data center computer rack temperature data and maintaining a status of each rack in the intermediate state. Whenever three consecutive temperatures with 100 degrees or above are encountered, the rack status will be upgraded to the warning level. This example will use the `mapGroupsWithState` API.

- The second example is about user sessionization, which will keep track of the user state based on interactions with a website. This example will use the `flatMapGroupsWithState` API.

Regardless of which API will be used to perform arbitrary state processing for your use cases, a common set of steps is needed, which includes the following:

- Define a few classes to represent the input data, the intermediate state, and the output.

- Define two functions. The first one is the callback function for Structured Streaming to call. The second function contains arbitrary state processing logic on the data of each group as well as the logic to maintain state.

- Decide on a timeout type and an appropriate value for it.

Extracting Patterns with mapGroupsWithState

The goal of this use case is to identify a particular pattern in the data center computer rack temperature data. The pattern of interest is three consecutive temperature readings with 100 degrees or above from the same rack, and the time difference between two consecutive high temperature readings must be within 60 seconds. When such a pattern is detected, the status of that particular rack is upgraded to warning status. If the next incoming temperature reading falls below the 100-degree threshold, then the rack status is downgraded to normal.

The data for this example is located in the directory <path>/chapter7/data/ iot_pattern in three files; their content is shown in Listing 7-11. The content of file1. json shows the temperature of rack1 is alternating between just below and above 100 degrees. File file2.json shows the temperature of rack2 is heating up. In file file3. json, rack3 is heating up as well, but the temperature readings are more than one minute apart.

Listing 7-11. Temperature Data in file1.json, file2.json, and file3.json

```
// file1.json
{"rack":"rack1","temperature":99.5,"ts":"2017-06-02T08:01:01"}
{"rack":"rack1","temperature":100.5,"ts":"2017-06-02T08:02:02"}
{"rack":"rack1","temperature":98.3,"ts":"2017-06-02T08:02:29"}
{"rack":"rack1","temperature":102.0,"ts":"2017-06-02T08:02:44"}

// file2.json
{"rack":"rack1","temperature":97.5,"ts":"2017-06-02T08:02:59"}
{"rack":"rack2","temperature":99.5,"ts":"2017-06-02T08:03:02"}
{"rack":"rack2","temperature":105.5,"ts":"2017-06-02T08:03:44"}
{"rack":"rack2","temperature":104.0,"ts":"2017-06-02T08:04:06"}
{"rack":"rack2","temperature":108.0,"ts":"2017-06-02T08:04:49"}
```

```
// file3.json
{"rack":"rack2","temperature":108.0,"ts":"2017-06-02T08:06:40"}
{"rack":"rack3","temperature":100.5,"ts":"2017-06-02T08:06:20"}
{"rack":"rack3","temperature":103.7,"ts":"2017-06-02T08:07:35"}
{"rack":"rack3","temperature":105.3,"ts":"2017-06-02T08:08:53"}
```

Next you are going to prepare a few classes and two functions to apply pattern detection logic to the previous data. For this use case, the rack temperature input data is represented by class RackInfo, and both the intermediate state and output are represented by the same class called RackState. Listing 7-12 shows the code.

Listing 7-12. Scala Case Classes for the Input and Intermediate State

```
case class RackInfo(rack:String, temperature:Double, ts:java.sql.Timestamp)

// notice the constructor arguments are defined to be modifiable so we can
update them
// the lastTS variable is used to compare the time between previous and
current temperature reading
case class RackState(var rackId:String, var highTempCount:Int,
                     var status:String, var lastTS:java.sql.Timestamp)
```

Next you define two functions. The first one is called updateRackState, which contains the core logic of the pattern detection of three consecutive high temperature readings that happen within 60 seconds of each other. The second function is called updateAcrossAllRackStatus, which is the callback function that will be passed into the mapGroupsWithState API. This function makes sure the rack temperature readings are processed according to the order of their event time. See Listing 7-13 for the code.

Listing 7-13. The Functions for Performing Pattern Detection

```
import org.apache.spark.sql.streaming.GroupState

// contains the main logic to detect the temperature pattern described above

def updateRackState(rackState:RackState, rackInfo:RackInfo) : RackState = {
    // setup the conditions to decide whether to update the rack state
    val lastTS = Option(rackState.lastTS).getOrElse(rackInfo.ts)
    val withinTimeThreshold = (rackInfo.ts.getTime - lastTS.getTime) <= 60000
```

```scala
  val meetCondition = if (rackState.highTempCount < 1) true else
  withinTimeThreshold
  val greaterThanEqualTo100 = rackInfo.temperature >= 100.0

(greaterThanEqualTo100, meetCondition) match {
  case (true, true) => {
    rackState.highTempCount = rackState.highTempCount + 1
    rackState.status = if (rackState.highTempCount >= 3) "Warning" else
    "Normal"
  }
  case _ => {
    rackState.highTempCount = 0
    rackState.status = "Normal"
  }
}
  rackState.lastTS = rackInfo.ts
  rackState
}

// call-back funcion to provide mapGroupsWithState API
def updateAcrossAllRackStatus(rackId:String, inputs:Iterator[RackInfo],
                  oldState: GroupState[RackState]) : RackState = {

  // initialize rackState with previous state if exists, otherwise create
     a new state
  var rackState = if (oldState.exists) oldState.get else RackState
  (rackId, 5, "", null)

  // sort the inputs by time stamp in ascending order
  inputs.toList.sortBy(_.ts.getTime).foreach( input => {
    rackState = updateRackState(rackState, input)
    // very important to update the rackState in the state holder class
       GroupState
    oldState.update(rackState)
  })
  rackState
}
```

The setup step is now complete, so now you will wire the callback function into mapGroupsWithState in the Structured Streaming application in Listing 7-14. The steps to simulate the streaming data are similar to one of the previous examples, as shown here:

- Create a directory called input under the directory
  <path>/chapter7/data. Remove all files in this directory
  if it already exists.

- Run the code in Listing 7-14.

- Copy file1.json to the input directory and then observe the output.
  Repeat this same step with file2.json and file3.json.

Listing 7-14. Using Arbitrary State Processing to Detect Patterns in a Streaming Application

```
import org.apache.spark.sql.streaming.{GroupStateTimeout, OutputMode}
import org.apache.spark.sql.types._
import org.apache.spark.sql.functions._

// schema for the IoT data
val iotDataSchema = new StructType().add("rack", StringType, false)
                                    .add("temperature", DoubleType, false)
                                    .add("ts", TimestampType, false)

val iotSSDF = spark.readStream.schema(iotDataSchema).json("<path>/chapter7/
data/input")

val iotPatternDF = iotSSDF.as[RackInfo]
                          .groupByKey(_.rack)
                          .mapGroupsWithState[RackState,RackState]
                          (GroupStateTimeout.NoTimeout)
                          (updateAcrossAllRackStatus)

// setup the output and start the streaming query
val iotPatternSQ = iotPatternDF.writeStream
                              .format("console")
                              .outputMode("update")
                              .start()
```

```
// after file3.json is copied over to "input" directory, run the line below
stop the streaming query
iotPatternSQ.stop

// the output after processing file1.json
+-------+-------------+-------+-------------------+
| rackId| highTempCount| status|             lastTS|
+-------+-------------+-------+-------------------+
|  rack1|            1| Normal| 2017-06-02 08:02:44|
+-------+-------------+-------+-------------------+

// the output after processing file2.json
+-------+-------------+--------+-------------------+
| rackId| highTempCount|  status|             lastTS|
+-------+-------------+--------+-------------------+
|  rack1|            0|  Normal| 2017-06-02 08:02:59|
|  rack2|            3| Warning| 2017-06-02 08:04:49|
+-------+-------------+--------+-------------------+

// the output after processing file3.json
+-------+-------------+-------+-------------------+
| rackId| highTempCount| status|             lastTS|
+-------+-------------+-------+-------------------+
|  rack3|            1| Normal| 2017-06-02 08:08:53|
|  rack2|            0| Normal| 2017-06-02 08:06:40|
+-------+-------------+-------+-------------------+
```

rack1 has a few temperature readings over 100 degrees; however, they are not consecutive, and therefore the output status is at the normal level. In file file2.json, rack2 has three consecutive temperature readings over 100 degrees, and the time gap between each one and the one before is less than 60 seconds; therefore, the status of rack2 is at the warning level. rack3 has three consecutive temperature readings over 100 degrees; however, the time gap between each one and the one before is more than 60 seconds. Therefore, its status is at the normal level.

User Sessionization with flatMapGroupsWithState

This use case performs user sessionization using the flatMapGroupsWithState API, which supports the ability to output more than one row per group. In this example, the sessionization processing logic is based on the user activities. A session is created when the login action is taken, and a session is ended when the logout action is taken. A session will be automatically ended when there are no user activities for a duration of 30 minutes. You will leverage the timeout feature described earlier to perform this detection. In terms of the output, whenever a session starts or ends, that information will be sent to the output. The output information consists of user ID, session start and end times, and the number of visited pages.

The data for this use case is located in the directory <path>/chapter7/data/ sessionization, which consists of three files. Their content is shown in Listing 7-15. File file1.json contains the activities of user1, and it includes a login action, but there is no logout action. File file2.json contains all the activities of user2 including both login and logout actions. File file3.json contains only the login action for user3. The timestamp of the user activities in three files is set up in such a way that the session of user1 will be timed out when file3.json is processed. This is because by then the amount of time user1 has been idled is more than 30 minutes.

Listing 7-15. User Activity Data

```
// file1.json
{"user":"user1","action":"login","page":"page1", "ts":"2017-09-06T08:08:53"}
{"user":"user1","action":"click","page":"page2", "ts":"2017-09-06T08:10:11"}
{"user":"user1","action":"send","page":"page3", "ts":"2017-09-06T08:11:10"}

// file2.json
{"user":"user2","action":"login", "page":"page1", "ts":"2017-09-06T08:44:12"}
{"user":"user2","action":"view", "page":"page7", "ts":"2017-09-06T08:45:33"}
{"user":"user2","action":"view", "page":"page8", "ts":"2017-09-06T08:55:58"}
{"user":"user2","action":"view", "page":"page6", "ts":"2017-09-06T09:10:58"}
{"user":"user2","action":"logout","page":"page9", "ts":"2017-09-06T09:16:19"}

// file3.json
{"user":"user3","action":"login", "page":"page4", "ts":"2017-09-06T09:17:11"}
```

Next you are going to prepare a few classes and two functions to apply the user sessionization logic to the previous data. For this use case, the user activity input data is represented by class `UserActivity`. The intermediate state of the user session data is represented by the class `UserSessionState`, and the user session output is represented by the class `UserSessionInfo`. Listing 7-16 shows the code for all these three classes.

Listing 7-16. Scala Case Classes for Input, Intermediate State, and Output

```
case class UserActivity(user:String, action:String, page:String, ts:java.
sql.Timestamp)

// the lastTS field is for storing the largest user activity timestamp and
   this information is used
// when setting the timeout value for each user session
case class UserSessionState(var user:String, var status:String, var
startTS:java.sql.Timestamp,
                           var endTS:java.sql.Timestamp, var lastTS:java.
                           sql.Timestamp,
                           var numPage:Int)

// the end time stamp is filled when the session has ended.
case class UserSessionInfo(userId:String, start:java.sql.Timestamp,
end:java.sql.Timestamp,  numPage:Int)
```

Next you define two functions. The first one is called `updateUserActivity`, which is responsible for updating the user session state based on a single-user activity. It appropriately updates either the session start or the end time based on the action the user has taken. In addition, it updates the latest activity timestamp. The second function is called `updateAcrossAllUserActivities`, and it is the callback function that will be passed into the `flatMapGroupsWithState` function. This function has two main responsibilities. The first one is to handle the timeout of the intermediate session state, and it updates the user session end time when such a condition arises. The other responsibility is to determine when and what to send to the output. The desired output is one row when a user session is started and another one when a user session is ended. See Listing 7-17 for the logic of these two functions.

Listing 7-17. The Functions for Performing User Sessionization

```scala
import org.apache.spark.sql.streaming.GroupState
import scala.collection.mutable.ListBuffer

def updateUserActivity(userSessionState:UserSessionState,
userActivity:UserActivity) : UserSessionState = {
    userActivity.action match {
      case "login" => {
        userSessionState.startTS = userActivity.ts
        userSessionState.status = "Online"
      }
      case "logout" => {
        userSessionState.endTS = userActivity.ts
        userSessionState.status = "Offline"
      }
      case _ => {
        userSessionState.numPage += 1
        userSessionState.status = "Active"
      }
    }

    userSessionState.lastTS = userActivity.ts
    userSessionState
}

def updateAcrossAllUserActivities(user:String,
inputs:Iterator[UserActivity],
                    oldState: GroupState[UserSessionState]) :
                    Iterator[UserSessionInfo] = {

  var userSessionState = if (oldState.exists) oldState.get else
  UserSessionState(user, "",
   new java.sql.Timestamp(System.currentTimeMillis), null, null, 0)

  var output = ListBuffer[UserSessionInfo]()
```

```scala
inputs.toList.sortBy(_.ts.getTime).foreach( userActivity => {
  userSessionState = updateUserActivity(userSessionState, userActivity)
  oldState.update(userSessionState)

  if (userActivity.action == "login") {
    output += UserSessionInfo(user, userSessionState.startTS,
                             userSessionState.endTS, 0)
  }
})

val sessionTimedOut = oldState.hasTimedOut
val sessionEnded = !Option(userSessionState.endTS).isEmpty
val shouldOutput = sessionTimedOut || sessionEnded

shouldOutput match {
 case true => {
    if (sessionTimedOut) {
        userSessionState.endTS = new java.sql.Timestamp(oldState.
        getCurrentWatermarkMs)
    }
    oldState.remove()
    output += UserSessionInfo(user, userSessionState.startTS,
                             userSessionState.endTS, userSessionState.
                             numPage)

 }
 case _ => {
   // extend sesion
   oldState.update(userSessionState)
   oldState.setTimeoutTimestamp(userSessionState.lastTS.getTime,
   "30 minutes")
 }
 }

 output.iterator
}
```

The setup step is now complete, so you will wire the callback function into the flatMapGroupsWithState function in the Structured Streaming application in Listing 7-18. In this example, it will leverage the timeout feature, and therefore setting up a watermark and event-time timeout type is required. The steps to simulate the streaming data are similar to one of the previous examples, as shown here:

1. Create a directory called input under the directory <path>/chapter7/ data. Remove all the files in this directory if it already exists.

2. Run the code in Listing 7-18.

3. Copy file1.json to the input directory and then observe the output. Repeat this same step with file2.json and file3.json.

Listing 7-18. Using Arbitrary State Processing to Perform User Sessionization in a Streaming Application

```
import org.apache.spark.sql.streaming.{GroupStateTimeout, OutputMode}
import org.apache.spark.sql.types._
import org.apache.spark.sql.functions._

val userActivitySchema = new StructType().add("user", StringType, false)
                                         .add("action", StringType, false)
                                         .add("page", StringType, false)
                                         .add("ts", TimestampType, false)

val userActivityDF = spark.readStream.schema(userActivitySchema).
json("<path>/chapter7/data/input")

// convert to DataSet of type UserActivity
val userActivityDS = userActivityDF.withWatermark("ts", "30 minutes").
as[UserActivity]

// specify the event-time timeout type and wire in the call-back function
val userSessionDS = userActivityDS.groupByKey(_.user)
                                  .flatMapGroupsWithState[User
                                  SessionState,UserSessionInfo]
                                  (OutputMode.Append,Group
                                  StateTimeout.EventTimeTimeout)
                                  (updateAcrossAllUser
                                  Activities)
```

```
// setup the output and start the streaming query
val userSessionSQ = userSessionDS.writeStream
                                .format("console")
                                .option("truncate",false)
                                .outputMode("append")
                                .start()
```

```
// only run this line of code below after done copyng over file3.json
userSessionSQ.stop
```

```
// the output after processing file1.json
```

userId	start	end	numPage
user1	2017-09-06 08:08:53	null	0

```
// the output after processing file2.json
```

userId	start	end	numPage
user2	2017-09-06 08:44:12	null	0
user2	2017-09-06 08:44:12	2017-09-06 09:16:19	3

```
// the output after processing file3.json
```

userId	start	end	numPage
user1	2017-09-06 08:08:53	2017-09-06 08:46:19	2
user3	2017-09-06 09:17:11	null	0

After processing the user activities in `file1.json`, you see there is one row in the output. This is expected because whenever function `updateAcrossAllUserActivities` sees a `login` action in the user activities, it will add an instance of the `UserSessionInfo` class to the output `ListBuffer`. There are two rows in the output after processing `file2.json`. One is for the `login` action, and the other one is for the `logout` action. Now `file3.json` contains only one user activity for `user3` with the action `login`, but the output contains two rows. The row for `user1` is the result of detecting that the `user1` session has timed out, which means the watermark has passed the timeout value of that particular session because of the lack of activity from `user1`.

As demonstrated in the previous two use cases, the arbitrary stateful processing feature in Structured Streaming provides flexible and powerful ways to apply user-defined processing logic on each group with total control of what to send to the output and when.

Handling Duplicate Data

Deduplicating data is a common need in the world of data processing, and it is not too difficult to do that in batch processing. In stream processing, though, it is more challenging because of the unbounded nature of streaming data. Data duplication in real-time streaming data happens when data producers send the same piece of data multiple times, and this may happen because they operate in an unreliable network connection and they want to err on the side of making sure a particular piece of data is sent and processed.

Luckily, Structured Streaming makes it easy for streaming applications to perform data duplication, and therefore these applications can guarantee exactly once processing by dropping duplicate data as it arrives. The data duplication feature that Structured Streaming provides can work in conjunction with a watermark or without it. One key thing to note, though, when performing data duplication without specifying a watermark is that the state that Structured Streaming needs to maintain will grow infinitely over the lifetime of your streaming application, and this may lead to out-of-memory issues. With watermarking, late data older than the watermark will be automatically dropped to avoid any possibility of duplicates.

The API to tell Structured Streaming to perform data deduplication is simple, and it has only one input, which is a list of column names to use to uniquely identify each row. The value of these columns will be used to perform duplicate detection, and Structured Streaming will store them as intermediate state. The sample data that will be used to demonstrate the data deduplication feature has the same schema as the mobile event data. The count aggregation will be based on the grouping of the id column. Both the id and ts columns are used as the user-defined keys for the deduplication purpose. The data for this example is located in <path>/chapter7/data/deduplication, which contains two files: file1.json and file2.json. The content of these files is displayed in Listing 7-19.

Listing 7-19. Sample Data for the Data deduplication Example

```
// file1.json - each line is unique in term of id and ts columns
{"id":"phone1","action":"open","ts":"2018-03-02T10:15:33"}
{"id":"phone2","action":"open","ts":"2018-03-02T10:22:35"}
{"id":"phone3","action":"open","ts":"2018-03-02T10:23:50"}

// file2.json - the first two lines are duplicate of the first two lines in
    file1.json above
// the third line is unique
// the fourth line is unique, but it arrives late, therefore it will not be
    processed
{"id":"phone1","action":"open","ts":"2018-03-02T10:15:33"}
{"id":"phone2","action":"open","ts":"2018-03-02T10:22:35"}
{"id":"phone4","action":"open","ts":"2018-03-02T10:29:35"}
{"id":"phone5","action":"open","ts":"2018-03-02T10:01:35"}
```

To simulate the data deduplication, first create a directory called input under the directory <path>/chapter7/data. Then run the code in Listing 7-20. The next step is to copy the file1.json file to the input directory and examine the output. The final step is to copy the file2.json file to the input directory to examine the output.

Listing 7-20. Deduplicating Data Using the dropDuplicates API

```
import org.apache.spark.sql.types._
import org.apache.spark.sql.functions._

val mobileDataSchema = new StructType().add("id", StringType, false)
                                       .add("action", StringType, false)
```

```
                                    .add("ts", TimestampType, false)

// mobileDataSchema is defined in previous example
val mobileDupSSDF = spark.readStream.schema(mobileDataSchema)
                                .json("<path>/chapter7/data/
                                deduplication")

val windowCountDupDF = mobileDupSSDF.withWatermark("ts", "10 minutes")
                                .dropDuplicates("id", "ts")
                                .groupBy("id").count

val mobileMemoryDupSQ = windowCountDupDF.writeStream
                                    .format("console")
                                    .option("truncate", "false")
                                    .outputMode("update")
                                    .start()
// output after copying file1.json to input directory
+-------+------+
|     id| count|
+-------+------+
| phone3|     1|
| phone1|     1|
| phone2|     1|
+-------+------+

// output after coping file2.json to input directory
+-------+------+
|     id| count|
+-------+------+
| phone4|     1|
+-------+------+
```

As expected, after file2.json is copied to the input directory, only one line is displayed in the console. The reason is the first two lines are duplicates of the first two lines in file1.json, and therefore they were filtered out. The last line has a timestamp of 10:10, which is considered late data since that timestamp is older than the ten-minute watermark threshold. Therefore, the last line was not processed and dropped.

Fault Tolerance

One of the most important considerations when developing important streaming applications and deploying them to production is failure recovery. According to Murphy's law, anything that can go wrong will go wrong. Machines will fail, and software will have bugs. Luckily, Structured Streaming provides a way to restart or recover your streaming application when there is a failure, and it will continue where it left off. To take advantage of this recovery mechanism, you need to configure your streaming applications to use checkpointing and write-ahead logs by specifying a checkpoint location when setting up streaming queries. Ideally the checkpoint location should be a path on a reliable and fault-tolerant file system like HDFS or S3. Structured Streaming will periodically save all the progress information such as the offset details of the data being processed and the intermediate state values to the checkpoint location. Adding a checkpoint location to a streaming query is straightforward. You just need to add an option to your streaming query with `checkpointLocation` as the name and the path as the value. See Listing 7-21 for an example.

Listing 7-21. Adding the checkpointLocation Option to a Streaming Query

```
val userSessionSQ = userSessionDS.writeStream.format("console")
                                    .option("truncate",false)
                                    .option("checkpointLocation",
                                     "/reliable/location")
                                    .outputMode("append")
                                    .start()
```

If you take a peek into the specified checkpoint location, you should see the following subdirectories: `commits`, `metadata`, `offsets`, `sources`, and `stats`. The information in these directories is specific to a particular streaming query; hence, each one must use a different checkpoint location.

Just like most software applications, streaming applications will evolve over time because of the need to improve the processing logic or performance or to fix bugs. It is important to keep in mind how this might affect the information saved in the checkpoint location and to know what changes are considered safe to make. Broadly speaking, there are two categories of changes. One is the change to streaming application code, and the other is the change to the Spark runtime.

Streaming Application Code Change

The information in the checkpoint location is designed to be somewhat resilient to the changes of streaming applications. There are a few kind of changes that will be considered incompatible changes. The first one is about changing the way the aggregation is done by either changing the key column, adding more key columns, or removing one of the existing key columns. The second one is changing the class structure that was used for storing the intermediate state, for example, when a field is removed or the type of a field is changed from string to integer. When incompatible changes are detected during a restart, Structured Streaming will let you know via an exception. In this case, you must either use a new checkpoint location or remove the content in the previous checkpoint location.

Spark Runtime Change

The checkpoint format is designed to be forward compatible such that streaming applications should be able to restart from an old checkpoint across patch versions or minor version updates of Spark (i.e., upgrading from Spark 2.2.0 to 2.2.1 or from Spark 2.2.x to 2.3.x). The only exception to the rule is when there are critical bug fixes. It is good to know that when incompatible changes are introduced by Spark, it will be clearly documented in the release notes.

If it is not possible to start a streaming application with an existing checkpoint location because of incompatibility issues, then you will need to use a new checkpoint location, and perhaps you will also need to seed your applications with some information about the offset to read data from.

Streaming Query Metrics and Monitoring

Similar to other long-running applications such as online services, it is important to have some insights into your streaming applications regarding the progress it is making, the incoming data rate, or the amount of memory being consumed by the intermediate state. Structured Streaming provides a few APIs to extract the information about recent execution progress and an asynchronous way of monitoring all streaming queries in a streaming application.

Streaming Query Metrics

The most basic useful information about a streaming query at any moment in time is its current status. You can retrieve and display this information in a human-readable format by calling the StreamingQuery.status function. The returned object is of type StreamingQueryStatus, and it can easily convert the status information into JSON format. Listing 7-22 shows an example of what the status information looks like.

Listing 7-22. Query Status Information in JSON Format

```
// use a streaming query from the example above
userSessionSQ.status

// output
res11: org.apache.spark.sql.streaming.StreamingQueryStatus =
{
  "message" : "Waiting for data to arrive",
  "isDataAvailable" : false,
  "isTriggerActive" : false
}
```

Clearly the previous status provides basic information about what's going on in a streaming query at the moment the status function is called. To get additional details from recent progress such as the incoming data rate, the processing rate, the watermark, the offsets of the data source, and some information about the intermediate state, you can call the StreamingQuery.recentProgress function. This function returns an array of instances of the StreamingQueryProgress class, which can convert the details into JSON format. By default, each streaming query is configured to retain 100 progress updates, and this number can be changed by updating the Spark configuration called spark.sql.streaming.numRecentProgressUpdates. To see the most recent streaming query progress, you can call the function StreamingQuery.lastProgress. Listing 7-23 shows a sample of a streaming query progress.

Listing 7-23. Streaming Query Progress Details

```
{
  "id" : "9ba6691d-7612-4906-b64d-9153544d81e9",
  "runId" : "c6d79bee-a691-4d2f-9be2-c93f3a88eb0c",
  "name" : null,
  "timestamp" : "2018-04-23T17:20:12.023Z",
  "batchId" : 0,
  "numInputRows" : 3,
  "inputRowsPerSecond" : 250.0,
  "processedRowsPerSecond" : 1.728110599078341,
  "durationMs" : {
    "addBatch" : 1548,
    "getBatch" : 8,
    "getOffset" : 36,
    "queryPlanning" : 110,
    "triggerExecution" : 1736,
    "walCommit" : 26
  },
  "eventTime" : {
    "avg" : "2017-09-06T15:10:04.666Z",
    "max" : "2017-09-06T15:11:10.000Z",
    "min" : "2017-09-06T15:08:53.000Z",
    "watermark" : "1970-01-01T00:00:00.000Z"
  },
  "stateOperators" : [ {
    "numRowsTotal" : 1,
    "numRowsUpdated" : 1,
    "memoryUsedBytes" : 16127
  } ],
  "sources" : [ {
    "description" : "FileStreamSource[file:<path>/chapter7/data/input]",
    "startOffset" : null,
    "endOffset" : {
      "logOffset" : 0
    },
```

```
    "numInputRows" : 3,
    "inputRowsPerSecond" : 250.0,
    "processedRowsPerSecond" : 1.728110599078341
  } ],
  "sink" : {
    "description" : "org.apache.spark.sql.execution.streaming.
    ConsoleSinkProvider@37dc4031"
  }
}
```

Looking at the details in the sample streaming progress shown previously, there are
a few important key metrics to pay attention to. The input rate represents the amount of
incoming data flowing into a streaming application from an input source. The process
rate tells you how fast a streaming application can process the incoming data. In an
ideal state, the processing rate should be higher than the input rate, and if that is not
the case, then you need to consider scaling up the number of nodes in a Spark cluster.
If a streaming application is maintaining state either implicitly through the groupBy
transformation or explicitly through the arbitrary state processing APIs, then it is
important to pay attention to the metrics in the stateOperators section.

The Spark UI provides a rich set of metrics at the job, stage, and task levels. Each
trigger in a streaming application is mapped to a job in Spark UI, where the query plan
and task durations can be easily inspected.

Note   The streaming query status and progress details are available through
an instance of a streaming query. While your streaming application is running in
production, you don't have the luxury of having access to those streaming queries.
What if you would like to see that information from a remote host? One option is
to embed a small HTTP server inside your streaming application and expose a few
simple URLs to retrieve that information.

Monitoring Streaming Queries

Structured Streaming provides a callback mechanism to asynchronously receive events and the progress of the streaming queries in a streaming application. This is done via the StreamingQueryListener interface, which tells when a streaming query is started, when it has made some progress, and when it is terminated. An implementation of this interface can control what to do with the provided information. One obvious implementation would be to send this information to a Kafka topic or some other publish-subscribe system for offline analysis or for another streaming application to process. Listing 7-24 contains a simple implementation of the StreamingQueryListener interface; it prints out the information to the console.

Listing 7-24. A Simple Implementation of the StreamingQueryListener Interface

```
import org.apache.spark.sql.streaming.StreamingQueryListener
import org.apache.spark.sql.streaming.StreamingQueryListener.
{QueryStartedEvent, QueryProgressEvent, QueryTerminatedEvent}

class ConsoleStreamingQueryListener extends StreamingQueryListener {
    override def onQueryStarted(event: QueryStartedEvent): Unit = {
      println(s"streaming query started: ${event.id} - ${event.name} -
                                    ${event.runId}")
    }

    override def onQueryProgress(event: QueryProgressEvent): Unit = {
      println(s"streaming query progess: ${event.progress}")
    }

    override def onQueryTerminated(event: QueryTerminatedEvent): Unit = {
      println(s"streaming query terminated: ${event.id} - ${event.runId}")
    }
}
```

Once you have an implementation of StreamingQueryListener, the next step is to register it with StreamQueryManager, which can handle multiple listeners. See Listing 7-25 for how to register and unregister a listener.

Listing 7-25. Registering and Unregistering an Instance of StreamingQueryListener with StreamQueryManager

```
Val listener = new ConsoleStreamingQueryListener

// to register
spark.streams.addListener(listener)

// to unregister
spark.streams.removeListener(listener)
```

One thing to remember is each listener receives the streaming query events from all the streaming queries in a streaming application. If there is a need to apply specific event processing logic to a certain streaming query, then it can leverage the streaming query name.

Summary

The Spark Structured Streaming engine provides many advanced features and the flexibility to build complex and sophisticated streaming applications.

- Any serious streaming processing engine must support the ability to process incoming data by the event time. Structured Streaming not only supports the ability to do this but also supports window aggregation based on fixed and sliding windows. In addition, it will automatically maintain the intermediate state in a fault-tolerant manner.

- Maintaining the intermediate state introduces the risk of running out of memory as streaming applications process more and more data. A watermark was introduced to make it easier to reason about late data as well as to remove no longer needed intermediate state.

- Arbitrary stateful processing enables a user-defined way of processing the values of each group and maintaining its intermediate state. Structured Streaming provides an easy way of doing this via a callback API, and there is a flexibility in generating one or more rows per group to the output.

- Structured Streaming provides an end-to-end, exactly-once guarantee. This is achieved by using the checkpointing and write-ahead log mechanisms. Both of them can be turned on easily by providing a checkpoint location that resides on a fault-tolerant file system. Streaming applications can be easily restarted and pick up from where they left off before the failure by reading the information saved in the checkpoint location.

- Production streaming applications require the ability to get insights into the status and metrics of streaming queries. Structured Streaming provides a short summary of the streaming query status as well as the detailed metrics about incoming data rate, processing rate, and some details about the intermediate state memory consumption. To monitor the lifecycle of all streaming queries and their detailed progresses, you can register one or more instances of the StreamingQueryListener interface.

CHAPTER 8

Machine Learning with Spark

There has been a lot of excitement around artificial intelligence (AI), machine learning (ML), and deep learning (DL) in recent years. AI experts and researchers have predicted AI will radically transform the way humans live, work, and do business in the future. For businesses around the world, AI is considered to be one of the next steps in their journey of digital transformation, and some are more far along than others in incorporating AI into their business strategies. Businesses expect AI to help solve their business problems efficiently and quickly as well as to create business value and improve their competitive advantages. Internet giants such as Google, Amazon, Microsoft, Apple, and Facebook are leading the pack in investing in, adopting, and incorporating AI into their product portfolios. In 2017, more than $15 billion of venture capital (VC) money went into investing in AI-related startup companies around the world, and this trend is expected to continue in 2018.

AI is a broad area of computer science that tries to make machines seem like they have intelligence. It is an audacious goal to help advance humankind. One of the subfields within AI is machine learning, which focuses on teaching computers to learn without being explicitly programmed. The learning process involves analyzing a large number of datasets using algorithms and building a model to explain the world. These algorithms can be categorized into different groups based on the task they are designed for. One of the things these algorithms have in common is they learn through an iterative process of refining their internal parameters to achieve an optimal outcome.

Deep learning (DL) is one of the machine learning methods that is inspired by the way the human brain works, and it has proven to be really good at learning complex patterns from data by representing them as a nested hierarchy of concepts. With the combination of the availability of large and curated datasets and the advancement in graphical processing units (GPUs), DL has proven to be effective at solving problems in areas such as object recognition, image recognition, speech recognition, and machine

© Hien Luu 2018
H. Luu, *Beginning Apache Spark 2*, https://doi.org/10.1007/978-1-4842-3579-9_8

translation. In fact, it has proven itself at one of the image classification challenges called ImageNet, where a computer system trained using a DL method was able to beat a human at classifying images. The implication of this achievement and similar ones is that now computer systems can see, recognize objects, and hear at the same level as their creators. Figure 8-1 illustrates the relationship between AI, ML, and DL as well their timelines.

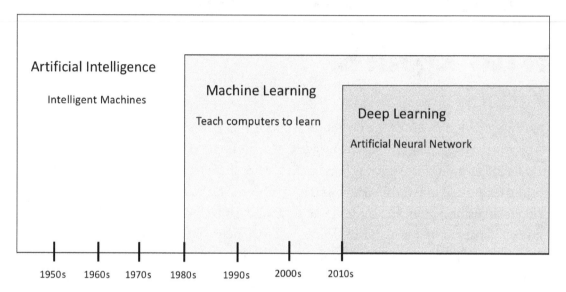

Figure 8-1. *Relationship between AI, ML, and DL and their timelines*

One of the motivations behind the creation of Spark was to help applications run iterative algorithms efficiently at scale. Over the last few versions of Spark, the MLlib library has steadily increased its offerings to make ML scalable and easy to use by providing a set of commonly used ML algorithms and a set of tools to facilitate the process of building and evaluating ML models.

To appreciate the features that the MLlib library provides, it is necessary to have a fundamental understanding of the process of building ML applications. This chapter starts by providing that information and proceeds to introducing the features and APIs that are available in the MLlib library so that you can apply them to building your intelligent applications using machine learning.

Machine Learning Overview

The goal of this section to provide a brief overview about machine learning and the typical process used to develop ML applications. It is not meant to be exhaustive; feel free to skip it if you are already familiar with ML.

ML is a vast and fascinating field of study, which combines parts of other fields of studies such as mathematics, statistics, and computer science. It is a method of teaching computers to learn patterns and derive insights from historical data, often for the purpose of making decisions or predictions. Unlike traditional, hard-coded software, ML gives you only probabilistic outputs based on the imperfect data you provide. The more data you can provide to ML algorithms, the more accurate the output will be. ML can solve much more interesting and difficult problems than traditional software can, and these problems are not specific to any industry or business domain. Examples of these relevant areas are image recognition, speech recognition, language translation, fraud detection, product recommendations, robotics, autonomous driving cars, speeding up the drug discovery process, medical diagnosis, customer churn prediction, recommendations, and many more.

Given that the goal of AI is to make machines seem like they have intelligence, one of the best ways to measure that is by comparing machine intelligence against human intelligence. There are a few well-known and publicized demonstrations of such comparisons in recent decades. The first one was a computer system called Deep Blue that defeated the world chess champion in 1997 under strict tournament regulations. This example demonstrates that computer machines can think faster and better than a human in a game that has a vast but limited set of possible moves. The second one was a computer system called Watson that competed on the Jeopardy game show against two legendary champions in 2011 and won the first price of $1 million. The example demonstrates computer machines can understand human language in a specific question-and-answer structure and then tap into their vast knowledge base to come up with probabilistic answers. The third one is about a computer program called AlphaGo that defeated a world champion in the game of Go in a historic match in 2016. This example demonstrates a great leap in the advancement of the AI field because Go is considered to be a complex board game that requires intuition and creative and strategic thinking, and it is not feasible to perform an exhaustive move search because of the number of possible moves it has is greater than the number of atoms in the universe.

Machine Learning Terminologies

Before going deeper into ML, it is important to learn a few basic terms in the ML language. This will be helpful in future sections when this terminology is mentioned. To ideally make it easier to understand these terms, the explanations are provided in the context of the canonical ML example called the spam email classification example.

- Observation

    - This term comes from the statistics field. An *observation* is an instance of the entity that is used for learning. For example, emails are considered observations.

- Label

    - A value used to label an observation. For example, "spam" or "not spam" are two possible values used to label emails.

- Features

    - These are important attributes about observations that most likely have the strongest influence in the output of the prediction. Examples are the email sender IP address, the number words, the number of capital words, and so on.

- Training data

    - This is a portion of the observations used to train a chosen ML algorithm to produce a model. A general practice in the industry is to split the collected data into three portions: training data, validation data, and test data. The test data portion is roughly about 70 percent or 80 percent of the original data set.

- Validation data

    - This is a portion of the observations used to evaluate the performance of the ML model during the model tuning process.

- Test data

    - This is a portion of the observations used to evaluate the performance of the ML model after the tuning process is finalized.

- ML algorithm

  - This is a collection of steps that run in an iterative manner to extract insights or patterns from given test data. The main goal of an ML algorithm is to learn a mapping from inputs to outputs. There is already a well-known set of ML algorithms to choose from. The challenge is in selecting the right algorithm to use to solve a particular ML problem. For the email spam detection problem, one might pick the naive Bayes algorithm.

- Model

  - After an ML algorithm learns from the given input data, it produces a model, which is used to perform predictions or make decisions on the new data. A model is represented by a mathematical formula. The goal is to produce a generalized model and perform well against any new data it has not seen before.

The relationship between ML algorithm, data, and model is best illustrated in Figure 8-2.

model = algorithm(data)

Figure 8-2. *Relationship between ML algorithm, data, and model*

One important point to remember when applying machine learning is to never train an ML algorithm with test data because that will defeat the purpose of producing a generalized ML model. Another important point to note is that ML is a vast field, and as you dig deeper into this field, undoubtedly you will discover many more terms and concepts. Ideally this basic set of terminologies will help you get started on this journey of learning ML.

Machine Learning Types

As mentioned earlier, ML is about teaching machines to learn patterns from previous data for the purpose of making decisions or predictions. These tasks are widely applicable to many different types of problem, and each problem type requires a different way of learning. Broadly speaking, there are three types of learning, as shown in Figure 8-3.

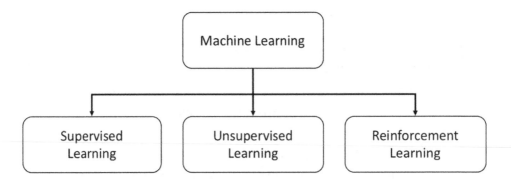

Figure 8-3. *Different machine learning types*

Supervised Learning

Among the different learning types, this one is widely used and more popular because it can help solve a large class of problems in the area of classification and regression.

Classification is about classifying the observations into one of the discrete or categorical classes of labels. Examples of classification problems include predicting whether an email is a spam email; whether a product review is positive or negative; whether an image contains a dog, cat, dolphin, or bird; whether the topic of a news article is about sports, medicine, politics, or religion; whether a particular handwritten digit is a 1 or 2; and whether the revenue for Q4 will meet expectations. When the result of the classification has only two discrete values, that is called *binary classification*, and when it has more than two discrete values, that is called *multiclass classification*.

Regression is about predicting real values from observations. Unlike classification, the predicted value is not discrete, but rather it is continuous. Examples of regression problems include predicting the house price based on their location and size, predicting the stock price of a company, predicting the income of a person based the background and education of a set of people, and so on.

One key distinguishing factor between this type of learning from the others is each observation in the training data must contain a label, whether that is discrete or continuous. In other words, the correct answers are provided to the algorithm so it can learn by iterating and incrementally improving its predictions on the training data, and it will stop once an acceptable error margin is achieved.

A simple mental model to use to distinguish classification from regression is that classification is about separating the data into various buckets and regression is about fitting the best line to the data. See Figure 8-4 for the visual representation of this mental model.

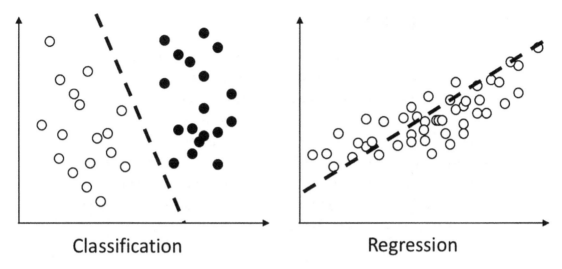

Classification   Regression

Figure 8-4. *Mental model of classification and regression*

There is a large collection of algorithms that are designed to solve the classification and regression machine learning problems. This chapter will focus on only the ones that are supported in the Spark MLlib component, as listed in Table 8-1.

Table 8-1. *Supervised Learning Algorithms in MLlib*

Tasks	Algorithms
Classification	Logistic regression
	Decision tree
	Random forest
	Gradient-boosted tree
	Linear support vector machine
	Naive Bayes
Regression	Linear regression
	Generalized linear regression
	Decision tree regression
	Random forest regression
	Gradient-boosted regression

Unsupervised Learning

The name of this learning method implies there is no supervision; in other words, the data used to train the ML algorithm wouldn't contain the labels, and it is up to the learning algorithm to come up with its own findings. This learning type is designed to solve a different class of problem, that is, to discover the hidden structure or patterns inside the data, and it is up to us, the humans, to interpret the meaning behind those insights. As it turns out, a certain type of hidden structure called *clustering*, which is an exploratory analysis technique in data analytics, is a good method for structuring information to derive meaningful relationships or find similarities of the observations within the clusters. Figure 8-5 depicts examples of clusters.

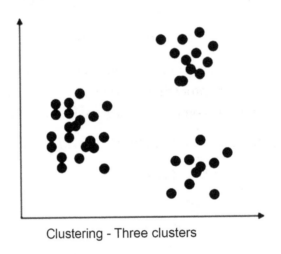

Clustering - Three clusters

Figure 8-5. *Visualization of clustering*

Surprisingly, there are many practical problems that can be solved by this type of learning method. Let's say there is a large collection documents, and there is no prior knowledge of which topic a particular document belongs to; you can use unsupervised learning to discover the clusters of related documents, and from there you can assign a topic to each of the clusters. Another interesting and common problem that the unsupervised learning method can help solve is in the area of credit card fraud detection, which is a type of anomaly detection. After the grouping of user credit card transactions into clusters, it is not too difficult to spot the outliers, which might represent the abnormal credit card transactions after it was stolen by a thief.

Table 8-2 lists the supported algorithms for the unsupervised learning method.

Table 8-2. *Unsupervised Learning Algorithms in MLlib*

Tasks	Algorithms
Clustering	K-means
	Latent Dirichlet allocation
	Bisecting k-means
	Gaussian

Reinforcement Learning

Unlike the first two types of learning, this one doesn't learn from data. Instead, it learns from interacting with an environment through a series of actions, and the feedback loop provides the information it uses to make adjustments with the goal of maximizing some reward. In other words, it learns from its own experience.

Until recently, this type of learning hasn't gotten as much attention as the first two because it has not yet had significant practical success beyond computer games. In 2016, Google DeepMind was able to successfully apply this learning type to play an Atari game and then went on to incorporate it into its AlphaGo program, which defeated a world champion in the game of Go.

At this point, Spark MLlib doesn't include any reinforcement learning algorithms. The following sections will focus on the first two types of learnings.

Note   The term *supervised* metaphorically refers to a teacher (human) who "supervises" the learner, which is the ML algorithm, by specifically providing the answers (labels) along with a set of examples (training data).

Machine Learning Process

To be effective at applying machine learning to the development of intelligent applications, you should consider studying and adopting a set of best practices that most ML practitioners follow. It has been said that applying machine learning effectively is a craft, half-science and half-art. Fortunately, there is a well-known and structured process that consists of a series of steps to help with providing reasonable repeatability and consistency, which is depicted in Figure 8-6.

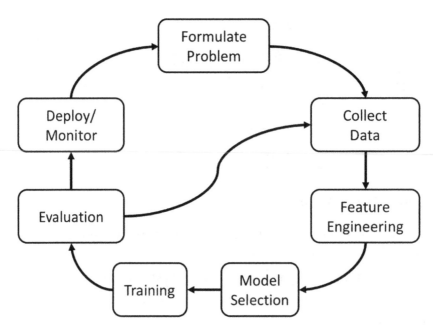

Figure 8-6. *Machine learning application development process*

It may be obvious, but the first step in this process is to clearly understand the business objective or challenge that you think ML can help you with. It is beneficial to evaluate alternative solutions to ML to understand the cost and trade-offs. Sometimes it is faster to go with a simple rule-based solution to start with. If a strong confidence has established that ML is a better choice in terms of delivering valuable business insights efficiently, quickly, and broadly across many scenarios without humans in the loop, then proceed to the next step. After the problem is clearly understood, the next part is to establish a set of success metrics that all stakeholders can agree on.

The next step is to identify and collect the necessary types of and an appropriate amount of data to support the problem at hand. The quality and quantity of the collected data will have a direct impact on the performance of the trained ML model. One important point to keep in mind is to make sure the collected data is as much as possible representative of the problem you are trying to solve. The phrase "garbage in, garbage out" is still very much applicable in characterizing a key limitation in ML.

Feature engineering is one of the most important and time-consuming steps in this process. This step is mainly about data cleaning and using domain knowledge to identify key attributes or features about observations that will be useful to the ML algorithms to learn the direct relationship between the training data and provided labels. The data cleaning task is usually done using the exploratory data analysis framework to gain a better understand of the data in terms of data distribution, correlations, outliers, and so on. Feature engineering is a fairly expensive step because of the need of involving humans in the loop and using their domain knowledge of the problem that is being solved. DL has shown to be a superior learning method over ML because it can automatically extract features with human intervention.

The next step after feature engineering is selecting an appropriate ML model or algorithm and training it. Given that there are many available algorithms to solve similar ML tasks, the question is, what is the best model or models to use? Like most things, deciding on the best one requires a combination of having a good understanding of the problem at hand, having good working knowledge of the various characteristics of each algorithm, and having the experience to apply them to similar problems in the past. In other words, it is half-science and half-art when it comes to selecting the best algorithm. It may require some experimentation to arrive at the best algorithm. Once an algorithm is selected, then let it learn from the data produced in the feature engineering step. The expected output is a model, and you then proceed to perform model evaluation to see how well it performs. The goal of all the previous steps is to produce a model that is generalized, meaning that it performs well on data it has never seen before.

Another important step in the ML development process is the model evaluation task. It is both necessary and challenging. The goal of this step is to not only answer the question of how well a model performs but also to know when to stop tuning the model because its performance has reached the established success metrics in the first step. The evaluation process can be done offline and online. The former case refers to evaluating the model using the training data, and the latter case refers to evaluating the model using live or new data. There is a set of commonly used metrics to understand the model performance, for example, precision, recalls, F1 score, AUC, and so on. The art part of this step is to understand which metrics are applicable for certain ML tasks. The result of the model performance determines whether to proceed to the production deployment step or to go back to the step of collecting more data or a different type of data.

This information is meant to provide an overview of the ML development process and not meant to be comprehensive. It can easily take a whole chapter to adequately cover the inner details of each step and the best practices.

Spark Machine Learning Library

The remaining sections of this chapter will cover the main features inside the Spark MLlib component and provide examples of applying ML algorithms in Spark to each of the following ML tasks: classification, regression, clustering, and recommendations.

Note   In the Python world, scikit-learn is one of the most popular open source machine learning libraries. It is built on top of the NumPy, SciPy, and matplotlib libraries, and it provides a set of supervised and unsupervised learning algorithms. It is designed to be simple and efficient tool; therefore, it is a perfect tool to learn and practice machine learning on a single machine. The moment the size of the data exceeds the storage capacity of a single machine, that's when it is time to switch to Spark MLlib.

There are many ML libraries to choose from. In the era of big data, there are two reasons to pick Spark MLlib over the other options. The first one is the ease of use. Spark SQL provides a user-friendly way of performing data exploratory analysis, and the MLlib library provides a means to build, manage, and persist complex ML pipelines. The second reason is performing ML at scale. The combination of the Spark unified data analytic engine and the MLlib library can support training machine learning models with billions of observations and thousands of features.

Machine Learning Pipelines

As you can see from the previous section, the ML process is essentially a pipeline that consists of a series of steps that run in a sequential manner and that usually need to be repeated several times to arrive at an optimal model. Aligning with the goal of making practical machine learning easy, Spark MLlib provides a set of abstractions to help simplify the steps of data cleaning, featuring engineering, model training, model tuning, and evaluation as well as organizing them into a pipeline to make it easy to understand, maintain, and repeat. The pipeline concept is actually inspired from the scikit-learn library mentioned earlier.

There are four main abstractions to form an end-to-end ML pipeline: transformers, estimators, evaluators, and pipelines. They provide a set of standard interfaces to make it easy to understand someone else's pipeline. Figure 8-7 depicts the similarity between the core steps in the ML process and the main abstractions MLlib provides.

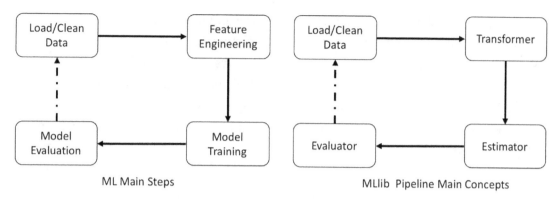

Figure 8-7. *Similarity between ML main steps and MLlib pipeline main concepts*

The one thing in common across these abstractions is that their inputs and output are mostly DataFrames, which means it is necessary to convert the input data into a DataFrame to work with these abstractions.

Note   Like other components within the Spark unified data analytics engine, MLlib is switching to DataFrame-based APIs to provide more user-friendly APIs and to take advantage of the optimizations the Spark SQL engine provides. The new APIs are available in the package `org.apache.spark.ml`. The first MLlib version was developed on RDD-based APIs, and it is still supported, but it is in maintenance mode only. The old APIs are available in the package `org.apache.spark.mllib`. Once the feature parity is reached, then the RDD-based APIs will be deprecated.

Transformers

Transformers are designed to transform data in the DataFrame by manipulating one or more columns during the feature engineering step and the model evaluation step. The transforming process is in the context of building features that will be consumed by the ML algorithm to learn. This process usually involves adding or removing columns (features), converting the column values from text to numerical value, or normalizing the values of a particular column.

There is a strict requirement about working with ML algorithms in MLlib; they require all features to be in the Double data type, including the label.

From a technical perspective, a transformer has a function called `transform` that performs transformations on the input column, and the result is stored in the output column. The input column and output column names can be specified during the construction of a transformer. If they are not specified, the default column names ("`inputCol`", "`outputCol`") are used. Figure 8-8 depicts what a transformer looks like; the shaded column in DF1 represents the input column, and the darker shaded column in DF2 represents the output column.

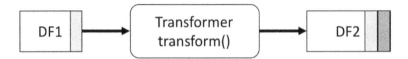

Figure 8-8. *Transformer input and output*

There are many types of data transformations for each data type; therefore, it is not surprising there are roughly about 30 transformers available in MLlib. Table 8-3 shows the various transformers for each type of data transformation.

Table 8-3. *Transformers for Different Transformation Types*

Type	Transformers
General	SQLTransformer
	VectorAssembler
Numeric data	Bucketizer
	QuantileDiscretizer
	StandardScaler
	MixMaxScaler
	MaxAbsScaler
	Normalizer
Text data	IndexToString
	OneHotEncoder
	Tokenizer, RegexTokenizer
	StopWordsRemover
	NGram
	HashingTF

The following section will cover a few commonly used transformers.

The Binarizer transformer simply transforms the values of an input column into two groups. The first group contains the values that are less than or equal to the specified threshold, and the value in the output column will be zero. The value in the output column will 1 for the other values. The input column must be of type double or VectorUDT. Listing 8-1 transforms the temperature column values into two buckets.

Listing 8-1. Using the Binarizer Transformer to Convert the Temperature into Two Buckets

```
import org.apache.spark.ml.feature.Binarizer

val arrival_data = spark.createDataFrame(Seq(("SFO", "B737", 18, 95.1, "late"),
                                     ("SEA", "A319", 5, 65.7, "ontime"),
                                     ("LAX", "B747", 15, 31.5, "late"),
                                     ("ATL", "A319", 14, 40.5, "late") ))
                                     .toDF("origin", "model", "hour",
                                     "temperature", "arrival")

val binarizer = new Binarizer().setInputCol("temperature")
                          .setOutputCol("freezing")
                          .setThreshold(35.6)
binarizer.transform(arrival_data).show

// show the current values of the parameters in binarizer transformer
binarizer.explainParams

inputCol: input column name (current: temperature)
outputCol: output column name (default: binarizer_60430bb4e97f__output,
current: freezing)
threshold: threshold used to binarize continuous features (default: 0.0,
current: 35.6)

// show the transformation result
binarizer.transform(arrival_data).select("temperature", "freezing").show
+------------+---------+
| temperature| freezing|
+------------+---------+
|        95.1|      1.0|
```

```
|           65.7|         1.0|
|           31.5|         0.0|
|           40.5|         1.0|
+-----------+---------+
```

The Bucketizer transformer is a general version of the Binarizer where it can transform the column values into buckets of your choice. The way to control the number of buckets as well as the range of values for each bucket is by specifying a list of bucket borders in the form of an array of double values. This transformer is useful in the scenario where the values of a column are continuous values, and you want to transform them into an easier-to-understand representation. For example, you have a column that contains the income amount of each person who lives in a particular state, and you want to bucket their incomes into the following buckets: high income, middle income, low income, and so on.

The value bucket border array must be of type double, and they must abide by the following requirements:

- The smallest bucket border value must be less than the minimum value in the input column in the DataFrame.

- The largest bucket border value must be greater than the maximum value in the input column in the DataFrame.

- There must be at least three bucket borders in the input array, which creates two buckets.

In the case of a person's income, it is fairly easy to know the smallest income amount is 0; then the smallest bucket border value can just be something less than 0. If it is not possible to predict the minimum column value, then specify negative infinity. Similarly, if it is not possible to predict the maximum column value, then specify positive infinity. See Listing 8-2 for an example of using this transformer to bucket the temperature column into three buckets, which means the bucket border array must contain at least four values. The output is sorted by the temperature column to make it easier to see.

Listing 8-2. Using the Bucketizer Transformer to Convert the Temperature into Three Buckets

```
import org.apache.spark.ml.feature.Bucketizer

val bucketBorders = Array(-1.0, 32.0, 70.0, 150.0)
```

```
val bucketer = new Bucketizer().setSplits(bucketBorders)
                                .setInputCol("temperature")
                                .setOutputCol("intensity")

val output = bucketer.transform(arrival_data)

output.select("temperature", "intensity")
        .orderBy("temperature")
        .show
```

```
+------------+----------+
| temperature| intensity|
+------------+----------+
|        31.5|       0.0|
|        40.5|       1.0|
|        65.7|       1.0|
|        95.1|       2.0|
+------------+----------+
```

The OneHotEncoder transformer is commonly used when working with numeric categorical values. If the categorical values are of string type, then first apply the StringIndexer estimator to convert them to a numerical type. The OneHotEncoder transformer essentially maps a numeric categorical value into a binary vector to purposely remove the implicit ranking of the numeric categorical values. For example, the following data represents student majors, and each major is assigned an ordinal value, which seems to suggest a certain major is higher than the others. To remove such unintended bias during the ML training step, this transformer is used to convert the ordinal value into an vector. See Listing 8-3 for an example of using this transformer.

Listing 8-3. Using the OneHotEncoder Transformer to Convert the Ordinal Value of the Categorical Values

```
import org.apache.spark.ml.feature.OneHotEncoder

val student_major_data = spark.createDataFrame(Seq(("John", "Math", 3),
                                    ("Mary", "Engineering", 2),
                                    ("Jeff", "Philosophy", 7),
                                    ("Jane", "Math", 3),
                                    ("Lyna", "Nursing", 4) ))
```

```
                                          .toDF("user", "major",
                                          "majorIdx")

val oneHotEncoder = new OneHotEncoder().setInputCol("majorIdx")
                                    .setOutputCol("majorVect")
oneHotEncoder.transform(student_major_data).show()

+----+------------+---------+---------------+
|user|       major| majorIdx|      majorVect|
+----+------------+---------+---------------+
|John|        Math|        3|  (7,[3],[1.0])|
|Mary| Engineering|        2|  (7,[2],[1.0])|
|Jeff|  Philosophy|        7|      (7,[],[])|
|Jane|        Math|        3|  (7,[3],[1.0])|
|Lyna|     Nursing|        4| ( 7,[4],[1.0])|
+----+------------+---------+---------------+
```

Another common need when working with string categorical values is to convert them into ordinal values, which can be done using the StringIndexer estimator. This estimator will be described in the "Estimators" section.

There are many interesting machine learning use cases where the input is in free-form text. It requires a few transformations to convert free-form text into a numerical representation that ML algorithms can consume. Among them are tokenization and counting word frequency.

Most likely you can guess what the Tokenizer transformer does. It performs the tokenization on a string of words that are separated by spaces and returns an array of words. If there is a need to perform tokenization with a different delimiter, then you can use RegexTokenizer. See Listing 8-4 for an example of using the Tokenizer transformer.

Listing 8-4. Using the Tokenizer Transformer to Perform Tokenization

```
import org.apache.spark.ml.feature.Tokenizer
import org.apache.spark.sql.functions._

val text_data = spark.createDataFrame(Seq(
                          (1, "Spark is a unified data analytics
                          engine"),
                          (2, "It is fun to work with Spark"),
```

```
                              (3, "There is a lot of exciting
                              sessions at upcoming Spark summit"),
                              (4, "mllib transformer estimator
                              evaluator and pipelines")  )
                   ).toDF("id", "line")

val tokenizer = new Tokenizer().setInputCol("line").setOutputCol("words")
val tokenized = tokenizer.transform(text_data)

tokenized.select("words").withColumn("tokens", size(col("words"))).
show(false)
```

```
+--------------------------------------------------------------------+
|   words                                                  | tokens|
+--------------------------------------------------------------------+
|[spark, is, a, unified, data, analytics, engine]          |      7|
|[spark, is cool, and, it, is, fun, to, work, with,        |     11|
|[there, is, a, lot, of, exciting, sessions, at,           |
|  upcoming, spark, summit]                                |     11|
|[mllib, transformer, estimator, evaluator, and, pipelines]|      6|
+--------------------------------------------------------------------+
```

Stop words are the commonly used words in a language. In the context of natural language processing or machine learning, stop words tend to add unnecessary noises rather than provide any meaningful contributions. Therefore, it is common that the stop word removal step is done immediately after the tokenization step. The StopWordsRemover transformer is designed to help with this step. As of Spark 2.3, the stop words for the following languages are included in the Spark distribution for you to use: Danish, Dutch, English, Finnish, French, German, Hungarian, Italian, Norwegian, Portuguese, Russian, Spanish, Swedish, and Turkish. It is designed to be flexible such that it can use a set of user-provided stop words by reading them from a provided directory path. To use the stop words of a particular language, first call StopWordsRemover.loadDefaultStopWords(<language in lower case>) to load them and then provide them to an instance of StopWordsRemover. Additionally, you can request this transformer to perform stop word filtering with case insensitivity if necessary. See Listing 8-5 for an example of using the StopWordsRemover transformer to remove English stop words.

Listing 8-5. Using the StopWordsRemover Transformer to Remove English Stop Words from the Words in the Tokenization Example

```
import org.apache.spark.ml.feature.StopWordsRemover

val enStopWords = StopWordsRemover.loadDefaultStopWords("english")

val remover = new StopWordsRemover().setStopWords(enStopWords)
                                    .setInputCol("words")
                                    .setOutputCol("filtered")

// use the tokenized from Listing 8-5 example
val cleanedTokens = remover.transform(tokenized)

cleanedTokens.select("words","filtered").show(false)
```

```
+------------------------------------------------------------------------+-------------------------------------------------------------+
|words                                                                   |filtered                                                     |
+------------------------------------------------------------------------+-------------------------------------------------------------+
|[spark, is, a, unified, data, analytics, engine]                        |[spark, unified, data, analytics, engine]                    |
|[spark, is, cool, and, it, is, fun, to, work, with, spark]              |[spark, cool, fun, work, spark]                              |
|[there, is, a, lot, of, exciting, sessions, at, upcoming, spark, summit]|[lot, exciting, sessions, upcoming, spark, summit]           |
|[mllib, transformer, estimator, evaluator, and, pipelines]             |[mllib, transformer, estimator, evaluator, pipelines]        |
+------------------------------------------------------------------------+-------------------------------------------------------------+
```

The HashingTF transformer is used to transform the words into a numeric representation by computing the frequency of each word in each line. Each word is mapped into an index by applying a hash function called MurmurHash3. This approach is efficient, but it suffers from a potential hash collision, meaning multiple words may map into the same index. One way to minimize the collision is by specifying a large number of buckets that is a power of 2 to help with evenly distributing the words. The example in Listing 8-6 will feed the filtered column from the example in Listing 8-6 into the HashingTF transformer.

Listing 8-6. Using the HashingTF Transformer to Transform Words into a Numerical Representation via Hashing and Counting

```
import org.apache.spark.ml.feature.HashingTF

val tf = new HashingTF().setInputCol("filtered")
                        .setOutputCol("TFOut")
                        .setNumFeatures(4096)

val tfResult = tf.transform(cleanedTokens)
tfResult.select("filtered", "TFOut").show(false)
```

```
+-------------------------------------------------+-------------------------------------------------------------------------+
|filtered                                         |TFOut                                                                    |
+-------------------------------------------------+-------------------------------------------------------------------------+
|[spark, unified, data, analytics, engine]        |(4096,[991,1185,1461,3377,3717],[1.0,1.0,1.0,1.0,1.0])                    |
|[spark, cool, fun, work, spark]                  |(4096,[251,1185,1575,2435],[1.0,2.0,1.0,1.0])                             |
|[lot, exciting, sessions, upcoming, spark, summit]|(4096,[724,1185,1255,1962,2966,3023],[1.0,1.0,1.0,1.0,1.0,1.0])          |
|[mllib, transformer, estimator, evaluator, pipelines]|(4096,[994,2132,2697,3522,3894],[1.0,1.0,1.0,1.0,1.0])               |
+-------------------------------------------------+-------------------------------------------------------------------------+
```

The last transformer this section covers is VectorAssembler, which simply combines
a set of columns into a vector column. In machine learning terminology, that is the
equivalent of combining individual features into single-vector features for the ML
algorithm to learn. The type of the individual input column must be one of the following
types: numeric, boolean, or vector. The output vector column contains the values of all
the columns in the specified order. This transformer is used practically in every single
ML pipeline, and its output will be passed into an estimator. See Listing 8-7 for an
example of using the VectorAssembler transformer.

Listing 8-7. Using the VectorAssembler Transformer to Combine Features into a
Vector Feature

```
import org.apache.spark.ml.feature.VectorAssembler

val arrival_features  = spark.createDataFrame(Seq(
                                       (18, 95.1, true),
                                       (5, 65.7, true), (15, 31.5,
                                       false),
                                       (14, 40.5, false) ))
                                  .toDF("hour", "temperature",
                                  "on_time")

val assembler = new VectorAssembler().setInputCols(Array("hour",
"temperature", "on_time"))
                                  .setOutputCol("features")

val output = assembler.transform(arrival_features)
output.show
```

```
+-----+-----------+--------+---------------+
| hour| temperature| on_time|        features|
+-----+-----------+--------+---------------+
|   18|        95.1|    true| [18.0,95.1,1.0]|
|    5|        65.7|    true| [5.0,65.7,1.0]|
```

```
|    15|          31.5|   false|  [15.0,31.5,0.0]|
|    14|          40.5|   false|  [14.0,40.5,0.0]|
+-----+-----------+--------+----------------+
```

Knowing how the transformers work and the available transformers in MLlib plays an important role in the feature engineering step of the ML development process. Generally, the output of a VectorAssembler transformer will be consumed by an estimator, which will be covered in the next section.

Estimators

The next concept is the estimators, which are an abstraction for either an ML learning algorithm that trains on data or any other algorithm that operates on data. It is rather confusing that an estimator can be one of two kinds of algorithm. An example of the first type is the ML algorithm called LinearRegression, which is used for a regression task such as predicting house prices. An example of the second algorithm is StringIndexer, which encodes categorical values of a column into indices, such that the index value for each categorical value is based on the frequency it appears in the entire input column of a DataFrame. At a high level, this kind of estimator transforms the values of a column into another column; however, it requires two passes over the entire DataFrame to produce the expected output.

From a technical perspective, an estimator has a function called fit that applies an algorithm on the input column, and the result is encapsulated in an object type called Model, which is a Transformer type. The input column and output column names can be specified during the construction of an estimator. Figure 8-9 depicts what an estimator looks like and its input and output.

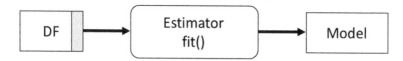

Figure 8-9. *Estimator and its input and output*

To give a sense of the two types of estimator, Table 8-4 provides a subset of the available estimators in MLlib.

Table 8-4. *Sample of Available Estimators in MLlib*

Type	Estimators
Machine learning Algorithms	LogisticRegression
	DecisionTreeClassifier
	RandomForestClassifier
	LinearRegression
	RandomForestRegressor
	KMeans
	LDA
	BisectingKMeans
Data Transformation algorithms	IDF
	RFormula
	StringIndexer
	OneHotEncoderEstimator
	StandardScaler
	MixMaxScaler
	MaxAbsScaler
	Word2Vec

The following section provides a few examples of commonly used estimators when working with text and numeric data.

RFormula is an interesting and general-purpose estimator where the transformation logic is expressed declaratively. It can handle both numeric and categorial values, and the output it produces is a vector of features. MLlib borrows the idea of this estimator from the R language, and currently it supports only a subset of the operators available in R. The basic and supported operators are listed in Table 8-5. It will take a little bit of time to understand the transformation language to take full advantage of the flexibility and power of the RFormula estimator.

Table 8-5. *Supported Operators in the RFormula Transformer*

Operator	Description
~	Delimiter between the target and the terms.
+	Concatenate terms.
-	Remove a term.
:	Interaction between other terms to create new feature. Multiplication will be used for numeric value and binarized for categorical values.
.	All columns except the target.

The following example specifies the label is the arrival column and uses all the remaining columns as features. In addition, it creates a new feature using the interaction between the hour and temperature columns. Since these two columns are of numeric type, their values will be multiplied. Listing 8-8 contains the code for the example described earlier.

Listing 8-8. Using the RFomula Transformer to Create a Feature Vector

```
import org.apache.spark.ml.feature.RFormula
val arrival_data = spark.createDataFrame(Seq(("SFO", "B737", 18, 95.1, "late"),
                                ("SEA", "A319", 5, 65.7, "ontime"),
                                ("LAX", "B747", 15, 31.5, "late"),
                                ("ATL", "A319", 14, 40.5, "late") ))
                                .toDF("origin", "model", "hour",
                                "temperature", "arrival")

val formula = new RFormula().setFormula("arrival ~ . + hour:temperature")
                        .setFeaturesCol("features")
                        .setLabelCol("label")

// call fit function first, which returns a model (type of transformer),
then call transform
val output = formula.fit(arrival_data).transform(arrival_data)

output.select("*").show(false)
```

```
+------+-----+----+-----------+-------+------------------------------------------+-----+
|origin|model|hour|temperature|arrival|features                                  |label|
+------+-----+----+-----------+-------+------------------------------------------+-----+
|SFO   |B737 |18  |95.1       |late   |(8,[0,5,6,7],[1.0,18.0,95.1,1711.8])      |0.0  |
|SEA   |A319 |5   |65.7       |ontime |[0.0,0.0,1.0,1.0,0.0,5.0,65.7,328.5]      |1.0  |
|LAX   |B747 |15  |31.5       |late   |(8,[4,5,6,7],[1.0,15.0,31.5,472.5])       |0.0  |
|ATL   |A319 |14  |40.5       |late   |[0.0,1.0,0.0,1.0,0.0,14.0,40.5,567.0]     |0.0  |
+------+-----+----+-----------+-------+------------------------------------------+-----+
```

One of the commonly used estimators for working with text is the IDF estimator. Its name is an acronym for *inverse document frequency*. This estimator is often used right after the text is tokenized and term frequency is computed. The idea behind this estimator is to compute the importance or weight of each word by counting the number of documents it appears in. The intuition behind this idea is that a word with high occurrence and wide prevalence would be less important, for example, the word *the*. Inversely, a word with high occurrence and appearing in only a few documents would indicate a higher importance, for example, the world *classification*. In the context of a DataFrame, a document refers to a row. A keen reader would figure out that it requires going through every single row in order to compute the importance of each word, and therefore IDF is an estimator, not a transformer. The example in Listing 8-9 will chain the Tokenizer and HashingTF transformers together with the IDF estimator. The fit function of an estimator is an eager evaluation function that will trigger job.

Listing 8-9. Using the IDF Estimator to Compute the Weight of Each Word

```
import org.apache.spark.ml.feature.Tokenizer
import org.apache.spark.ml.feature.HashingTF
import org.apache.spark.ml.feature.IDF

val text_data = spark.createDataFrame(Seq(
                        (1, "Spark is a unified data analytics
                        engine"),
                        (2, "Spark is cool and it is fun to
                        work with Spark"),
                        (3, "There is a lot of exciting
                        sessions at upcoming Spark summit"),
                        (4, "mllib transformer estimator
                        evaluator and pipelines")  )
                ).toDF("id", "line")
```

```
val tokenizer = new Tokenizer().setInputCol("line")
                                .setOutputCol("words")

// the output column of the Tokenizer transformer is the input to HashingTF
val tf = new HashingTF().setInputCol("words")
                        .setOutputCol("wordFreqVect")
                        .setNumFeatures(4096)

val tfResult = tf.transform(tokenizer.transform(text_data))

// the output of the HashingTF transformer is the input to IDF estimator
val idf = new IDF().setInputCol("wordFreqVect")
                   .setOutputCol("features")

// since IDF is an estimator, call the fit function
val idfModel = idf.fit(tfResult)
// the returned object is a Model, which is of type Transformer
val weightedWords = idfModel.transform(tfResult)

weightedWords.select("label", "features").show(false)

weightedWords.printSchema

 |-- id: integer (nullable = false)
 |-- line: string (nullable = true)
 |-- words: array (nullable = true)
 |    |-- element: string (containsNull = true)
 |-- wordFreqVect: vector (nullable = true)
 |-- features: vector (nullable = true)

// the feature column contains a vector for the weight of each word, since
it is long, the output is not included //below
weightedWords.select("wordFreqVect", "features").show(false)
```

A good estimator to know when working with text data that contains categorical values is the StringIndexer estimator. It encodes a categorical value into an index based on its frequencies such that the most frequent categorical value gets an index value of 0 and so on. For this estimator to come up with an index value for a categorical value, it first has to count the frequency of each one of those and finally assign an index value; in other words, it must see all the values of the input column in the DataFrame. If the input column is numeric, this estimator will cast it string type before computing its frequency. Listing 8-10 provides an example of using the StringIndexer estimator to encode the movie genre.

Listing 8-10. Using the StringIndex Estimator to Encode the Movie Genre

```
import org.apache.spark.ml.feature.StringIndexer

val movie_data = spark.createDataFrame(Seq(
                                        (1, "Comedy"),
                                        (2, "Action"),
                                        (3, "Comedy"),
                                        (4, "Horror"),
                                        (5, "Action"),
                                        (6, "Comedy")  )
                              ).toDF("id", "genre")

val movieIndexer = new StringIndexer().setInputCol("genre")
                                .setOutputCol("genreIdx")

// first fit the data
val movieIndexModel = movieIndexer.fit(movie_data)

// use returned transformer to transform the data
val indexedMovie = movieIndexModel.transform(movie_data)

indexedMovie.orderBy("genreIdx").show()
+---+-------+---------+
| id|  genre| genreIdx|
+---+-------+---------+
|  3| Comedy|      0.0|
|  6| Comedy|      0.0|
|  1| Comedy|      0.0|
|  5| Action|      1.0|
|  2| Action|      1.0|
|  4| Horror|      2.0|
+---+-------+---------+
```

As shown earlier, this estimator assigns the index based on the descending order of the frequency. This default behavior can be easily changed to ascending order of the frequency; in fact, it supports two other ordering types: descending

353

alphabet and ascending alphabet. To change the default ordering type, simply call the setStringOrderType("<ordering type>") function with one of the following values: frequencyDesc, frequencyAsc, alphabetDesc, alphabetAsc.

Another useful estimator for working with categorical values is OneHotEncoderEstimator, which encodes the index of a categorical value as a binary vector. The OneHotEncoder transformer has been deprecated starting with Spark 2.3.0 because of its stateless nature, which makes it not usable on new testing data where the number of categories may differ from the training data. This estimator is often used in conjunction with the StringIndexer estimator where the output of StringIndexer becomes the input of this estimator. Listing 8-11 demonstrates using StringIndexer and OneHotEncoderEstimator together.

Listing 8-11. OneHotEncoderEstimator Consumes the Output of the StringIndexer Estimator

```
import org.apache.spark.ml.feature.OneHotEncoderEstimator

// the input column genreIdx is the output column of StringIndex in
listing 8-9
val oneHotEncoderEst = new OneHotEncoderEstimator().setInputCols
(Array("genreIdx"))
                                .setOutputCols(Array("genreIdxVector"))

// fit the indexedMovie data produced in listing 8-10
val oneHotEncoderModel = oneHotEncoderEst.fit(indexedMovie)

val oneHotEncoderVect = oneHotEncoderModel.transform(indexedMovie)

oneHotEncoderVect .orderBy("genre").show()

+---+-------+---------+---------------+
| id| genre | genreIdx| genreIdxVector|
+---+-------+---------+---------------+
|  5| Action|     1.0|  (2,[1],[1.0])|
|  2| Action|     1.0|  (2,[1],[1.0])|
|  3| Comedy|     2.0|      (2,[],[])|
|  6| Comedy|     2.0|      (2,[],[])|
|  1| Comedy|     2.0|      (2,[],[])|
|  4| Horror|     0.0|  (2,[0],[1.0])|
+---+-------+---------+---------------+
```

Another interesting estimator to know when working in free text is the Word2Vec estimator, which stands for *words to vector*. This estimator utilizes a well-known technique, called *word embeddings*, that converts word tokens into numeric vector representations such that semantically similar words are mapped to nearby points. The intuition behind this technique is that similar words tend to occur together and have similar context. In other words, two different words that have similar neighboring words are probably quite similar in meaning or are related. This technique has proven to be quite effective in a number of natural language processing applications such as word analogies, word similarities, entity recognition, and machine translation.

The Word2Vec estimator has a few important configurations, and appropriate values need to be provided to control the output that is based on the input. Table 8-6 describes the configurations.

Table 8-6. *Word2Vec Configurations*

Name	Default Value	Description
vectorSize	100	This is the size of the output vector.
windowSize	5	This is the number of words to be used as the context.
minCount	5	This is the minimum number of times a token must appear to be included in the output.
maxSentenceLength	1000	This specifies interaction between other terms to create a new feature. Multiplication will be used for numeric values, and binarized will be used for categorical values.

The example in Listing 8-12 demonstrates how to use the Word2Vec estimator and shows how to find similar words.

Listing 8-12. Using the Word2Vec Estimator to Compute Word Embeddings and Find Similar Words

```
import org.apache.spark.ml.feature.Word2Vec

val documentDF = spark.createDataFrame(Seq(
                        "Unified data analytics engine Spark".
                        split(" "),
                        "People use Hive for data analytics".
                        split(" "),
```

```
                              "MapReduce is not fading away".split(" ")
                          ).map(Tuple1.apply)).toDF("word")

val word2Vec = new Word2Vec().setInputCol("word")
                          .setOutputCol("feature") .setVectorSize(3)
                          .setMinCount(0)

val model = word2Vec.fit(documentDF)
val result = model.transform(documentDF)

result.show(false)
```

```
+-------------------------------------------+------------------------------------------------------------------------------------+
|word                                       |feature                                                                             |
+-------------------------------------------+------------------------------------------------------------------------------------+
|[Unified, data, analytics, engine, Spark]  |[-0.04857720620930195,-0.039790508151054386,-0.0047628857195377355] |
|[People, use, Hive, for, data, analytics]  |[-0.019269779634972412,-0.0019863341003656387,0.04896292210711787]  |
|[MapReduce, is, not, fading, away]         |[0.09048619866371155,0.02390633299946785,0.004982998222112656]      |
+-------------------------------------------+------------------------------------------------------------------------------------+
```

```
// find similar words to Spark, the result shows both Hive and MapReduce
are similar.
model.findSynonyms("Spark", 3).show
```

```
+----------+--------------------+
|      word|          similarity|
+----------+--------------------+
|    engine| 0.9133241772651672|
| MapReduce| 0.7623026967048645|
|      Hive| 0.7179173827171326|
+----------+--------------------+
```

```
// find similar words to Hive, the result shows Spark is similar
model.findSynonyms("Hive", 3).show
```

```
+-------+--------------------+
|   word|          similarity|
+-------+--------------------+
|  Spark| 0.7179174423217773|
| fading| 0.5859972238540649|
| engine| 0.43200281262397766|
+-------+--------------------+
```

The next estimators are about normalizing and standardizing numeric data. The reason for using these estimators is to ensure that learning algorithms that use distance as a measure don't place more weight on a feature with large values than another feature with smaller values.

Normalizing numeric data is the process of mapping its original range into a range from zero to one. This is especially helpful when observations have more than one attribute with different ranges. For example, say you have an employee's salary and their height. The value for salary is in the thousands, and the value for height is a single digit. This is what the MinMaxScaler estimator is designed for. This estimator linearly rescales each feature (column) individually to a common range of values of min and max using the column summary statistics. If the min value is 0.0 and max value is 3.0, then all the values will fall in that range. Listing 8-13 provides an example of working with MinMaxScaler using the employee_data dataset that has salary and height information. The magnitude between the values of these two features is pretty big, but after running through the MinMaxScaler, that is not the case anymore.

Listing 8-13. Using MinMaxScaler to Rescale Features

```
import org.apache.spark.ml.feature.MinMaxScaler
import org.apache.spark.ml.linalg.Vectors

val employee_data = spark.createDataFrame(Seq(
                              (1, Vectors.dense(125400, 5.3)),
                              (2, Vectors.dense(179100, 6.9)),
                              (3, Vectors.dense(154770, 5.2)),
                              (4, Vectors.dense(199650, 4.11))))
                          .toDF("empId", "features")

val minMaxScaler = new MinMaxScaler().setMin(0.0)
                              .setMax(5.0)
                              .setInputCol("features")
                              .setOutputCol("scaledFeatures")

val scalerModel = minMaxScaler.fit(employee_data)

val scaledData = scalerModel.transform(employee_data)

println(s"Features scaled to range: [${minMaxScaler.getMin},
${minMaxScaler.getMax}]")
```

Features scaled to range: [0.0, 5.0]

```
scaledData.select("features", "scaledFeatures").show(false)
```

```
+---------------+-------------------------------------+
|       features|                       scaledFeatures|
+---------------+-------------------------------------+
|  [125400.0,5.3]|         [0.0,2.1326164874551963]|
|  [179100.0,6.9]|         [3.616161616161616,5.0]|
|  [154770.0,5.2]| [1.9777777777777779,1.9534050179211468]|
|  [199650.0,4.11]|                       [5.0,0.0]|
+---------------+-------------------------------------+
```

Besides the numeric data normalizing, another operation that is often used for working with numeric data is called *standardization.* This operation is especially applicable when the numeric data has a distribution that is closed to a bell-shaped curve. The standardization operation can help shift the data to a normalized form where data will be in a range of -1 and 1, with a mean of 0. The reason for doing this is to help certain ML algorithms work better when the data has a good distribution around the mean of 0. The StandardScaler estimator is designed for the standardization operation. The example in Listing 8-14 uses the same input data set as in Listing 8-13. The output shows the values of the features are now centered around 0, with one unit of standard deviation.

Listing 8-14. Use StandardScaler to Standardize the Features Around the Mean of Zero

```
import org.apache.spark.ml.feature.StandardScaler
import org.apache.spark.ml.linalg.Vectors

val employee_data = spark.createDataFrame(Seq(
                            (1, Vectors.dense(125400, 5.3)),
                            (2, Vectors.dense(179100, 6.9)),
                            (3, Vectors.dense(154770, 5.2)),
                            (4, Vectors.dense(199650, 4.11))))
                        .toDF("empId", "features")

// set the unit standard deviation to true and center around the mean
val standardScaler = new StandardScaler().setWithStd(true)
                            .setWithMean(true)
```

```
                                              .setInputCol("features")
                                              .setOutputCol("scaledFeatures")

val standardMode = standardScaler.fit(employee_data)

val standardData = standardMode.transform(employee_data)

standardData.show(false)
+------+----------------+----------------------------------------------+
| empId|        features|                                scaledFeatures|
+------+----------------+----------------------------------------------+
|     1| [125400.0,5.3]| [-1.2290717420781212,-0.06743742573177587]|
|     2| [179100.0,6.9]|   [0.4490658767775897,1.3248191055048935]|
|     3| [154770.0,5.2]| [-0.3112523404805006,-0.15445345893406737]|
|     4| [199650.0,4.11]|   [1.091258205781032,-1.102928220839048]|
+------+----------------+----------------------------------------------+
```

There are many more estimators available in MLlib to perform numerous data transformations and mappings, and they all follow a standard abstraction that fits the input data and produces an instance of a model. The previous examples are meant to illustrate how to work with these estimators. Examples of the second kind of estimators, which are about ML algorithms, will be covered in the following sections.

Pipeline

In machine learning, it is common to run a sequence of steps to clean and transform data, then train one or more ML algorithms to learn from the data, and finally tune the model to achieve the best possible performance. The pipeline abstraction in MLlib is designed to make this workflow easier to develop and maintain. From the technical perspective, MLlib has a class called Pipeline, which is designed to manage a series of stages, and each one is represented by PipelineStage. A PipelineStage can be either a transformer or an estimator. The abstraction Pipeline is a type of estimator.

The first step in setting up a pipeline is to create a series of stages and then create an instance class Pipeline and configure it with an array of stages. The Pipeline will run those stages in the specified order. If a stage is a transformer, the transform() function is called. If a stage is an estimator, the fit() function is called to produce a transformer, and its tranform() function is called. Let's walk through a small workflow of processing text using the transformer and estimators covered in the previous sections. The small pipeline depicted in Figure 8-10 consists of two transformers and one estimator. When the `Pipeline.fit()` function is called, the input DataFrame that contains raw text will be passed into the `Tokenizer` transformer, and its output will be passed into the `HashingTF` transformer, which converts the words into features. The `Pipeline` recognizes that `LogisticRegression` is an estimator, so it will invoke the `fit` function with the computed features to produce a `LogisticRegressionModel`.

The code for the `Pipeline` depicted in Figure 8-10 is in Listing 8-15. Remember a `Pipeline` abstraction is an estimator. So once an instance of `Pipeline` is created and configured, the `fit()` function must be called with the training data as the input to trigger the execution of the stages, and it will be an instance of `PipelineModel`, which is a type of transformer. At this point, you can call the `transform()` function with the test data to perform predictions.

MLlib provides a feature called *ML persistence* that makes it easy to persist a pipeline or a model to disk and load it later for use. The cool thing is the persistence feature is designed to save the information in a language-neutral format such that a pipeline or model that is persisted in Scala can be read back in Java or Python, and vice versa.

Real-life production pipelines consist of many stages. When the number of stages gets large, it is difficult to understand the flow as well as challenging to maintain. MLlib pipeline abstraction can really help with these areas. Another key point to note is that both the `Pipeline` and `PipelineModel` objects are designed to help ensure both the training and test data flow through identical feature processing steps.

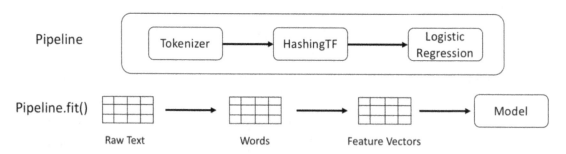

Figure 8-10. Example of a small pipeline

Listing 8-15. Using a Pipeline to Create a Small Workflow

```
import org.apache.spark.ml.{Pipeline, PipelineModel}
import org.apache.spark.ml.classification.LogisticRegression
import org.apache.spark.ml.feature.{HashingTF, Tokenizer}
```

```
val text_data = spark.createDataFrame(Seq(
                            (1, "Spark is a unified data analytics
                            engine", 0.0),
                            (2, "Spark is cool and it is fun to work
                            with Spark", 0.0),
                            (3, "There is a lot of exciting sessions
                            at upcoming Spark summit", 0.0),
                            (4, "signup to win a million dollars",
                            0.0)  )
                            ).toDF("id", "line", "label")

val tokenizer = new Tokenizer().setInputCol("line").setOutputCol("words")

val hashingTF = new HashingTF().setInputCol(tokenizer.getOutputCol)
                        .setOutputCol("features")
                        .setNumFeatures(4096)

val logisticReg = new LogisticRegression().setMaxIter(5)
                                    .setRegParam(0.01)

val pipeline = new Pipeline().setStages(Array(tokenizer, hashingTF,
logisticReg))
val logisticRegModel = pipeline.fit(text_data)

// persist model and pipeline
logisticRegModel.write.overwrite().save("/tmp/logistic-regression-model")
pipeline.write.overwrite().save("/tmp/logistic-regression-pipeline")

// load model and pipeline
val prevModel = PipelineModel.load("/tmp/spark-logistic-regression-model")
val prevPipeline = Pipeline.load("/tmp/logistic-regression-pipeline")
```

Model Tuning

The goal of the model tuning step is to train a model with the right set of parameters to achieve the best performance to meet the object defined in the first step of the ML development process. This step is usually tedious, repetitive, and time-consuming because it may involve trying different ML algorithms or a few sets of parameters. The purpose of this section is to describe a few tools MLlib provides to help with the laborious part of the model tuning step. It is not the intention of this section to show how to perform model tuning.

Before going into the details of the two tools that MLlib provides, let's first have a clear understanding of the following terminologies, where one of them is an input to the model tuning process.

- Model hyperparameters are

  - Configurations that are used to govern the machine learning algorithm training process

  - Configurations that are external to the model and can't be learned from the training data

  - Configurations that are provided by the machine learning practitioners before the training process starts

  - Configurations that are tuned for a given machine learning task through an iterative manner

- Model parameters are

  - Properties that are not provided by the machine learning practitioners

  - Properties of the training data that are learned during the training process

  - Properties that will be optimized during the training process

  - Properties of the model that are used to perform predictions

Examples of model hyperparameters include the number of clusters in the K-means clustering algorithm or the amount of regularization to apply in the logistic regression algorithm or the learning rate.

Examples of the model parameters include the coefficients in a linear regression model or the branch locations in the decision tree model.

The two commonly used classes in MLlib to help with model tuning are CrossValidator and TrainValidationSplit, and both them are of type Estimator. These classes are also known as *validators*. They both require the following inputs for them to work properly:

- The first input is about specifying what needs to be tuned, which can be either an ML algorithm or an instance of `Pipeline`. In other words, it must be of type `Estimator`.

- The second input is a set parameters to be used to tune the provided estimator. These parameters are also known as a *parameter grid* to search to find the best model. A convenient utility called `ParagramGridBuilder` is available to help with building the parameter grid.

- The last input is an evaluator to evaluate the performance of a model based on the held-out test data. For each different machine learning task, MLlib provides a specific evaluator, which can produce one or more evaluation metrics for you to understand the model performance. Commonly used machine learning metrics are supported, such as root mean square error, precision, recall, and accuracy.

At a high level, the aforementioned validators will perform the following steps with the given inputs:

1. The input data that contains the features is split into training and test based on the specified ratio.

2. For each training and test pair, the following steps are applied to each pair.

    - For each combination in the "parameter grid," the given estimator is fitted with the training data and the parameter combination. The output model is then evaluated by the specified evaluator against the test data. The performance metric is recorded and compared.

3. The model producing the best performance is returned along with the set of parameters that was used.

The previous steps are illustrated in Figure 8-11, which makes it easier to visualize what's going on inside the validator.

Validator

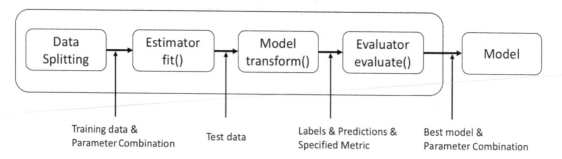

Figure 8-11. *Inside a validator*

The first validator I am going to discuss is TrainValidationSplit, which splits the given input data into a training and validation dataset pair based on the specified ratio and then trains and evaluates the dataset pair against each of the parameter combinations. For example, if the given parameter set has six combinations, then the given estimator is trained and evaluated six times, each time with a different parameter combination. Listing 8-16 provides an example of using TrainValidationSplit to tune a linear regression estimator with a parameter grid of six parameter combinations. Since the focus of this example is about TrainValidationSplit, there is an assumption that the feature engineering has already been done to the input data and it has a column called features.

Listing 8-16. Example of TrainValidationSplit

```
import org.apache.spark.ml.{Pipeline, PipelineModel}
import org.apache.spark.ml.classification.LogisticRegression
import org.apache.spark.ml.feature.{HashingTF, Tokenizer}
import org.apache.spark.ml.tuning.{ParamGridBuilder, TrainValidationSplit}
import org.apache.spark.ml.evaluation.BinaryClassificationEvaluator

val text_data = spark.createDataFrame(Seq(
                        (1, "Spark is a unified data analytics
                        engine", 0.0),
                        (2, "Spark is cool and it is fun to work
                        with Spark", 0.0),
                        (3, "There is a lot of exciting sessions
                        at upcoming Spark summit", 0.0),
```

```
                     (4, "signup to win a million dollars",
                     0.0)  )
                  ).toDF("id", "line", "label")

val tokenizer = new Tokenizer().setInputCol("line").setOutputCol("words")

val hashingTF = new HashingTF().setInputCol(tokenizer.getOutputCol)
                         .setOutputCol("features")

val logisticReg = new LogisticRegression().setMaxIter(5)

val pipeline = new Pipeline().setStages(Array(tokenizer, hashingTF,
logisticReg))

// the first parameter has 3 values and second parameter has 2 values,
// therefore the total parameter combinations is 6
val paramGrid = new ParamGridBuilder().addGrid(hashingTF.numFeatures,
Array(10, 100, 250))

                              .addGrid(logisticReg.regParam,
                              Array(0.1, 0.05))
                              .build()

// setting up the validator with required inputs - estimator, evaluator,
parameter grid and train ratio
val trainValidationSplit = new TrainValidationSplit().
setEstimator(pipeline)

                                      .setEvaluator(new
                                      BinaryClassificationEvaluator)
                                      .setEstimatorParamMaps(paramGrid)
                                      .setTrainRatio(0.8)
// train the linear regression estimator
val model = trainValidationSplit.fit(training)
```

The next validator I will discuss is the CrossValidator, which is an implementation of a widely used technique in the machine learning practitioner community to help with the model tuning step. This technique maximizes the amount of data for training and validation by randomly dividing the observations into k groups, or folds, of approximately the same size. The first fold is used for validation purposes, and the remaining folds are used for training purposes. This process is repeated k times, and each time the estimator is trained and evaluated against randomly divided training and validation folds. Figure 8-12 illustrates this process. The k value is chosen such that each training and validation group is statistically representative of the available observation, and each fold has roughly the same amount of sample data.

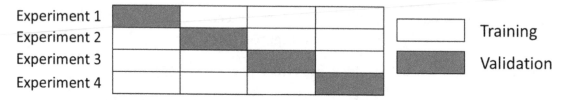

Figure 8-12. *K-fold example with k=4*

One must be mindful about the expensiveness of using this validator with a sizeable number of parameter combinations. This is because each experiment described in Figure 8-12 is performed against each the parameter combinations. For example, if k is 4 and the number of parameter combination is 6, then the total number of times the estimator will be trained and evaluated is 24. Listing 8-17 replaces `TrainValidationSplit` in 8-16 with an instance of `CrossValidator` that is configured with a k value of 2. In practice, the value for k is usually is 10 or higher. The example in Listing 8-17 ends up training and evaluating the estimator 12 times.

Listing 8-17. Example of CrossValidator

```
import org.apache.spark.ml.tuning.CrossValidator

val crossValidator = new CrossValidator().setEstimator(pipeline)
                                .setEvaluator(new
                                BinaryClassificationEvaluator)
                                .setEstimatorParamMaps(paramGrid)
                                .setNumFolds(2)

val model = crossValidator.fit(text_data)
```

Machine Learning Tasks in Action

This section tries to bring all the concepts and tools that MLlib provides together and apply them by working through the following machine learning tasks: classification, regression, and recommendation. By working through the machine learning development process with real datasets, ideally it will become more obvious as to how all the pieces fit, and it is always good to see the working code.

This section is not meant to comprehensively cover the hyperparameters of each machine learning algorithm, and the model tuning step is left as an exercise for you.

Classification

Classification is one of the most widely studied and used machine learning tasks because of its ability to help solve many real-life classification-related problems. For example, is this a fraudulent credit card transaction? Is this email a spam email? Is this an image of a cat or dog or bird?

There are three types of classification.

- *Binary classification*: This is where the label to predict has only two possible classes (for example, fraud or not fraud, conference paper is accepted or not, tumor is benign or malignant).

- *Multiclass classification*: This is where the label to predict has more than two possible classes (for example, whether an image is a dog, cat, or bird).

- *Multilabel classification*: This is where each observation can belong to more than one class. Movie genres are a good example of this. A movie can be classified as both action and comedy. MLlib doesn't natively support this type of classification.

MLlib provides a few machine learning algorithms for the classification tasks. They are listed here:

- Logistic regression

- Decision tree

- Random forest

- Gradient-boosted tree

367

- Linear support vector machine

- One versus rest

- Naïve Bayes

Model Hyperparameters

The logistic regression algorithm will be used in the following example, and the following is a subset of its model hyperparameters. Every single model hyperparameter has a default value.

- `family`: The possible values are `auto`, `binomial`, and `multinomial`. The default value is `auto`, which means the algorithm will automatically select the family to be either `binomial` or `multinomial` based on the values in the `label` column. `binomial` is for binary classification. `multinomial` is for the multiclass classification.

- `regParam`: This is the regularization parameter that is used to control the overfitting. The default value is 0.0.

Example

The following example tries to predict which Titanic passengers survived the tragedy. This is a binary classification machine learning problem, and as a starting point the logistic regression algorithm is the chosen algorithm. This example is based on a competition on kaggle.com, and the information and the data are available at `https://www.kaggle.com/c/titanic`. The data is provided in CSV format, and there are two files: `train.csv` and `test.csv`. The `train.csv` file contains the `label` column.

The provided data contains many interesting features; however, the code in Listing 8-18 will use only age, gender, and `ticket_class` as features.

Listing 8-18. Using the Logistic Regression Algorithm to Predict the Survival of Titanic Passengers

```
import org.apache.spark.ml.Pipeline
import org.apache.spark.ml.feature.StringIndexer
import org.apache.spark.ml.feature.VectorAssembler
import org.apache.spark.ml.classification.LogisticRegression
import org.apache.spark.ml.evaluation.BinaryClassificationEvaluator
```

```
val titanic_data = spark.read.format("csv").option("header", "true")
                                    .option("inferSchema","true")
                                    .load("/<folder>/train.csv")

// explore the schema
titanic_data.printSchema
 |-- PassengerId: integer (nullable = true)
 |-- Survived: integer (nullable = true)
 |-- Pclass: integer (nullable = true)
 |-- Name: string (nullable = true)
 |-- Sex: string (nullable = true)
 |-- Age: double (nullable = true)
 |-- SibSp: integer (nullable = true)
 |-- Parch: integer (nullable = true)
 |-- Ticket: string (nullable = true)
 |-- Fare: double (nullable = true)
 |-- Cabin: string (nullable = true)
 |-- Embarked: string (nullable = true)

// to start out with, we will use only three features
// filter out rows where age is null
val titanic_data1 = titanic_data.select('Survived.as("label"), 'Pclass.
as("ticket_class"),
                              'Sex.as("gender"), 'Age.as("age"))
                              .filter('age.isNotNull)

// split the data into training and test with 80% and 20% split
val Array(training, test) = titanic_data1.randomSplit(Array(0.8, 0.2))

println(s"training count: ${training.count}, test count: ${test.count}")

// estimator:  to convert gender string to numbers
val genderIndxr = new StringIndexer().setInputCol("gender").
setOutputCol("genderIdx")

// transfomer: assemble the features into a vector
val assembler = new VectorAssembler().setInputCols(Array("ticket_class",
"genderIdx", "age"))
                              .setOutputCol("features")
```

```
// estimator: the algorithm
val logisticRegression = new LogisticRegression().setFamily("binomial")

// set up the pipeline with three stages
val pipeline = new Pipeline().setStages(Array(genderIndxr, assembler,
logisticRegression))

// train the algorithm with the training data
val model = pipeline.fit(traininng)

// perform the predictions
val predictions = model.transform(test)

// perform the evaluation of the model performance, the default metric is
the area under the ROC
val evaluator = new BinaryClassificationEvaluator()
evaluator.evaluate(predictions)
res10: Double = 0.8746657754010692

evaluator.getMetricName
res11: String = areaUnderROC
```

The metric produced by BinaryClassificationEvaluator has a value of 0.87, which is decent performance for just using three features. The previous example doesn't explore the various hyperparameters and training parameters.

Regression

Another popular machine task is called *regression*, which is designed to predict a real number or continuous value. For example, you want to predict the sales revenue for next quarter, the income amount of a population, and the amount of rain in a certain region of the world.

MLlib provides a few machine learning algorithms for the regression tasks. They are listed here:

- Linear regression

- Generalized linear regression

- Decision trees

- Random forest

- Gradient-boosted trees

- Isotonic regression

Model Hyperparameters

The LinearRegression algorithm will be used in the following example, and its subset of model hyperparameters is shown here:

- *regParam*: This is the regularization parameter that is used to control the overfitting. The default value is 0.0.

- *fitIntercept*: This parameter is used to determine whether to fit the intercept. The default value is true.

Example

The following example will try to predict the house price based on a set of information about the house. The details and the data are available on kaggle.com at https://www.kaggle.com/c/house-prices-advanced-regression-techniques/data. The data is provided in CSV format, and there are two files, train.csv and test.csv. The label column in the train.csv file is called SalePrice.

The provided data contains many interesting features; however, the code in Listing 8-19 will use only a subset of them.

Listing 8-19. Using the Linear Regression Algorithm to Predict Home Prices

```
import org.apache.spark.sql.functions._
import org.apache.spark.ml.Pipeline
import org.apache.spark.ml.feature.StringIndexer
import org.apache.spark.ml.feature.VectorAssembler
import org.apache.spark.ml.regression.LinearRegression
import org.apache.spark.ml.feature.RFormula
import org.apache.spark.ml.evaluation.RegressionEvaluator
import org.apache.spark.mllib.evaluation.RegressionMetrics

val house_data = spark.read.format("csv").option("header", "true")
                                .option("inferSchema","true")
                                .load("<path>/train.csv")
```

```
// select columns to use as features
val cols = Seq[String]("SalePrice", "LotArea",  "RoofStyle",
                       "Heating", "1stFlrSF", "2ndFlrSF", "BedroomAbvGr",
                       "KitchenAbvGr", "GarageCars", "TotRmsAbvGrd",
                       "YearBuilt")
val colNames = cols.map(n => col(n))

// select only needed columns
val skinny_house_data = house_data.select(colNames:_*)

// create a new column called "TotalSF" by adding the value of "1stFlrSF"
and "2ndFlrSF" columns
// cast the "SalePrice" column to double
val skinny_house_data1 = skinny_house_data.withColumn("TotalSF", col("1stFlrSF") +
                                                          col("2ndFlrSF"))
                                                      .drop("1stFlrSF",
                                                          "2ndFlrSF")
                  .withColumn("SalePrice", $"SalePrice".cast("double"))

// examine the statistics of the label column called "SalePrice"
skinny_house_data1.describe("SalePrice").show
```

```
+--------+-------------------+
| summary|          SalePrice|
+--------+-------------------+
|   count|               1460|
|    mean| 180921.19589041095|
|  stddev|  79442.50288288663|
|     min|            34900.0|
|     max|           755000.0|
+--------+-------------------+
```

```
// create estimators and transformers to setup a pipeline

// set the invalid categorical value handling policy to skip to avoid error
// at evaluation time
val roofStyleIndxr = new StringIndexer().setInputCol("RoofStyle")
                                       .setOutputCol("RoofStyleIdx")
                                       .setHandleInvalid("skip")
```

```
val heatingIndxr = new StringIndexer().setInputCol("Heating")
                                      .setOutputCol("HeatingIdx")
                                      .setHandleInvalid("skip")

val linearRegression = new LinearRegression().setLabelCol("SalePrice")


// assembler to assemble the features into a feature vector
val assembler = new VectorAssembler().setInputCols(
                                Array("LotArea", "RoofStyleIdx",
                                "HeatingIdx",
                                        "LotArea", "BedroomAbvGr",
                                        "KitchenAbvGr", "GarageCars",
                                        "TotRmsAbvGrd", "YearBuilt",
                                        "TotalSF"))
                                .setOutputCol("features")

// setup the pipeline
val pipeline = new Pipeline().setStages(Array(roofStyleIndxr, heatingIndxr,
assembler, linearRegression))

// split the data into training and test pair
val Array(training, test) = skinny_house_data1.randomSplit(Array(0.8, 0.2))

// train the pipeline
val model = pipeline.fit(training)

// perform prediction
val predictions = model.transform(test)

val evaluator = new RegressionEvaluator().setLabelCol("SalePrice")
                                        .setPredictionCol("prediction")
                                        .setMetricName("rmse")

val rmse = evaluator.evaluate(predictions)
rmse: Double = 37579.253919082395
```

RMSE stands for the *root-mean-square error*. In this case, the RMSE value is around $37,000, which indicates there is a lot of room for improvement.

Recommendation

The recommender system is one of the most intuitive and well-known machine learning applications. Maybe that is the case because almost everyone has seen examples of recommender systems in action on popular web sites such as Amazon and Netflix. In fact, almost every single popular website on the Internet has one or more examples of recommender systems. Popular examples of recommender systems are songs you may like on Spotify, people you want to follow on Twitter, courses may you like on Coursera or Udacity, and so on. The cool thing is recommender systems bring benefits to both users and the company behind that website. Users will be delighted to find or discover items that they like without expending too much effort. Companies will be happy because of the increased user engagement and loyalty as well as their bottom line. If a recommender system is designed and performs well, it is a win-win situation.

The common approaches to building recommender systems include content-based filtering, collaborative filtering, and a hybrid of the two. The first approach requires collecting information about the items being recommended and the profile of each user. The second approach requires collecting only user activities or behavior via explicit or implicit means. Examples of explicit behavior include rating a movie or an item on Amazon. Examples of implicit behavior including viewing the movie trailer or description. The intuition behind the second approach is the "wisdom of the crowd" concept where the people who agreed in the past will tend to agree in the future.

This section will focus on the collaborative filter approach, and one of the popular algorithms for this approach is called ALS, which stands for *alternate-least-square*. The only input this algorithm needs is the user-item rating matrix, which is used to discover user preferences and item properties through a process called *matrix factorization*. Once these two pieces of information are found, then they are used to predict the user's preference on items not seen before. MLlib provides an implementation of the ALS algorithm.

Model Hyperparameters

The ALS algorithm implementation in MLlib has a few important hyperparameters that you need to be aware of. The following section contains just a subset. Please consult the documentation at `https://spark.apache.org/docs/latest/ml-collaborative-filtering.html`.

- *rank*: This parameter specifies the number of latent factors or properties about users and items that will be learned during the training process. An optimal value for rank is usually determined by experimentation as well as an intuition about the number of properties needed to accurately describe an item. The default value is 10.

- *regParam*: This is the amount of regularization to deal with overfitting. An optimal value for this parameter is usually determined by experimentation. The default is 0.1.

- *implicitPrefs*: ALS algorithms support both explicit and implicit user activities or behavior. This parameter is used to tell which one the input data represents. The default is false, meaning the activities or behavior are explicit.

Example

The example you are going to work through is to build a movie recommender system using the movie ratings data set from grouplens.com at `https://grouplens.org/datasets/movielens/`. The specific dataset that will be used is the latest MovieLens 100k dataset at `http://files.grouplens.org/datasets/movielens/ml-latest-small.zip`. This dataset contains roughly about 100,000 ratings by 700 users across 9,000 movies. There are four files included in the zip file: `links.csv`, `movies.csv`, `ratings.csv`, and `tags.csv`. Each row in file `ratings.csv` represents one rating of one movie by one user, and it has this format: `userId`, `movieId`, `rating`, `timestamp`. The rating is on a scale from 0 to 5 with half-star increments.

The code in Listing 8-20 trains the ALS algorithm with one set of parameters and then evaluates the model performance based on the RMSE metric. In addition, it will call a few interesting provided APIs in the `ALSModel` class to get recommendations for movies and users.

Listing 8-20. Building a Recommender System Using the ALS Algorithm Implementation in MLlib

```
import org.apache.spark.mllib.evaluation.RankingMetrics
import org.apache.spark.ml.evaluation.RegressionEvaluator
import org.apache.spark.ml.recommendation.ALS
import org.apache.spark.ml.tuning.{ParamGridBuilder, CrossValidator}
```

```
import org.apache.spark.sql.functions._

// we don't need the timestamp column, so drop it immediately
val ratingsDF = spark.read.option("header", "true")
                          .option("inferSchema", "true")
                          .csv("<path>/ratings.csv").drop("timestamp")

// quick check on the number of ratings
ratingsDF.count

res14: Long = 100004

// quick check who are the active movie raters
val ratingsByUserDF = ratingsDF.groupBy("userId").count()
ratingsByUserDF.orderBy($"count".desc).show(10)

+-------+------+
| userId| count|
+-------+------+
|    547|  2391|
|    564|  1868|
|    624|  1735|
|     15|  1700|
|     73|  1610|
|    452|  1340|
|    468|  1291|
|    380|  1063|
|    311|  1019|
|     30|  1011|
+-------+------+

println("# of rated movies: " +ratingsDF.select("movieId").distinct().count)
# of rated movies: 9066

println("# of users: " + ratingsByUserDF.count)
# of users: 671

// analyze the movies largest number of ratings
val ratingsByMovieDF = ratingsDF.groupBy("movieId").count()
```

```
ratingsByMovieDF.orderBy($"count".desc).show(10)

+--------+------+
| movieId| count|
+--------+------+
|     356|   341|
|     296|   324|
|     318|   311|
|     593|   304|
|     260|   291|
|     480|   274|
|    2571|   259|
|       1|   247|
|     527|   244|
|     589|   237|
+--------+------+

// prepare data for training and testing
val Array(trainingData, testData) = ratingsByUserDF.randomSplit(Array(0.8, 0.2))

// setting up an instance of ALS
val als = new ALS().setRank(12)
                   .setMaxIter(10)
                   .setRegParam(0.03)
                   .setUserCol("userId")
                   .setItemCol("movieId")
                   .setRatingCol("rating")

// train the model
val model = als.fit(trainingData)

// perform predictions
val predictions = model.transform(testData).na.drop

// setup an evaluator to calcuate the RMSE metric
val evaluator = new RegressionEvaluator().setMetricName("rmse")
                                         .setLabelCol("rating")
                                         .setPredictionCol("prediction")
```

```
val rmse = evaluator.evaluate(predictions)
println(s"Root-mean-square error = $rmse")
Root-mean-square error = 1.06027809686058
```

The ALSModel class provides two sets of useful functions to perform recommendations. The first set is for recommending the top n items to all users or a specific set of users. The second set is for recommending the top n users to all items or a specific set of items. Listing 8-21 provides an example of calling these functions.

Listing 8-21. Using ALSModel to Perform Recommendations

```
// recommend the top 5 movies for all users
model.recommendForAllUsers(5).show(false)

// active raters
val activeMovieRaters = Seq((547), (564), (624), (15), (73)).toDF("userId")

model.recommendForUserSubset(activeMovieRaters, 5).show(false)

+------+-----------------------------------------------------------------+
|userId|    recommendations                                              |
+------+-----------------------------------------------------------------+
|    15| [[363, 5.4706035], [422, 5.4109325], [1192, 5.3407555],        |
|       [1030, 5.329553], [2467, 5.214414]]                             |
|   547| [[1298, 5.752393], [1235, 5.4936843], [994, 5.426885],         |
|       [926, 5.28749], [3910, 5.2009006]]                              |
|   564| [[121231, 6.199452], [2454, 5.4714866], [3569, 5.4276495],     |
|       [1096, 5.4212027], [1292, 5.4203687]]                           |
|   624| [[1960, 5.4001703], [1411, 5.2505665], [3083, 5.1079946],      |
|       [3030, 5.0170803], [132333, 5.0165534]]                         |
|    73| [[2068, 5.0426316], [5244, 5.004793], [923, 4.992707],         |
|       [85342, 4.979018], [1411, 4.9703207]]                           |
+------+-----------------------------------------------------------------+

// recommend top 3 users for each movie
val recMovies = model.recommendForAllItems(3)

// read in movies data set so you can see the movie title
val moviesDF = spark.read.option("header", "true")
```

```
                   .option("inferSchema", "true")
                   .csv("<path>/movies.csv")

val recMoviesWithInfoDF = recMovies.join(moviesDF, "movieId")

recMoviesWithInfoDF.select("movieId", "title", "recommendations").show(5,
false)
```

```
+-------+-----------------------------+-----------------------------+
|movieId|                        title|              recommendations|
+-------+-----------------------------+-----------------------------+
|   1580| Men in Black (a.k.a. MIB) (1997)| [[46, 5.6861496], [113,
                                         5.6780157], [145, 5.3410296]]|
|   5300|          3:10 to Yuma (1957)| [[545, 5.475599], [354,
                                         5.2230153], [257, 5.0623646]]|
|   6620|      American Splendor (2003)| [[156, 5.9004226], [83,
                                         5.699677], [112, 5.6194253]] |
|   7340|    Just One of the Guys (1985)| [[621, 4.5778027], [451,
                                         3.9995837], [565, 3.6733315]]|
|  32460| Knockin' on Heaven's Door (1997)| [[565, 5.5728054], [298,
                                         5.00507], [476, 4.805148]]   |
+-------+-----------------------------+-----------------------------+
// top rated movies
val topRatedMovies = Seq((356), (296), (318), (593)).toDF("movieId")

// recommend top 3 users per movie in topRatedMovies
val recUsers =  model.recommendForItemSubset(topRatedMovies, 3)

recUsers.join(moviesDF, "movieId").select("movieId", "title",
"recommendations").show(false)
```

```
+-------+-----------------------------+-----------------------------+
|movieId|                        title|              recommendations|
+-------+-----------------------------+-----------------------------+
|    296|          Pulp Fiction (1994)| [[4, 5.8505774], [473,
                                         5.81865], [631, 5.588397]]   |
|    593| Silence of the Lambs, The (1991)| [[153, 5.839533], [586,
                                         5.8279104], [473, 5.5933723]] |
|    318| Shawshank Redemption, The (1994)| [[112, 5.8578305], [656,
                                         5.8488774], [473, 5.795221]]  |
```

```
|    356|              Forrest Gump (1994)| [[464, 5.6555476], [58,
                                           5.6497917], [656, 5.625555]]|
+-------+-----------------------------+-----------------------------+
```

In Listing 8-20, an instance of the ALS algorithm was trained with one set of parameters, and the RSME you got is about 1.06. Let's try retraining that instance of the ALS algorithm with a set of parameter combinations using CrossValidator to see whether you can lower the RSME value. The code in Listing 8-22 sets up grid search with a total of 4 parameter combinations for the two model hyperparameters (als.regParam and als.rank) and a CrossValidator with three folds. This means the ALS algorithm will be trained and evaluated 12 times, and therefore it will take a minute or two to finish on a laptop.

Listing 8-22. Using CrossValidator to Tune the ALS Model

```
val paramGrid = new ParamGridBuilder().addGrid(als.regParam,
Array(0.05, 0.15))
                              .addGrid(als.rank, Array(12,20))
                              .build

val crossValidator = new CrossValidator().setEstimator(als)
                              .setEvaluator(evaluator)
                              .setEstimatorParamMaps(paramGrid)
                              .setNumFolds(3)
// print out the 4 hyperparameter combinations
crossValidator.getEstimatorParamMaps.foreach(println)
{
      als_d2ec698bdd1a-rank: 12,
      als_d2ec698bdd1a-regParam: 0.05
}
{
      als_d2ec698bdd1a-rank: 20,
      als_d2ec698bdd1a-regParam: 0.05
}
{
      als_d2ec698bdd1a-rank: 12,
      als_d2ec698bdd1a-regParam: 0.15
}
```

```
{
     als_d2ec698bdd1a-rank: 20,
     als_d2ec698bdd1a-regParam: 0.15
}

// this will take a while to run through more than 10 experiments
val cvModel = crossValidator.fit(trainingData)

// perform the predictions and drop the
val predictions2 = cvModel.transform(testData).na.drop

val evaluator2 = new RegressionEvaluator().setMetricName("rmse")
                                    .setLabelCol("rating")
                                    .setPredictionCol("prediction")

val rmse2 = evaluator2.evaluate(predictions2)
rmse2: Double = 0.9881840432547675
```

You have successfully lowered the RMSE by leveraging CrossValidator to help with tuning the model. It may take a while to train the best model, but MLlib makes it easy to experiment with a set of parameter combinations.

Deep Learning Pipeline

This chapter would be incomplete if there is no reference to the deep learning topic, which is one of the hottest topics in the artificial intelligence and machine learning landscapes. There are already lots of resources available in the form of books, blogs, courses, and research papers to explain every aspect of deep learning. In terms of technology, there are a lot of innovations from the open source community, universities, and large companies such as Google, Facebook, Microsoft, and others that are coming up with deep learning frameworks. Here is the current list of deep learning frameworks:

- TensorFlow is an open source framework created by Google.

- MXNet is a deep learning framework developed by a group of universities and companies.

- Caffe is a deep learning framework developed by UC Berkeley.

- CNTK is an open source deep learning framework developed by Microsoft.

- Theano is an open deep learning framework developed by the University of Montreal.

- PyTorch is an open source deep learning framework developed by Facebook.

- BigDL is an open source deep learning framework developed by Intel.

From the Apache Spark's side, Databricks is driving the effort of developing a project called Deep Learning Pipelines, which is not another deep learning framework, but rather it is designed to work on top of the existing popular deep learning frameworks listed earlier. In the spirit of Spark and MLlib, the Deep Learning Pipelines project provides high-level and easy-to-use APIs for building scalable deep learning applications in Python with Apache Spark. This project is currently being developed outside of the Apache Spark open source project, and eventually it will be incorporated into the main trunk. At the time of this writing, the Deep Learning Pipelines project provides the following features:

- Common deep learning use cases implemented in just a few lines of code

- Working with images in Spark

- Applying pretrained deep learning models for scalable predictions

- The ability to do transfer learning, which adapts a model trained for a similar task to the current ask

- Distributed hyperparameter tuning

- Easily exposing deep learning models so others can use them as a function in SQL- to make predictions

You can find more details about the exciting Deep Learning Pipelines project at `https://github.com/databricks/spark-deep-learning`.

Summary

The adoption of artificial intelligence and machine learning is steadily increasing, and there will be many exciting breakthroughs in the coming years. Building on top of the strong foundation of Spark, the MLlib component is designed to help with building intelligent applications in an easy and scalable manner.

- Artificial intelligence is a broad field, and its goal is to make machines seem like they have intelligence. Machine learning is one of the subfields; it focuses on teaching machines to learn by training them with data.

- The process of building machine learning applications is an iterative one and involves a few steps that are usually followed in a certain sequence.

- The Spark MLlib component consists of tools for feature engineering, constructing, evaluating, and tuning machine learning pipelines as well as a set of well-known machine learning algorithms such as classification, regression, clustering, and collaborative filtering.

- The core concepts the MLlib component introduces to help with building and maintaining complex pipelines are transformers, estimators, and pipeline. A pipeline is the orchestrator that ensures both training and test data flow through identical feature processing steps.

- Model tuning is a critical step in the machine learning application development process. It is tedious and time-consuming because it involves training and evaluating one or models over a set of parameter combinations. Combined with the pipeline abstraction, MLlib provides two tools to help: `CrossValidator` and `TrainValidationSplit`.

Index

© Hien Luu 2018
H. Luu, *Beginning Apache Spark 2*, https://doi.org/10.1007/978-1-4842-3579-9

CPSIA information can be obtained
at www.ICGtesting.com
Printed in the USA
LVHW061743040819
626457LV00003B/6/P